After the
Darkest Hour

After the Darkest Hour

HOW SUFFERING

BEGINS THE JOURNEY

TO WISDOM

Kathleen A. Brehony, Ph.D.

AN OWL BOOK

HENRY HOLT AND COMPANY

NEW YORK

Henry Holt and Company, LLC
Publishers since 1866
115 West 18th Street
New York, New York 10011

Henry Holt ® is a registered trademark of
Henry Holt and Company, LLC.

Library of Congress Cataloging-in-Publication Data

Brehony, Kathleen A.
    After the darkest hour : how suffering begins the
journey to wisdom / Kathleen Brehony.—1st ed.
        p.   cm.
    Includes bibliographical references.
    ISBN 0-8050-6436-2
        1. Suffering.   2. Life change events—Psychological aspects.
    3. Adjustment (Psychology).   4. Self-actualization (Psychology).   I. Title.

BF 789.S8 B74   2000
155.9'3—dc21
                                                                    00-029577

First published in hardcover in 2000 by Henry Holt and Company.

First Owl Books Edition 2001

Printed in the United States of America

1   3   5   7   9   10   8   6   4   2

This book is lovingly dedicated to

TERESA KELLY MUNN

my beloved aunt, my second mother,

my warrior friend.

Vocatus ataque non vocatus, Deus aderit.
("Called or not called, God will be there.")

—Engraved in stone over the front door of
Carl Jung's home near Kusnacht, Switzerland

Contents

*After the
Darkest Hour*

PART ONE

Reflections on Suffering

Introduction

What does not destroy me, makes me stronger.

—Friedrich Nietzsche

When I was a child, I looked forward to Sunday mornings. My family lived in Avenel, New Jersey, and often would spend Saturday nights with my grandparents at their home in Newark. With my mother, father, and brother sleeping upstairs, I would get up early with Nana. She made those mornings magical with stories of life as she saw it and treats only the two of us would share. My grandmother, Anna Kelly, used to tell me stories about Ireland and how the blue hydrangeas in her yard came up bluer every year when she mixed coffee grounds into the dirt around them and about her old dog Skippy who would eat nothing but Wheaties with heavy cream and a half a cup of sugar. We would talk as we made our way to seven-thirty mass, and afterward as we stopped by the Italian bakery near Ivy Street and lugged home bags of crullers, jelly doughnuts, and hard rolls. On these special mornings my Nana would give me a cup of coffee that was more coffee-flavored milk than the real thing. She said that's how French people drink coffee and besides, she leaned in and cautioned, it was more for dunking than drinking. Still, it'd be better not to mention it to my mother and father.

I loved our shared secrets and how her confidences made me feel so grown-up. We'd dunk our crullers into the coffee-milk until they were soppy and talk for hours before anyone else woke up and came into her warm kitchen for a big family breakfast. She'd tell me stories about when my mother and her brothers and sisters were kids. My mother was Mary and she and her sisters, Teresa and Jeannie, were all so close that when one had a problem, they'd all cry even when two didn't have a clue as to what the tears were about. During World War II, Nana told me, they all worked on their victory garden and raised chickens for food. My favorite episode in this period was about my Uncle Jimmy. He was in charge of the chickens, but he was so softhearted that he named each one and tried to keep them all as pets. When my grandfather told him that the family needed these birds for food, Jimmy couldn't bear it. He liberated every one of them except a special black hen he named—for reasons no one has ever known—Bard Rock the Third. He kept that old Bard Rock in his room for almost three weeks before she was discovered. He'd sneak food up to her and clean up her messes and feathers. Nana claimed she couldn't remember what happened to the hen after her cover was blown. That was okay with me. I didn't really want to know the final outcome.

But I learned more than family lore on those mornings. Nana introduced me to her family's homeland in Ireland and all of its spirits, faeries, and saints—Brigid was my favorite. Nana told me stories about the Kellys from County Cork and how my father's mother, Mary Geraghty, was born near Galway Bay and could foretell the future by reading tea leaves. I remember my grandmother telling me one tale again and again on those mornings. It was about a magical Irish bird that could raise itself up from its own ashes by flapping its wings and pulling itself together before soaring off into the sky. The story, she said, reminded her that no matter how bad things ever get in our lives, we can always find the strength and will to rise above them and go on.

I was quite a bit older when I recognized Nana's story was more Greek than Irish, though it's said that every culture has some representation of a mythological creature with the power to be reborn from its own ashes. The Greeks called this bird the Phoenix. The Egyptians named it Benu, and for them it personified the all-powerful sun god Atum, or Re, whose name literally means "to rise in brilliance." The myths of many cultures tell how the sun—in fact, light itself—first entered the world in the form of a sacred heronlike bird. Chinese, Sumerian, Assyrian, Incan, Aztec, and, yes, even the Irish Celts, all looked upon this light-bearing bird as a powerful emblem of resurrection and immortality. As an adult, I became more interested in Jungian psychology and archetypal symbols, and studied many different ones and their meanings. I always found myself drawn to the Phoenix. Maybe it was my early exposure to it that has given the Phoenix such resonance with me. I find it best and most beautifully represents the inner ability each of us has to emerge transformed out of our self-imposed limitations and life's greatest suffering. No matter what comes our way down the path of life, we have the power to overcome the obstacles, realize our full potential, and go on to achieve our greatest emotional, creative, and spiritual goals.

The Irish have a history of hardship and persecution, and so it's difficult to be of Irish descent and not consider the question of suffering. Our history, music, and literature carry it as a prominent theme. You can see how I was introduced to it before I was ten, and I just thought I was having a good time with my grandmother. As I've grown older, I've wanted to understand more about how and why we suffer and what factors make us bitter versus better as a result of our experiences. The Phoenix brings up an enduring question about suffering for me: Why is it that some people seem to have this bird's symbolic strength to rise above the flames of loss and pain in their lives while others settle into the ashes, becoming bitter, jaded, and hard? But my thoughts have always been broad and free-floating, never focused enough to make any conclusions regarding these questions that have rattled around in my head since those early morning talks over jelly doughnuts.

Until the summer of 1998. An instant of crunching metal and shattering glass changed everything about an ordinary, even pleasant, Tuesday afternoon and every day that has followed.

My father and stepmother, Jim and Deanne Brehony, were driving on Route 270 South, a six-lane interstate that snakes through the foothills of the Blue Ridge Mountains and meanders through Maryland farm country, ending bluntly at the Capitol Beltway near Washington, D.C. They had been visiting Deanne's daughter and son-in-law, Shelley and Dick Riley, in West Virginia, left their house around ten in the morning, and set aside the whole day for an easy trip home to northern Virginia. Around one-thirty they stopped for a sandwich at the Alpine Pantry, a favorite Amish store, and bought a jar of homemade apple butter as a gift for the neighbor who had watched their house while they were away. Then they got back on the road expecting nothing more than a leisurely two-hour drive home on that clear, dry afternoon.

But something else came down the road of life that day. An hour later, a Buick sedan spun out of control on the far-right northbound lane near Hyattstown, Maryland. It weaved at high speed across two lanes of traffic, careened over thirty yards of grassy median, and slammed head-on into their Toyota Camry. In the end, it took three men using the "jaws of life" more than an hour to get them out of that smoking tangle.

"Air bags saved your lives," the state trooper who soon arrived on the scene told my dad and stepmom. Both of them were conscious but seriously hurt. However, as they were stuck in the wreck and bleeding, no one would know what their injuries were until they reached a hospital. The accident and rescue were rough, but Dad and Deanne were soon to be separated from each other, which was a challenge they hadn't even considered. Paramedics asked if either had any special medical conditions. My dad told them that he was a liver transplantee, so they sent him off by medical helicopter to the bustling, inner-city Washington Hospital Center—the most sophisticated trauma center in the area. Deanne was flown by separate helicopter to the quiet Suburban Hospital in Bethesda. For more than five hours, neither my father nor Deanne could find out anything about each other's condition. They didn't even know whether the other one would live through the night. Later, both would agree that this period of not-knowing was the most terrifying part of their ordeal.

I was home in Norfolk when I got the call from an E.R. nurse about the car accident my father and stepmother had been in. I shoved some clothes in an overnight bag and was on my way out the door when the phone rang again. "The doctors don't know yet if there's been any damage to Dad's liver. If there has been, they're going to transport him by helicopter to UVA," my brother, J.P., said in out-of-character measured tones that were useless attempts to cover the terror in his voice. Just three years earlier, my father had been given a new liver by the medical team at the University of Virginia Medical Center in Charlottesville, and it was understandable that he would need their special expertise if his liver had been seriously damaged.

Since Charlottesville is midway between Norfolk and Washington, I had no idea if I should go to UVA or drive to the Washington Hospital Center. I was afraid that I'd get to one hospital only to find that we'd crossed paths along the way and Dad was at the other. Through our network of cell phones and digital beepers, I knew that Deanne's daughter, Shelley, and son-in-law, Dick, were already en route to Suburban Hospital. Deanne would have family there. My brother and sister-in-law, Deborah, were on the way to the Washington Hospital Center. My heart was pounding out of my chest. I needed a decision, the more conscious or intuitive the better. Without the guidance of either, my partner and I flipped a coin and went to Washington. As luck would have it, Dad was there.

When we arrived, doctors had already told my father that Deanne had survived, that her injuries were serious but not life-threatening, and that she was in a hospital thirty minutes away. That was all we knew. Dad was in excruciating physical pain, but the news that Deanne was alive brought him great relief. He described his pain to us, saying that it felt like hot knives were continuously slicing through his legs and feet. The sharp pain came in surging waves that we saw literally took his breath away, but Dad said he could bear this much more easily now that he knew Deanne was safe and would recover. The doctors told us that they could only give my father minimal medication for pain. They were counting on its wrenching compass to help them diagnose the full extent of his injuries. The doctors told us that at this point the only things they knew were that the air bag had, indeed, saved Dad's life and liver, and that every bone below each knee in both legs had been crushed.

I stood next to my dad and held his hand. He was propped up in the hospital bed with IV drips flowing and four machines clicking away with red digital readouts and pulsing green lines. I kissed him. I wept. He smiled, squeezed my hand, and whispered through shuddering breaths, "Aren't we blessed? We're so lucky."

After visiting with my father, we raced to Deanne's hospital. She, too, was in great pain. She had broken three ribs, her sternum, and left ankle. She showed us that her chest and stomach were mottled yellow and red. Plum-colored bruises outlined a wide stripe where the seat belt had burned into her flesh on impact. In spite of the trauma of the past few hours Deanne looked nicely put together; she was wearing a pretty robe and had on makeup. She was smiling and then, unbelievably, she uttered the same words my father had earlier: "Aren't we blessed? We're so lucky."

Later that night, we all returned to my father and stepmother's house. I was walking with Dorothy, my beloved yellow Labrador retriever. She'd been locked in the car for hours in the cavernous parking lots of two hospitals and was happy to run freely around the backyard. A thunderstorm had raged through earlier and it was a cool night for August. The sky was clear and filled with stars. I relished that quiet moment with Dorothy far from the noise and pace of emergency rooms. I wasn't sure what the right prayer was for the occasion, but I remember looking toward the heavens and giving thanks that my father and Deanne were still alive. The paramedics told a man on the staff at the E.R. that he was astounded that anyone had come out of that twisted car alive. This man related that observation to Deborah when he handed her Deanne's purse, covered with a dried brown substance. Noticing Deborah's panicky expression, he assured her that the lab had analyzed the substance and that "it had been definitively and unequivocally proven to be apple butter." She took the purse.

The lights from the house burned warm and yellow against the dark night, making it clear that everyone was still up talking and relaxing over a cold beer. As I looked at the house and thought about the people it held, I considered what a bonding experience this has been for these two families—Deanne's and my own. There had been an immediate connection among all four of their adult children and their spouses when my father and Deanne told us they were going to get married. We liked each other for sure, but we lived all over the world—Deanne's son and his family lived in Germany, Shelley and Dick in West Virginia, J.P. and Deborah outside of D.C., and Nancy and I three hours south in Norfolk with a lot of time spent in L.A. We only gathered at holidays and family events, so there were very few opportunities to really get to know one another. Watching people in the house moving back and forth in front of the glass door in the den, I remembered an old Chinese proverb that goes something like "You will often forget those you have laughed with but you will never forget those you have cried with." Through the window I could see Deborah and Shelley sitting on the sofa, arms around each other, talking. In the kitchen, my partner, Nancy, and Dick were making sandwiches for the whole family—no one had eaten in the last twelve hours. My brother, J.P., was holding and rocking Shelley and Dick's baby son, Connor. He was snuggling with him. And though I couldn't hear it, by the movement of his mouth and the way he was swaying, I think my brother was singing.

As I looked into the house, I realized that my heart rate was finally near normal. This was the first moment I could say that since I had received the call from the E.R. nurse fourteen hours earlier. I could feel my body tingling, electric with the exhaustion that only comes from a long spell of outright fear and trembling. With this new calm, I was now quite sure I'd get some sleep tonight unless I kept thinking about what my dad and stepmother had said to me: "Aren't we blessed? We're so lucky."

Those simple words created a cascade of thoughts. They both felt blessed in spite of all the unexpected pain they had suffered and would be part of their recovery ahead. My father was seventy-two years old when the accident happened. Though he had had many good things in his life, the past five or six years had been full of suffering. He nursed my mother for two years, watching her waste away to nothing from leukemia. He and my mother met when they were just seventeen years old. They married after World War II when he returned home after serving with the Army Air Corps and had stayed that way for forty-seven years. Within months after her death, he began to get sick. A surgeon removed his gall bladder, thinking that was the problem. It wasn't. Then he met Deanne, and fell in love, something he never expected to do. He'd never even dated another woman besides my mom. In spite of his newfound happiness with Deanne, physically my dad continued to lose energy and was going downhill. A litany of medical tests didn't reveal a thing. One fall morning just before Thanksgiving in 1995, he was in such pain that Deanne rushed him to an emergency room. There, doctors finally discovered that his liver was basically worthless. It had been beaten down by years of undiagnosed hepatitis C, which he most likely contracted from a blood transfusion in his youth. He had to wait and wonder if he would live long enough to get a new liver and then go through major transplant surgery. Just a few years later, here he was in a hospital bed again. This time he was facing multiple surgeries and another long and painful recovery. Worse yet, the doctors couldn't say whether he'd ever get out of a wheelchair again. And he was talking about how he was blessed. How did he do it?

I think most people would agree that my father had every right to rail at the heavens and yell, "Why me? Isn't enough, enough?" Yet, instead, the first words he spoke to me were about blessings and luck. I started thinking all at once about Greek drama, independent films, and the myths that serve us as much today as they ever did. The muse was flowing wildly, I grant you, but it had been a difficult day. I knew any attempts on my part to stop the questions would be futile.

As Dorothy scrambled through the wet grass chasing some nocturnal critter, the questions wandering around my tired brain began to focus. What were my dad and stepmom talking about? How could they be lying in hospital beds with dozens of broken bones talking about blessings? Then I thought about the story of the Phoenix I'd first heard so long ago. My questions became more focused. Why is it that some people see blessings even in the darkest times? Why is it that they seem able to use their experiences of pain, suffering, or loss to become better people? Like a refiner's fire, these dark times seem to catapult them into higher levels of consciousness. They become stronger, wiser, more compassionate, and even spiritually awakened. I started reflecting on the many wise thinkers who have written about the power of suffering to change us for the better. That's when I started thinking about the Greeks.

Aeschylus, the sixth-century B.C.E. Greek dramatist, has been accurately dubbed the "Father of Tragedy"—because he again and again makes the point that the gods have decreed that the *only* true human path to wisdom is by way of suffering. In his many plays—*Prometheus Bound, Seven Against Thebes,* and the *Oresteia,* among others—it is the horrible, agonizing life experiences themselves that remove the shackles and hurl the protagonist from his limited and ordinary life into a heroic one.

Aeschylus was not alone in his thinking about the connections between suffering and enlightenment. Aristotle agreed with him, saying that the goal of comprehending the truth about life and the nature of reality was not to simply learn, but to learn through suffering. Every mystery school of the ancient world used metaphorical dramas and initiation rituals to emphasize that one can only be reborn in knowledge and wisdom when one is able to relinquish everything through suffering. This theme resounds in every myth of every culture. Without glamorizing suffering or reinforcing the misconception that the only human nobility lies in its ragged wounds, it's hard to miss the point that many wise thinkers believe that suffering contains remarkable gifts. Mystics of all spiritual and wisdom traditions agree that suffering is the only key that opens the door to transformation of the soul and psyche. It is by way of pain, they say, that we come to terms with our true destinies, our true selves, and form an authentic relationship with God. Spanish mystic John of the Cross called this process of enlightenment the "dark night of the soul." Thirteenth-century Sufi mystic Rumi declared that "pain is a treasure, for it contains mercies" and reminds us that "spring seasons are hidden in the autumns." Every religion teaches that pain and suffering are paths to God and self-enlightenment. The First Noble Truth of Buddhism states simply that "life is suffering." Zen master D. T. Suzuki amplifies this central tenet when he says, "The value of human life lies in the fact of suffering, for where there is no suffering, no consciousness of karmic bondage, there will be no power of attaining spiritual experience and thereby reaching the field of nondistinction. Unless we agree to suffer, we cannot be free of suffering." The Bible is also clear on this point: "Consider it all joy, my brethren, when you encounter various trials, knowing that the testing of your faith produces endurance" (James 1:2–3). In the fourth century, Rabbi Eleazar Ben Jacob eloquently put forth the Jewish theology of suffering when he wrote, "When sufferings come upon him man must utter thanks to God, for suffering draws man near unto the Holy One, blessed be He."

In the world of secular wisdom the similar theme, that suffering builds character and proffers wisdom, abounds. One of my most beloved heroes, the great humanitarian Helen Keller, lost her sight and her hearing at a very young age. Rather than cursing her fate, she instead attributed all her accomplishments to what she had learned as a result of her hardships. To Helen Keller, suffering was a mighty though savage teacher. "Character cannot be developed in ease and quiet," she said. "Only through experience of trial and suffering can the soul be strengthened, vision cleared, ambition inspired, and success achieved." The late-nineteenth-century Swiss writer Henri Amiel, who was best known for his "Journal," which was, and is, considered a masterpiece of self-examination, wrote, "Suffering was a curse from which man fled, now it becomes a purification of the soul, a sacred trial sent by Eternal Love, a divine dispensation meant to sanctify and ennoble us, an acceptable aid to faith, a strange initiation into happiness." British writer and prime minister Benjamin Disraeli recognized suffering as a critical element on the path to knowledge. "Seeing much, suffering much, and studying much are the three pillars of learning," he wrote. "The ultimate measure of man is not where he stands in moments of comfort," said Dr. Martin Luther King, Jr., "but where he stands at times of challenge and controversy." The idea that our pain can be a source of enlightenment is even acknowledged in a bumper sticker I saw recently that made me laugh: "Oh No! Not another one of life's lessons!"

As adults most of us do our best to avoid life's trials and tribulations, regardless of the lessons they might impart. After all, who wants to suffer? Even more so as parents we often strive to protect our children from any bump on the road of their development. And although obstacles in our path may not be thought of as "real" suffering, they teach us about the psychological strengths necessary for making the best out of challenging circumstances. Numerous research studies have shown that adversity and trials in childhood that don't overwhelm can strengthen a child's self-confidence and lay down the bedrock for future resiliency in life's difficult times. In the 1970s Freudian-trained Viennese psychoanalyst Heinz Kohut departed from more traditional views and offered a holistic theory about human personality development. One of the elements of his theory states that there is a level of difficulty—he called it "optimal frustration"—that actually helps a child to prepare him- or herself for the realities of living a human life. In his view, children who are given everything and protected from all challenges never learn the skills necessary to cope with the problems they will inevitably face in life. It's beneficial for a child to reach out and work at something to fulfill his or her own needs. Of course, the word *optimal* is critical here. Many of the world's children suffer hardships that far outweigh their abilities to cope. Starvation, violence, poverty, abuse, or devastating illnesses greatly exceed what might be thought of as "optimal." But in families in which a child's basic needs are met and he or she is loved and cherished, some struggle builds character.

According to Kohut, optimal frustration comes about when a child is left to attain a challenging goal in a nurturing environment. This encourages the child to take over fulfilling needs for him- or herself as he or she develops. Optimal frustration is the infant sucking on her own thumb while waiting a few minutes for Mom to feed her. Optimal frustration is created by loving parents who stand at just the perfect distance—not too close and not too far away—while proudly watching their toddler learn to walk. Optimal frustration is created by your nail-biting patience as you watch your preteen daughter miss a hundred free throws before she sinks one and you high-five her yelling "Nothing but net." These challenging opportunities are a vaccine to children—they inoculate them against the false belief that one will never have to try hard in life in order to overcome obstacles and difficulties.

I'm pretty sure that Victor Maklyn of Philadelphia never read Kohut's theory, but he's allegedly brought a lawsuit against his wealthy parents based on its assumptions. This twenty-one-year-old is suing Mom and Dad—financier George Maklyn and his wife, Judith—for $100,000-a-year "alimony" because they spoiled him rotten. His attorneys claim that he became accustomed to an easy, comfortable lifestyle—one that he could never provide for himself with his limited experience and education.

"I spent twenty-one years living in the lap of luxury, driving my Porsche, wearing designer clothes, partying at the finest clubs, eating gourmet food in the family mansion. How am I supposed to get along on my own?" said Victor. I guess Victor's parents had never heard of the theory of optimal frustration. Here's the best part: "Mom and Dad made sure I never had to lift a finger. They never made me get a summer job. They offered to get me into a top college, but I didn't feel like doing all that studying. It seemed like an awful lot of work, so I said no. They should have insisted but they didn't." Victor asks plaintively, "What am I supposed to do, flip burgers? Wash cars?"

Truthfully, I'm not certain of the accuracy of this story. I tried to find a number for the Maklyns but there was no listing. I admit that I read it in one of those weekly rags you find at the supermarket check-outs while waiting in the express line, the kind of publication with black-and-white photos of human/alien hybrids and at least one first-hand report of an Elvis sighting at a midwestern diner. "Always interesting, not always true" is my way of looking at most of those hot sheets, but this particular story resonated with me because it was an over-the-top version of the kind of blaming that I hear every day as a psychotherapist.

"My mother never taught me anything that I needed to know," one of my clients told me.[1] "She never made me stay in college. So all I've ever had are these rotten factory jobs. And now I'm injured and I can't go back to work." Evelyn is an intelligent woman who has had many opportunities to improve her situation. But, she doesn't see it that way. When pressed, she admits that she dropped out of college to travel around the country with her bass-playing boyfriend in spite of her mother's objections. Although her single-parent mother worked at two jobs to have the money to send her to college, Evelyn still blames her for not snatching her out of a dingy blues club and returning her to the dorm. Besides the obvious lack of personal responsibility Evelyn takes for her actions, college was a long time ago for her. Evelyn is now in her fifties and could have chosen to go back and finish her degree many times over the years. In fact, this current hardship has just opened this door to Evelyn once more. Two months ago, she was injured at work when a barrel of heavy, dry chemicals fell on her knee. The damage to the joint was significant and because she had already suffered knee injuries from playing sports as a teenager, her doctors recommended that Evelyn find another job that doesn't force her to be on her feet all day as her current one does. With this single restriction, Evelyn is expected to be able to walk normally and be free of pain.

In light of the medical advice she received, Evelyn's been offered education and training for a new career through Rehabilitative Services. The chance to get the education she needs to become the teacher she's told me she's always wanted to be is at hand and will be paid for by her Workmen's Comp and state resources. But, so far she's refused to embrace these options. I've tried to help Evelyn see that, although it is a terrible thing that she's suffered this injury, it has presented an opportunity that wasn't there before. She nods in agreement but then does nothing. In our sessions, Evelyn continues to share how she's furious at life and has told me that "it isn't fair" more times than I can count. How could anyone disagree? It's true that life isn't always fair. But Evelyn keeps playing this same tape over and over in her head, magnifying the injustice of it all. Not only is the tape playing for her but she also broadcasts it aloud so often to her friends that they're sick of it. She tells me they are tending to avoid her and her litany of negativity. Evelyn doesn't see that her actions have contributed to her growing solitude. Her isolation just reinforces her belief that no one has suffered as she has and nobody understands what she's going through.

My attempts to gently refocus Evelyn on what she can do now in spite of her loss fall on deaf ears. Evelyn seems to want only to use this painful time as an excuse to rationalize her anger, drink too much alcohol, and complain bitterly about the turn her life has taken. It seems to me that a great deal of Evelyn's suffering is self-created by her refusal to relinquish the role of victim at the hands of uncaring fate. It's true that she can't undo the damage to her knee, but I know that she could change her response to this unfortunate event. At the moment, I don't think that Evelyn is growing from her experience of suffering.

It makes me very sad that Evelyn is stuck in such suffering—even more so because her psychological pain seems to emanate from her worldview rather than from the unfortunate accident that broke her knee. Looking at a case like Evelyn's, I think that perhaps even to ask the questions about how we can grow through difficult, painful times suggests a certain amount of consciousness. Compassion is a central spiritual value, and we're not here to judge who deserves it and who doesn't. It's important to show kindness and patience with people who have become hard because they've suffered. But Evelyn—and lots of other people like her—demonstrate that it can't be the experience of suffering itself that gives rise to psychological and spiritual growth. Anne Morrow Lindbergh once said, "I do not believe that sheer suffering teaches. If suffering alone taught, all the world would be wise, since everyone suffers." Many people not only do not become wiser or grow in positive ways through suffering but, in fact, also lose ground in enlightenment and compassion. Instead of learning, they fall apart. Instead of growing, they become angry, jaded, self-pitying, pessimistic, and closed hearted—stuck forever in endless Sturm und Drang. Why? What are the differences between people who become bitter and those who become better through the gut-wrenching losses and anguish that everyone—sooner or later—will experience? What can each of us learn that will brace us for our next inevitable bout with suffering?

As I was remembering Evelyn and how an unfortunate but not-necessarily tragic event has catapulted her into depression and soul-numbing pessimism, I thought about an independent film I had seen a year or so earlier. At the 1996 Academy Awards, a beautiful young Asian woman, Jessica Yu, accepted the Best Short Subject Documentary Oscar for *Breathing Lessons*. I was struck by her acceptance speech that so whimsically highlighted the contrast between the grossly under-funded world of indie films and the glamour and money of Hollywood award ceremonies. "You know you've entered into new territory," she said, "when you realize your dress costs more than your film." As I net-worked around trying to find a copy of this movie, I also found out that Jessica Yu had directed an earlier short film that captured children's facial expression while eating really, really tart candy. It's called *Sour Death Balls*. I knew that I'd enjoy any movie made by someone with her outrageous sense of humor, and so I went out and rented her award-winning film. I was not disappointed.

Breathing Lessons is an unsentimental documentary about the life of severely disabled poet and writer Mark O'Brien. When he was six years old and just about to start the first grade, Mark was stricken with polio. He was one of the last of the baby boomers to contract this devastating disease. Mark was in a coma for more than two months and wasn't expected to survive, but he did. Life would never be the same for him, though. Polio left him paralyzed from the neck down, a condition that required him to spend every night in an iron lung in order to breathe.

The O'Brien family refused to place Mark in a nursing home and did whatever they could to help him live up to his fullest potential. Mark refers to his mother's care as "a miracle of love." "It showed what love can do to transform a person, to ennoble a person," he says. In spite of his tremendous physical limitations, Mark's parents fought to enroll him in a special disabled-students' program at the University of California. He learned to type by holding a stick in his mouth and was able to get around—with help—on an electric gurney. In 1982, Mark graduated from Berkeley with a B.A. in English, but his dream of going on to a master's in journalism was ended when he was struck again, this time by post-polio syndrome (PPS). This condition strikes polio sur-vivors anywhere from ten to forty years after recovery from the initial poliomyelitis virus. PPS delivers new and devastating symptoms of chronic fatigue, muscle and joint pain, slowly progressing muscle weakness, breathing difficulties, and muscle atrophy. Since the onset of this new challenge, Mark's had to spend all but three hours a month in his iron lung.

It would be easy to feel pity for Mark—a brilliant, vibrant man imprisoned in a body that isn't even able to breathe without help. But Mark would be the first to reject this overly limited and limiting view of his existence. "Being disabled is horrible. Monstrous," he told a reporter in 1997. "But it is still being alive, and there are possibilities." What he has done with those possibilities would be impressive for anyone in any full or limited physical condition.

Mark's world is encased in the rhythm of his machine. He lies flat on his back, his head at a permanent and wrenching right angle, his body wrapped in a tin can of a machine. Every three seconds, his iron lung—a 640-pound mechanical vacuum chamber that's almost as long as a subcompact car—exerts a push-pull motion on his helpless chest muscles. It pumps air into his lungs, and then releases it. Since worldwide vaccinations against polio have become a reality, there are only 150 iron lungs in use in the world. But it is the humming and whooshing sound of this machine that is the vibration of the life force to Mark. He has only moved his left knee, left foot, and head on his own since 1955. The iron lung allows his lungs to receive the air he needs to keep his heart pumping and blood flowing. Massage and physical therapists manipulate and massage the rest of his body. He's decorated the iron lung with pictures of his family, his girlfriend, the Virgin Mary—Mark is a devout Catholic—and Jessica Yu accepting the Oscar. A bright pink button is attached to his pillow. It simply says, "Not Dead Yet."[2]

In spite of his unmerciful disability, Mark reaches across the great divide toward other people—able-bodied and disabled—with a sure wit, a nimble mind, and a heart filled with a desire to communicate. He eloquently argues for the rights of disabled people and attests to the importance of independent living. He gives voice to his own savage experience in words both startling and often very funny. He writes evocatively and joyfully about his crushes on nurses, his penchant for cross-dressing, and his passion for baseball, especially for his home team, the San Francisco Giants. He fights for his life like a warrior, but his weapons are words—the offerings of a journalist and a poet. In his work and in each excruciating moment of getting through the day, Mark insists that we look past his body and into the meaning of his life and our own.

Mark describes the art of his breathing:

> *Grasping for straws is easier;*
> *You can see the straws.*
> *"This most excellent canopy, the air, look you,"*
> *Presses down upon me*
> *At fifteen pounds per square inch,*
> *A dense, heavy, blue-glowing ocean,*
> *Supporting the weight of condors*
> *That swim its churning currents.*
> *All I get is a thin stream of it,*
> *A finger's width of the rope that ties me to life*
> *As I labor like a stevedore to keep the connection.*
> *Water wouldn't be so circumspect;*
> *Water would crash in like a drunken sailor,*
> *But air is prissy and genteel,*
> *Teasing me with its nearness and pervading immensity.*
> *The vast, circumambient atmosphere*
> *Allows me but ninety cubic centimeters*
> *Of its billions of gallons and miles of sky.*
> *I inhale it anyway,*
> *Knowing that it will hurt*
> *In the weary ends of my crumpled paper bag lungs.*[3]

Mark O'Brien died in the early morning hours of July 4, 1999, just one day after his beloved Giants knocked the socks off the L.A. Dodgers (9–1) during a six-game winning streak.

⟊

In spite of his limitations and pain, it is clear that Mark O'Brien enriched his life with meaning. Maybe that's the key to enduring suffering in all its many forms. Twentieth-century psychiatrist Carl Jung insisted that it is not suffering itself but suffering without meaning that is the real scourge of human life. He believed that when we understand that we are all part of a world in which suffering is inevitable and universal, we can better understand how to grow through that pain. This is worth stating again: When we understand that we are all part of a world in which suffering is inevitable and universal, we can better understand how to grow through that pain. To Jung there were clear and significant differences between what he called "real" and "neurotic" suffering.

Real suffering is an authentic and realistic response to the ragged wounds of living a human life. It's also unavoidable and an essential part of *every* human life. Illness, loss of loved ones, disappointment, decline, death, limitations, and imperfections startle and shake us. But they awaken us to find meaning, dignity, and significance in our lives. They open the heart to pure compassion and newfound creative energy. Real suffering is useful. It propels us to new levels of consciousness and self-knowledge. It is through suffering and pain that we break down our habitual barriers between ourselves and others and allow for the entrance of a transpersonal, transcendent perspective: a full appreciation of our intimate and profound spiritual connections. Jungian analyst and writer James Hollis writes that suffering is an essential requirement for psychological and spiritual maturation, for without it one would remain "unconscious, infantile, and dependent."[4] The moments when we are stripped bare of our illusions and confront the realities of human existence introduce the most important questions we can ask ourselves: Who am I? What is my purpose here? Where do I find meaning in my life? What is my relationship to God or some higher, transpersonal power?

Jung saw the arrival of these questions as an important step in anyone's development. He believed they arose in light of the authentic suffering that he felt was essential to psychological health and the process of self-discovery he termed *individuation*. Instead of searching for happiness, he advised that people should search for *meaning*. He also understood that happiness is both an unattainable and incorrect goal because it will never last. He wrote in his autobiography, *Memories, Dreams, Reflections*, "The world into which we are born is brutal and cruel, and at the same time, one of divine beauty. Which element we think outweighs the other, whether meaninglessness or meaning, is a matter of temperament. If meaninglessness were absolutely preponderant, the meaningfulness of life would vanish to an increasing degree with each step in our development. But that is—or seems to me—not the case. Probably, as in all metaphysical questions, both are true: Life is—or has—meaning and meaninglessness. I cherish the anxious hope that meaning will preponderate and win the battle."[5]

In contrast to real, authentic suffering, Jung held that another kind of suffering, neurotic suffering, offers no meaning. Jung called it an "unconscious fraud" and declared neurotic suffering to be bogus and with no moral merit.[6] He saw neurotic suffering as a flight from the wounds of life and as an unconscious—and unsuccessful—attempt to heal them. On the one hand, symptoms such as anxiety, worry, ruminations, low self-esteem, depression, projections of unconscious complexes onto other people, addictions, and a sackcloth-and-ashes kind of guilt that causes people never to feel worthy are all aspects of neurotic suffering. On the other hand, deep anguish about our ordinary human imperfections and limitations is a symptom of real suffering. The pain that life will deliver in the form of loss, illness, or death can wake us up and deliver us to a state of consciousness in which we can make each moment count and find meaning in our existence. Neurotic suffering is completely different from the recognition of these existential truths. Neurotic suffering is a refusal to discover the meaning in our pain through a childish insistence that things should be as we want them to be and not as they are. Neurotic suffering expresses itself as self-pity and envy toward people whose lives seem better, less difficult, than our own. It seems to me that to suffer unnecessarily or through self-inflicted wounds is more masochistic than heroic. The difference between real and neurotic suffering to writer and Jungian analyst Marion Woodman is simple and clear. "Real suffering," she writes, "burns clean; neurotic suffering creates more and more soot."[7]

Neurotic suffering keeps pain going. While real suffering heals through mourning and meaning, neurotic suffering just rolls on and on and is self-imposed. It creates its own cycle of pain that is repetitive and endless, like a dog chasing its own tail. In *The Aion*, Jung wrote: "It is often tragic to see how blatantly a man bungles his own life and the life of others yet remains totally incapable of seeing how much the whole tragedy originates in himself, and how he continually feeds it and keeps it going."[8]

To Jung, neurosis "must be understood, ultimately, as the suffering of a soul which has not discovered its meaning."[9] Psychiatrist Viktor Frankl agrees. Frankl survived the horrors of the Nazi concentration camps, including Auschwitz and Dachau. His mother, father, brother, and wife did not; they died in the camps or the gas ovens. Except for Viktor and his sister, Stella, the entire family perished. In an instant, his whole former, comfortable life as a doctor encircled by a loving family vanished. His every possession was taken from him and he suffered from hunger, cold, and brutal beatings. For more than three years, death surrounded him at every moment like a filthy shroud. Soon after entering the camps, Frankl realized that he had "nothing to lose but his ridiculously naked life." However, in spite of the pain and torture that he experienced, Frankl refused to relinquish his humanity, his love, or his sense of responsibility to bear witness to the world. In spite of the atrocities around him, he remained courageous and filled with hope. In choosing "to be worthy of suffering"—as Dostoyevsky had once written—Frankl was able to rise above his outward fate, by making inner, conscious decisions about how he would respond to his circumstances. In his remarkable little book, *Man's Search for Meaning*, Frankl gives testimony to the existential belief that life is filled with suffering and that the only way to survive is to find meaning in it. "Once an individual's search for meaning is successful, it not only renders him happy but also gives him the capability to cope with suffering," he wrote.[10]

In his book, Frankl announces that he himself is filled with a "tragic optimism," a philosophy that allows him to say "yes" to life in spite of pain, suffering, and death. He has little patience with the nihilistic idea that being has no meaning and considers the common belief in that as a "mass neurosis." It is this philosophy, Frankl says, that served him in the camps and allowed him to maintain his dignity, grace, and compassion in spite of the unspeakable atrocities to which he was subjected. He holds that it is precisely man's search for meaning that is a primary motivation of our existence and one that gives us a reason to live in spite of life's tragedies.

To Frankl, meaning can be found in the fact that human beings are self-determining. Although we cannot always change the fact that terrible things will happen to us, we have every power to change how we will respond to those painful events in our lives. We do not simply exist but have the intrinsic authority—this "last of human freedoms"—to decide what our existence will be, what we will become in the next moment. "We must never forget that we may also find meaning in life even when confronted with a hopeless situation, when facing a fate that cannot be changed," he wrote. "For what then matters is to bear witness to the uniquely human potential at its best, which is to transform a personal tragedy into a triumph, to turn one's predicament into a human achievement. When we are no longer able to change a situation—just think of an incurable disease such as inoperable cancer—we are challenged to change ourselves."[11] Frankl was fond of quoting Nietzsche, who said, "He who has a *why* to live can bear with almost any *how*."

⌒

I finally went to bed that night after the accident thinking about Nietzsche and Frankl and Mark O'Brien and the Phoenix and my dad and Deanne and their banged-up bodies and still talking about blessings. Everyone else was sound asleep. Dorothy was snoring quietly on the floor, but my thoughts were still racing. My mother used to talk about my being "too tired to sleep" when I'd had a particularly wild day running on the beach and swimming in the ocean at the Jersey shore as a kid. That's how I was this night—too tired to sleep. I couldn't stop thinking about people I knew, in my private life and my professional one as a psychotherapist. I wondered about how many of the symptoms that I saw in them—anxiety, depression, isolation, addiction, relationship problems—resulted from the failure to accept the inevitability of suffering and to change our responses to it. I thought about how we have the choice to mourn while carrying hope within us, how we can feel sadness while being brave, how we can learn to live better, more joyfully, more courageously in spite of the hard times that life will inevitably foist upon us.

As dawn's gray light seeped into my room, it was obvious that sleep didn't fit into my schedule at this point. Dorothy opened her eyes briefly, then sighed and closed them again when I stepped past her on my way to the kitchen. The sun was already coming up, and we wanted to get an early start for the hospitals. I made a cup of tea and decided I'd be the first into the shower, then run out and get some bagels and fruit so that we could all have a quick breakfast. As the teakettle heated up, I sat and stared at a framed print that my niece Katelyn had left at the house. Most people call them "Magic Eyes," after the company best known for designing and retailing them. They're actually called "stereograms" (Single Image Random Dot Stereograms), and you've seen them in poster shops and bookstores throughout the country. They're computer-generated images. Their colorful, wild, wallpaper-like repetitive graphics contain an underlying three-dimensional picture. Some people can see the embedded image quite easily; others can stare for long moments before it becomes clear, and some can't ever seem to see it. I'm somewhere in the middle—If I'm patient I can usually discern the three-dimensional part, but I'm not as quick to pick it up as children so often are. I've reprinted one below:

Figure 1-1: Stereogram

Here are instructions from Magic Eye for the best viewing of the hidden image in the stereogram:

Hold the center of the image *right up to your nose* (it should be blurry). Stare as though you are looking *through* the image.

Very, very slowly move the image away from your face *until the two boxes above the image turn into three boxes!* If you see four boxes, move the image farther away from your face until you see three boxes. If you still see one or two boxes, start over! *When you have the three boxes, hold the image still* (try not to blink) and the hidden image will slowly appear!

Once you see the hidden image and depth, you can look around the entire 3-D image, and the *longer you look, the clearer it becomes.*[12]

In spite of my less-than-stellar ability to see the embedded image easily, I love these things. I find them to be an accurate and powerful metaphor for the way we come to consciousness. Something is right there in front of our faces and we don't get it, we don't see it. Then suddenly, and often for reasons we don't even understand, we get it. We finally get it. At that moment when this epiphany happens we can hardly believe that we couldn't see the embedded image right off the bat, but we didn't. And like consciousness, once we've seen it, new ones become easier to see in the future.

Take a moment to look at the stereogram shown here. Seeing the embedded, three-dimensional image depends on having the depth perception of two eyes. People with impaired depth perception, those with extremely dominant vision in one eye, or those who have sight in only one eye will have difficulty seeing the image hidden within the repetitive pattern. But if you have reasonable vision in both eyes, all you need is a calm attitude and patience. Let your eyes relax and stare as if you were looking through the image, actually focusing several inches beyond it. In a way, you are trying to see the hidden image without looking at it by "defocusing" your eyes. After a little while, a 3-D image will pop into view. Once you see it, you will be startled and in disbelief that you couldn't see it straightaway. Spend at least five minutes with this stereogram (read the specific directions that follow the image). Clues to the answer are found in the notes section for this chapter at the end of the book. If you fail to see it after spending some time and giving it a good try, turn to the notes section and then return to this page and look at it again. Those who see it right off or are patient in waiting for the image to come forward from the background won't have to look for a clue. The answer will be obvious.

Finding this "Magic Eye" on this particular morning seemed to be a bright moment of synchronicity. Maybe suffering could be better understood if we were able to bring it into a new kind of consciousness, into a new kind of focus. There's a lot to be learned from the great minds and bold spirits who have tackled hard questions about suffering and learned something in the process. This does not mean that we should feel bad about ourselves or guilty because we don't bear suffering as well as we might. I like to take the gentle approach with myself— learning rather than scolding. To be sure, most of us have had our share of neurotic, self-imposed suffering, myself included. Mostly it's much easier to ask "Why me?" than "Why not me?" when hard times present themselves. Transformation is always a struggle. But the experiences and wisdom of people who have grown from and found enlightenment in life's darkest moments could be our greatest teachers.

We're all bound to suffer. Some of us will experience great tragedies in our lives like the death of a loved one, the diagnosis of a serious illness, or a natural disaster that wipes away everything we've ever held dear. The loss of a relationship burns through our sense of well-being and can send us spiraling. Being fired or downsized or "outsourced" from a job engenders loss of confidence and outright fear about how we'll pay the bills. Isolation and loneliness often render a pain that chills the soul and swamps the spirit. It's clear to me that there are lots of ways to suffer and lots to learn. Being able to tell the difference between authentic suffering and the avoidable, unhealthy neurotic type would be a tremendous tool and provide a great potential for personal growth for all of us. For if we can master the art of suffering we'll very likely find our courage, our meaning, and a renewed sense of joy at the remarkable mystery of life. In the process of all that, we could very well find ourselves. Most important, we may just discover through this journey how intimately connected we are to all that is—to one another and to a higher, more transcendent reality. In doing so, we'll do much to confirm that—even in our greatest suffering—we are not alone.

✑

Over my tea, my stereogram, and my philosophical musings, I heard my family begin to stir. Dorothy came down the steps to the kitchen wagging her tail, eager for another trip outside. Shelley came into the kitchen holding Connor—just one year old and bright as a button. He laughed out loud, reached down to pet Dorothy, and shared a teething cookie that she found to be quite tasty. Slowly, everyone began to assemble in the kitchen. Someone made coffee, juice appeared, we discussed the best route to take to visit two distant hospitals and still avoid the D.C. rush-hour traffic. In the midst of everything that had happened the day before, there was life and love in this house. I felt the awe-inspiring presence of hope and I wondered whether this was one of the blessings that Dad and Deanne had talked about. It was in that gentle moment that the plan for this book was birthed.

The Truth about Life—
Everyone Lives a Drama

Life gives us magic
And life gives us tragedy
Everyone suffers some loss.
Still we have faith in it,
Childlike hope.
There's a reason that outweighs the cost.

—From "The Color of Roses"[1]

I was once conducting a group therapy session in a psychiatric hospital. The participants did not have long-term, serious mental illnesses but were generally functional people who had been experiencing a difficult time—often as a result of a significant loss in their lives such as a divorce, the death of a loved one, or a similar event that had knocked the pins out from under them and sent them reeling. In short, they were people who'd been overwhelmed by suffering.

"I know one of the secrets of life," I said to the group that day. "Really!" they declared, and I could hear them scooting their chairs closer to mine. They sat stone silent and wide-eyed, not wanting to miss a second of this self-proclaimed wisdom. "If you only live long enough," I said, "you will lose everything." There was a brief silence as the words sunk in, then the sound of screeching chairs cut through the air. They were falling all over themselves as they scrambled to put as much distance between us as possible. "We're already having a hard time," one woman yelled. "Why are you telling us this?!" "Because it's true," I said. "And because in understanding this you can learn to live better."

Because something is true does not mean that it is easy to understand, accept, or even to recognize. As with the stereogram, the hidden images of life's truths are there for us to see, but they often elude us. We can almost make out the hidden picture, then the colors blur and the image is lost again. When something is both true and painful, we have an even harder time acknowledging and accepting it. For in these cases we often do our best *not* to let the truth come to full light in hopes of trying to avoid the pain we anticipate it will bring. Figuratively, we all want to screech our chairs away from the notion that suffering is in store for every one of us. In fact, many of us choose to live our whole lives trying, in vain, to escape that truth. "There is nothing there!" we say, staring at the picture of life around us in which others are suffering loss and pain, smug in our conviction. "You may be suffering, but that doesn't mean I will!" we can think in our fortunate times, breathing a sigh of relief as we glance nervously over our shoulder. But the truth that suffering is a part of life remains, and only when we let that truth in will we be able to look beyond the suffering to its meaning. To see the image in the sterogram we must shift our perspective. To see and accept the truth about suffering requires a similar shift in consciousness.

First, in order to realize the fundamental truths about suffering, we must first understand that everyone suffers. And second, we must accept that suffering is the force that knocks out our illusionary beliefs about life and thrusts us toward new consciousness about ourselves and the true nature of reality. In spite of all the ways we try to deny the actuality of suffering, I believe most of us know these things in our heads. But that's not enough. We have to know these truths in our hearts—in the deepest, emotional places of our being. We have to feel them. It is only then that we can gather the rewards that they bring: the growth of consciousness, compassion, and courage. The stories that I've included here are ones that touch me with the truth and ground me during my own suffering. After my father and Deanne's accident I went back again and again, seeking the truth that is in plain sight.

I came across many stories, myths, and powerful examples from religion, history, my own life, and others I knew and some I heard of and then sought out that I found eloquently speak the truth about what it is to be human. These stories touch me in such a way that my head and my heart recognize the part that suffering plays and I can begin to allow it in. It is my hope, in writing this book, to seek the wisdom of the ages, to revisit and retell the stories that touch our hearts, shake off our illusions, and expand our consciousness. Gently, but with the power of truth, they call us to a new wakefulness. I hope they also help you begin to see the world, and your own life, with a new perspective. The story of Kisagotami is one such story that moved me when I first read it more than twenty years ago as I began to explore Eastern teachings and mystical experience. The tale is from the Buddhist *Dharma* and dates back more than two thousand years. This parable of a mustard seed takes place in India, but its lessons are universal.

Kisagotami was inconsolable. This young woman, married to the only son of a wealthy man, had birthed a beautiful son. Everything in her life was perfect; she was living a fairy tale. But just when her beloved son began to walk on his own, he was stricken with a terrible illness and suddenly died. The young mother, desperate in her grief, carried the dead child clasped to her bosom and went from house to house asking people for medicine or miracles: anything that would bring him back to life.

Naturally, all the people felt very sad for this grieving mother, but no one could help. Finally, one old man said, "My good girl, I myself have no such medicine as you ask for, but I think I know of one who has."

Kisagotami begged him for the name of the one who could restore her son to life.

"The Buddha can give you medicine. Go to him," the old man said.

So Kisagotami went to the great teacher, Gautama—the Buddha—and, with deep homage, begged him, "Master, do you know any medicine that can help me?"

Buddha listened with infinite compassion and gently said, "There is only one way to heal this affliction. Bring me back a mustard seed from a house that has never known death."

Relieved that so common a drug as a mustard seed could end her suffering, Kisagotami left and walked toward the city. Still clutching the body of her beloved son to her breast, she went in search of a mustard seed.

She stopped at the first house she came to and said, "I have been told by the Buddha to return with a mustard seed from a house that has never known death."

"Dear child, we will happily give you a mustard seed, but many people have died in this house. Just last month, we lost our beloved mother," she was told.

She went to the next house. "There have been countless deaths in our family," she heard.

She went to the houses of the rich and poor, the powerful and the meek. "We have also lost a son," said one. "We have lost our parents," said another. "The living are few, but the dead are many," said yet another. She went to every house in the city, until she realized that the Buddha's condition could never be fulfilled.

At last, not being able to find a single house where no one had died, her mind began to clear. She carried her dead son into the forest, buried him, and returned to the Buddha.

"Do you have the mustard seed?" he asked.

"No," she said. "But I understand the lesson you are teaching me. Grief made me blind and I thought that I was the only one that had suffered at the hands of death."

"Why have you come back?" asked the Buddha.

"I want to know the truth about life and death," she replied.

And so the Buddha began to teach her: "There is only one law in the universe that never changes, and that is that all things change, and that all things are impermanent. The death of your beloved child has helped you to see that. Your pain has opened your heart to the truth. I will show it to you."

The woman knelt at the Buddha's feet and followed his teachings for the rest of her life. Near the end of it, it is said, Kisagotami attained enlightenment.

The simple story of Kisagotami quietly speaks volumes to me about the true nature of reality. Kisagotami clearly experienced more than a "bump along the road of life" with the loss of her child. Her inability to accept her son's death was not neurotic suffering, it was the deep and fundamental pain brought on by real suffering. Kisagotami's story illustrates not only the way in which we often try to avoid suffering but also the fact that no one escapes it. Being human means that we will all suffer great pain. However, when we are in the midst of the searing grief of great loss—as Kisagotami was—it's easy to feel that we are the only human being ever to have had to endure such anguish, such loss, such vulnerability. Surely Mark O'Brien may have felt a singular loneliness, lying on his back, with a mechanical breath as his constant companion. We would all probably agree that he had every reason to feel isolated by his fate and be angry in light of it. We would most likely be able to relate to such feelings. But the archetypal drama that is played out through our individual lives is both ancient and commonplace. The losses we experience in our lives are different in their forms and arrival dates, but they inevitably come. Rarely are we not surprised. We all accept the reality of automobile accidents, yet nobody is prepared for the phone call on a Tuesday afternoon from an emergency room nurse who gently asks, "Is this Kathleen Brehony?" While everybody's life is unique, we are all subject to the mortal realities of aging, illness, and death ourselves and in those we love. Existence it seems is, as the German poet Rainer Maria Rilke wisely observed, "living our lives saying good-bye." But in spite of this, many of us don't accept the companion suffering is throughout our lives.

Kisagotami learned the hard way that death, loss, and suffering are universal experiences as she walked from house to house, unable to find one that sorrow had not visited. We would all like to believe, as Kisagotami did, that there is a house, or a place, or a group of people—preferably those we love—that lies beyond suffering's reach. Life often brutally reveals that this is just not so. And although philosophers and thinkers of all cultures have expressed the certainty of change and loss in many different ways, I find that Eastern traditions seem to emphasize the transient nature of existence more clearly than we do in the West. Time and again their poems and stories highlight that change is the natural order of the universe and that everything in our lives is subject to it. An ancient Buddhist text captures the nature of life with simple elegance:

> *This existence of ours is as transient as autumn clouds.*
> *To watch the birth and death of beings is like looking at the*
> *movements of a dance.*
> *A lifetime is like a flash of lightning in the sky,*
> *Rushing by, like a torrent down a steep mountain.*[2]

Surrounded by life's impermanence, still, we've evolved some curious explanations for why we lose those people and things we've become attached to and suffer as a result. Although there's no evidence that suffering is punishment for sin or retribution for "negative karma," we often imagine that such must be the case. This notion sprouts naturally from two flawed assumptions: one, that life should always be fair; and two, that people (especially other people) get what they deserve. What seductive concepts these are! They allow us to perceive the world as orderly and comprehensible. There is no mystery or chaos in this worldview—there is a God or some creative intelligence who has established rules that we can understand and manipulate. These ideas suggest that that if we are good and play by the rules we may be spared the kinds of sorrow and pain that others are subject to. If only that were true!

Such a view of life is not only false; it's dangerous. If we believe that life should be fair and we suffer only because of some misbehavior, then it becomes a pretty natural response to blame ourselves when we go through difficult, painful times. With this as a foundation for our reasoning, we can easily experience profound shame and guilt, asking, "What have I done to deserve this?" when life deals us one of its inescapable blows. This way of thinking also reinforces a false sense of separation, as if somehow we are different from everyone else in the world. Kisagotami had surely seen pain all around her as she grew up, but the notion that she could also be stricken with the loss of her beloved child was beyond her understanding or acceptance. With such a point of view, she suffered in a lonely place; she could not access the comfort that comes from a community of soul mates who would understand her loss because they had felt the same kind of pain. I had a similar response when my dad was hurt. Given all that my father—a nice guy, by the way—had been through in the past few years, I felt that he was getting "more than his share" of suffering as I stood by his hospital bed. I was angry and would have liked to vent my feelings, which would have sounded something like this: "Excuse me? Whom do I talk to about this? This does not coincide with my understanding of the rules!" This sense of entitlement to a pain-free existence and the alienation from one another and from the truth about life it breeds can be more isolating than suffering itself. And beyond the consequences of such willful naïveté, the assumption that suffering is the result of misbehavior does not fit the facts all around us. Quite simply, it can't explain the suffering of innocents, can't offer a believable explanation as to why terrible losses are so often bestowed on people who have done nothing wrong. How can we possibly offer the idea that pain and an early death are the just deserts for a three-year-old diagnosed with leukemia, a good man who dies while saving the life of a drowning person, the six million Jewish people annihilated in Nazi concentration camps, or the little children starving to death on the arid plains of Africa?

Suffering and loss are intrinsic and inevitable parts of living a human life in our less-than-perfect world. If we look at the way life unfolds around us with a clear view, we see suffering is a visitor upon the good and innocent people as well as upon the greatest sinner among us. Every religion and wisdom tradition teaches us that truth. In the New Testament, Matthew (5:45) reminds us that God "sends rain on the righteous and on the unrighteous."

In the Judeo-Christian tradition, suffering is brought about by a benevolent God who uses it as a tool to break down the outer man so that the Creator's love can be manifested and revealed to the believer. Suffering forms the ground for man's intimate, unencumbered union with God and occurs so that faith may be deepened, and so that both love and forgiveness can be most fully expressed. In this view, God has made a world that bestows suffering not as punishment but as a way to teach and redeem human beings.

Pain is a common way through which we come to understand that our life has a transcendent aspect, a larger dimension, and realize that "my life is not just about me." This transformed consciousness allows for the birth of true *compassion* (a word that literally means "to suffer with"). This heartfelt tenderness removes all barriers between oneself and others so that we can experience oneness with each other and the universe. I find that it is easy to recognize those who have true compassion; it is apparent in their interest in other people, their empathy, and in their eyes, which seem to look on the world and everything in it tenderly. What we also usually learn about truly compassionate people, as we come to know them, is that most often they have suffered some great loss.

These themes resonate most beautifully in the Old Testament story of Job. This is a familiar tale to most people raised in the Jewish or Christian traditions, but I'd like you to think of ways in which you have ever felt like Job as you read it.

Here's the story: Job is a very successful man by all accounts. If Job were living today he'd be driving a Mercedes and living in a mansion with a swimming pool. He has every bounty that life can bestow. But in spite of his wealth, he is not arrogant. He is a good man, always "blameless and upright." His life moves forward effortlessly until one day when Satan goes to visit Job's God—Yahweh. Yahweh points out Job to Satan and brags about just how good and loyal he is. Satan takes a look and isn't a bit impressed. Satan replies that it is quite easy for Job to worship him and turn away from evil since he's got everything he needs and more. Satan suggests a small wager. He bets Yahweh that Job wouldn't be quite so blameless and upright, so clear in his love for God, if things weren't so perfect in his life. In a way, Satan makes a good point. Isn't it easy to be "blameless and upright" when everything is going our way? Yahweh reluctantly agrees to let Satan test Job.

Soon after Satan and Yahweh make their bet, messengers report to Job that all his oxen and donkeys have been carried off by bandit tribes and all the servants have been killed. Another messenger arrives immediately thereafter and informs Job that a fire has fallen from heaven and burned up all the sheep. A new messenger follows to report that a different tribe has stolen all the camels. Before this messenger can even finish, yet another arrives to tell Job that a great wind came across the desert and struck the four corners of the house where all his children were eating and drinking wine. His seven strong sons and three beautiful daughters are dead.

Job is grief stricken but then rises above his anguish. He shaves his head, tears his robe, and falls to the ground and prays. He says, "Naked I came from my mother's womb, and naked shall I return there; the Lord gave and the Lord has taken away; blessed be the name of the Lord." In all this, Job does not sin or charge God with wrongdoing. In spite of his great losses, Job's faith is as strong as it has ever been.

The next day Satan comes again before Yahweh. He says that Job will relent in his integrity, will turn away from his worship of Yahweh, if his suffering increases to include his own flesh and bone. Satan asks to be allowed to give Job illness and physical pain. Yahweh reluctantly agrees to let Satan try this. This time Satan goes out and inflicts terrible sores on Job from the crown of his head to the soles of his feet.

In excruciating pain, Job finally calls out to his beloved Yahweh, "Why is this happening to me?" Job knows that he is not an evil man and has never done anything to deserve all the horrors that are raining down on his life. So now, he wants to die, which Yahweh will not allow. Failing that, Job wants answers. What is the justification for this kind of treatment by the Lord?

Job, like many others who suffer, lived his life honorably. He worshiped God and was thankful for all the blessings in his life. Yet, now, in spite of his good behavior, he endured one disaster after another. In spite of his anguish, Job continues to maintain his "integrity," his great faith in the omniscience and benevolence of God.

Hearing of his troubles, three friends arrive to counsel Job. They try to help him understand why all this is happening to him. They mean well, but they cannot tolerate the idea of an unfair or chaotic universe and look for rational answers to Job's plight. Three solutions come to their minds when they consider why a good man like Job should be suffering such a terrible fate: First, God is not as all-powerful as we have been led to believe. Second, God is not as good or as just as we've been told. Third, humanity is the source of evil and the cause of suffering. In other words: It's Job's fault.

Demanding clarity and order in the universe and informed by a theology of "retributive justice," Job's friends fixate on the third possible root of the problem. They offer glib platitudes and stock answers informed by orthodoxy and not by heart. "The reason that all these bad things are happening to you," they say, "is because you must have sinned." "What?!" Job says and refuses their conclusion. He knows he hasn't sinned. Instead, he decides that he's going to endure whatever he must until he learns the truth.

In spite of his continued suffering and lack of understanding it, Job never relinquishes his faith in God. Instead, he seeks a conversation, a union with God that will give him the relationship with that which he worships—if not the answers—that he yearns for. At last, God appears out of a whirlwind and shows all his power and majesty to Job. God points out all he's done and says something like "Where were you when I laid the foundation of the earth and put the stars in the heavens? Can you make snow and bears and mountain goats and clouds? Can you thunder with a voice like mine?" It is at this moment that Job is humbled. God never really gives a very clear answer as to why Job has suffered, but He invites Job into a warm and personal conversation and it is here that Job understands that he is loved and that God has suffered along with him. By accepting the freedom of will that God offers to him and all human beings, Job learns that he must open to the presence of an illogical and unjust universe. It is through his breaking down, his "dark night of the soul," that Job comes to a better understanding of these basic truths about life. In the end, like the rest of us, Job realizes he must resign himself to never fully knowing why he—a good man— suffers. He can only live with the paradox, experience the mystery.

Logical answers can never explain Job's suffering. But stripped of all that defined him, Job reached deeply into the well of his true Self—the soul—and came to know himself as a part of "all that is," in a direct and intimate relationship with God. In the process of breaking down and relinquishing his false self, Job comes to understand God's awesome power and his own relationship with Him. After all his travails, Job understands that it has been by trusting God in the midst of his suffering that he experienced his faith at the deepest level. So Job's devotion becomes more conscious, more alive, and God gives back to him twice what he had before. Job, now an awakened man with an even stronger character and faith, lives to be a hundred and forty years and sees four generations of his family grow and prosper. In the end, Job dies, "an old man and full of days."[3]

The drama of Job offers much to challenge and teach us all. But don't worry if you are still left with a nagging sense of the "unfairness" of Job's trials. The lessons of Job's story, and our own lives, are never fully learned. Here is the good news AND the bad news: Every life offers many "opportunities" to grapple with these questions, and to learn from loss. These lessons reflect such central mysteries of what it means to be human that all the world's religions and spiritual traditions share the same primary function: to answer the questions that emerge from the universal experiences of suffering. The story of how Buddhism began is another that deals with these same issues about suffering. But where the story of Job presents more questions than it answers, the story of Gautama Siddhartha may lead us to solutions and actions. I've discovered that with each retelling of this true story, I take something new away from it.

The historical Buddha was a wealthy prince named Gautama Siddhartha who was born in a northern province of India (in what is now present-day Nepal) in the sixth century B.C.E. Like Job, Gautama had many, many blessings. Gautama lived a pampered and sheltered life surrounded only by young, healthy friends, excellent food, the finest clothes, and every luxury that money could buy. He knew nothing of sickness, death, or human suffering until his curiosity about life got the better of him and he secretly slipped out of his father's royal compound with one of his servants. On his first trip beyond the walls of the kingdom, he saw a man begging on the side of the road. It was obvious that the man was sick and unable to walk. Gautama had never seen anything like this before and asked his servant about this man's situation. His servant explained that the man was sick and that illness is not an uncommon experience. On subsequent ventures out, Gautama saw a very old man, and his servant explained that this is what happens as people live—they age and wither. At last, he saw a funeral pyre. His servant explained that everyone dies. For the first time in his life, Gautama was shown the reality that human life inevitably contains illness, aging, and death. These realities disturbed him greatly. What could be the purpose of life, he thought, if it was so transient and so filled with suffering?

He was haunted by what he had seen and come to understand. One night, at the age of twenty-nine, Gautama kissed his wife and son goodbye, left his family's home, and set out to answer the question that plagued him. This has come to be known as the "Great Going Forth." He shaved his head, wore rags, and ate a single grain of rice a day as an ascetic in search of enlightenment. He traveled with wandering Hindu masters of the day studying philosophy and the way of *raja yoga*. He did everything he could think of to find the answer to the question of why people suffer.

Although Gautama tried many different paths to enlightenment, none satisfied him. He determined that he would sit and reflect on the truth about life until he found the answers. In fact, he vowed that he would not move from sitting in this one spot until illumination was his. It is said that the truth was revealed to him one night as he sat quietly meditating under a Bodi tree. He then dedicated his life to teaching others what he had learned. His followers called him "Buddha," which is based on the Sanskrit root word *budh* that simply means "to know" or "to wake up." Contemporary philosopher Huston Smith, one of the world's leading scholars on world religions, emphasizes Buddha's place—not as a god but as an enlightened, conscious man—when he describes the beginnings of the Buddhist tradition: "Buddhism begins with a man who shook off the daze, the doze, the dream-like inchoateness of ordinary awareness. It begins with the man who woke up."[4]

"Waking up" is a simple but powerful metaphor for consciousness. It suggests seeing the world anew—for the first time—as it really is. If we need a shift in consciousness to see the inevitability of suffering, we can understand how it takes the force and disruptiveness of suffering to wake us up to the truth about the nature of ourselves and of reality. In Buddha's case, his whole pursuit of enlightenment was propelled by the shock that he experienced when he encountered suffering for the first time. He saw his tidy, pleasant, overly indulged view of life as the false image it was. To me this story is so important, and I tell it often because it speaks directly to the shift in consciousness that suffering offers us. Through it we see that suffering is the way to wake up to the truths about ourselves and life itself. Of course, we cannot capture such enlightenment in an instant, though sometimes we get dashes of insight with blinding suddenness. We might not be able to see the world with the vision and clarity that Buddha did, but we can learn a great deal about it by knowing and applying the Four Noble Truths of Buddhism. They can act as a "wake-up call" to a new life of deeper meaning and purpose.

The Four Noble Truths of Buddhism emphasize the nature and inevitability of suffering as well as ways of transcending it. The First Noble Truth simply states that "life is suffering." The uninitiated may take this basic precept as evidence of a very pessimistic worldview, but nothing could be farther from the truth. The whole of Buddhist philosophy deals with discovering and accepting "what is." It aims at one single question, and that question is: How do we alleviate suffering?

The First Noble Truth is commonly translated into English incorporating the word *suffering*. But the Sanskrit word *dukkha* is not easy to translate. "Suffering" is not entirely accurate. *Dukkha*, actually, is better described as meaning "dissatisfaction" or "discontent." But really, even these words fail to convey the full meaning. *Dukkha* is used in Sanskrit and Pali—the languages in which Buddhist teachings were historically written—to describe a bone that has come out of its socket or an axle that is off center in relationship to its wheel. The word really implies that something has gone wrong or become "dislocated." Imagining the way a disjointed wheel on a cart would wobble and shake as the cart moved forward is the best way to understand the actual meaning of *dukkha*. A wheel such as this could be expected to create constant hardship and pain to the rider of the cart. And so, the First Noble Truth acknowledges our accurate human perception that things are "out of kilter" as we travel along on life's rocky road. Psychologist and author Polly Young-Eisendrath clearly explains the subtle, multifaceted nature of this concept when she writes: "When we begin to notice that we are not in control, that bad things happen no matter how much we try to be good and plan for the future, we are thrown into a noticeable state of *dukkha*—incompleteness, dissatisfaction, and confusion."[5]

What I have witnessed as a therapist who has accompanied many people during times of great suffering, and as a human being who has suffered, leads me to believe that a great deal of pain arises from a failure to understand—or maybe a refusal to accept—some basic truths about life that these stories and others from religion, wisdom traditions, and numerous philosophies try to teach us. In refusing to see the truth about suffering, we can expend our whole lives—the best of who we are, what we have to offer, and what time we have on earth—in willful denial.

Recognizing and accepting the truth about life—that *everyone suffers*—gives us a larger context, a framework, in which we can better understand our own suffering. This wisdom also reveals ways in which we can use our pain for personal transformation, to gain the experience of true compassion, and for greater ongoing spiritual and psychological growth. Some of the things I know to be true can be stated simply:

A Few True Things

1. Change is the natural order of the universe.
2. Change always incorporates loss.
3. Although we cannot always control the events of our life that create suffering, we can consciously determine our responses to them.
4. There are hidden gifts in the power and pain of suffering.

We can spend our lives approaching, confronting, and denying these truths or we can open our minds, hearts, and souls to them and let them ease our pain and enhance our experience of life in many ways.

Change: The Natural Order

The early Greek philosopher Heraclitus wrote: "No man ever steps in the same river twice, for it's not the same river and he's not the same man." Just as the rushing waters of a moving river are in constant flux and change, so are we. This is not a merely figurative notion. Quite literally, all the cells in our bodies will be replaced by new ones in just a few years' time. The leaves fall from trees, the seasons show their faces with cycles of snow and sun, infants grow into little girls into women into old ladies, and death is our inevitable destination. Such is the pervasiveness of change.

The commonly held idea (perhaps, even hope) that life is static, predictable—that we can hang on to our present realities forever—is both illusionary and false. Yet most of us live with, and expect life to conform to, the idea that continuity and permanence are the order of the day. In spite of all the evidence to the contrary, most of us see change as an interloper, a radical, often painful, departure from the way "things are supposed to be." Most of us live as if we will never have to let go of anything, and as though we can count on things staying the way they are now. So, when we experience what we consider to be a negative change such as illness, death of a loved one, divorce, or dismissal from a job that sets us back, we can't believe that this is happening to us. Even as you read this (or as I write it!), we may be "making our deals" with the greatest powers: "Well, that's all well and good provided this loss business does not include my beloved _____." Whether we fill in the blank with a spouse's name or a pet's, our financial status or professional security, we show our reluctance to accept fully the truth about life and loss. And when we refuse to accept the impermanence of all things, it's no wonder we feel sandbagged when life delivers one of its inevitable blows. It's no wonder that every time it happens we scream, "Why me?"

In spite of the many blessings that open to us by accepting the true nature of reality, many of us desperately want life to remain as we have come to know it: predictable, clear, and secure. Like the stereotyped residents of the fictional 1950s black-and-white TV town of Pleasantville from the film of that same name, we resist what is new, untested, unproved. We don't want anything to change our sense of what our lives are and will be like. Things are better, we surmise, if they are predictable and clearly defined. Desiring to remain safe on familiar terrain, we adhere to patterns, ideas, and ways of being that we adamantly refuse to relinquish in spite of their failure to accommodate the truth about the realities of life. Some of us try to anesthetize our fears with drugs, alcohol, or addictions to work, money, or questionable dogma: anything to insulate us from the truth about what it means to live as a human being. We run from our fear of change on the assumption that it brings loss and loss means suffering. In doing so we can forfeit any real experience of life we have in the short time we are here to live it. The truth is we suffer no matter what. Heraclitus spoke honest words again when he said, "Nothing endures but change." If we learn from our suffering instead of trying to run from it, we can enrich our lives.

Change Means Loss

As you might imagine, people have been struggling with the unpredictability of change in their lives probably since man came into existence. In fact, the idea that life is a constantly changing series of personal experiences, of fortune and misfortune, is found in every culture throughout time. Buddhists refer to *samsara* as the uncontrolled cycle of birth and death, this illusionary ocean of suffering in which human life takes place. Taoists revere the truth about fluid, flowing spirals of change as the nature of all things and explore the wisdom inherent in understanding this through spiritual teachings such as the *Tao te Ching* and the *I Ching*, or "Book of Changes." Native American cosmologies look to the rhythmic changes in nature's seasons as instruction for learning the truth about beginnings and endings and the undulating course that characterizes all existence. Like Buddhist monks in Tibet, the Navajo even create their greatest art in colored paintings made entirely of sand: Images of *Father Sky* and *Changing Woman* are painstakingly and lovingly trickled onto the earth, grain by grain, using a medium that is itself impermanent and will be swept away at the end of the day. The medium is their message: Life consists of never-ending cycles of creation and destruction. Images showing change and fate as having a wheel-like, constantly turning shape are widespread and found throughout every culture from mandala figures in the East to the Rota Fortuna at the center of the Tarot's Major Arcana in the Western esoteric tradition.

Have you ever considered, while watching or flicking past the television show *Wheel of Fortune*, that it is based on esoteric medieval symbolism that addresses one of the fundamentals of human existence? I didn't think so. But, long before popular television game shows of the same name, the "Wheel of Fortune" (sometimes called the "Wheel of Life") was in the hearts and minds of human beings as a convenient method of explaining how life works. Few people could read in the Middle Ages, and until the mid-fifteenth century when Johann Gutenberg invented the printing press there wasn't a whole lot to read anyway. Teaching often took place through pictures and symbols that presented complicated ideas and expressed them in ways that ordinary people could relate to and remember. This circular symbol called the "Wheel of Life" was ubiquitous throughout Europe. A variety of interpretations were delicately drawn in miniature in fine manuscripts, carved in the majestic granite walls of Europe's great medieval cathedrals, and colorfully depicted in stained glass in the rose windows at

Basel and Amiens. In every case, this popular image attempts to explain the cycle of change in life and the common psychological reactions to different stages of that cycle.

The late Roman philosopher Boethius, who lived in the early sixth century, strongly influenced people of the Middle Ages about the vicissitudes of life through his writings and offered the most popular interpretation of the "Wheel of Life." He was, and still is, considered to be a very important thinker who shaped a great deal of Western philosophy. But it was his own personal experiences, particularly those contained in his major work, *The Consolation of Philosophy*, that informed his understanding of how the wheel of life turns for everyone.

Boethius had a fabulous career at the court of Theoderic the Great, king of the Ostrogoths and the ruler of Rome. He was widely renowned as a gifted statesman, scholar, and orator and held an esteemed place in his society. In fact, Boethius was given the kind of attention that we give to present-day celebrities and movie stars. He was kind of the Warren Beatty of the sixth century. He was happily married and had equally brilliant sons, who were made consuls of the court. Like Job, Boethius was leading an absolutely charmed life. He was, that is, until certain advisers of the king began to speak against him and others, suggesting to the aging and somewhat nervous monarch that he had enemies in high places. Boethius, they said, was among them. Without warning Boethius's whole life changed. His brilliant career was finished. He was thrown into prison and charged with treason. And it is here that he raged at the slings and arrows of outrageous fortune. It is here that he was comforted by the Spirit of Philosophy and enlightened by the idea that life's greatest gifts are not due to Fortune, after all, because she is capricious and erratic in her bestowal of these. Instead, Boethius was reassured that there are other, more powerful forces that offer greater gifts to humankind.

In his dank prison cell, far from the high life he had enjoyed, Boethius came to understand that there are things of more importance in life than one's station, wealth, or position of power. "Honour is not accorded to virtue because of the office held, but to the office because of the virtue of the beholder," he wrote. He pointed out that short of death, the center, the only part of the wheel that does not move or change, is the only place where one can truly be protected from Fortune's fickle touch. This center contains deeper, more axial truths—the laws of God and nature—that remain untouched by Fortune's waxing and waning. These higher truths, to Boethius, revolve around a broad, transcendent perspective that identifies what is truly of value in life. In *The Consolation of Philosophy*, written as a dialogue between a character named Boethius and the magical Spirit of Philosophy who appears as a beautiful woman, the spirit reminds Boethius that man has a divine destiny and that he suffers not because of his situation but only because of his bad attitude and failure to endure his agony with a calm mind. In his wretched pain, he's forgotten who he is and what the divine aim of life is all about. Fortune owes him nothing just because she took back what she had loaned him, the Spirit tells him. Gems, servants, clothes, noble birth, power, money, and status are no good in and of themselves. To pursue them is to seek value in worthless things. Rather the true blessings in life—real goodness and happiness—come from knowing and mastering oneself, realizing our divine nature, and following the force of love. This is the core, the heart of the matter, untouchable by changeable Fortune. Residing in the hub of the wheel moves us away from our own self-absorbed nature and into a centered place in which we can experience the right relationship with something greater than ourselves no matter what happens in our lives.

Boethius's influence on the philosophy of the day was powerful. People in the Middle Ages needed a way of understanding the events of their lives, plagued as they were with war, slavery, and the "Black Death"—all life-threatening, horrific events that were entirely beyond their control. They greeted his interpretation with open arms. The "Wheel of Life" was depicted by artists and writers throughout the Middle Ages. Dante, in particular, offers an excellent description of the way that Fortune influences human lives. His images extend from earlier portrayals of Fortune as a woman standing on a globe and turning it with her feet. In the *Inferno,* he wrote:

> No mortal power may stay her spinning wheel.
> The nations rise and fall by her decree.
> None may foresee where she will set her heel:
> She passes, and things pass. Man's mortal reason

cannot encompass her. She rules her sphere
as the other gods rule theirs.
Season by season her changes change her changes endlessly,
and those whose turn has come press on her so,
she must be swift by hard necessity.[6]

The symbol of Fortune as a woman turning a globe with her feet gave way to a more modern one around the twelfth century. In this image (shown in Figure 2-1), the wheel is turned in a clockwise direction by the spirit of Fortune, still always portrayed as a woman, who stands beside a mechanical wheel, which she controls with a lever. Once again, the truths illustrated are simple: change is the natural

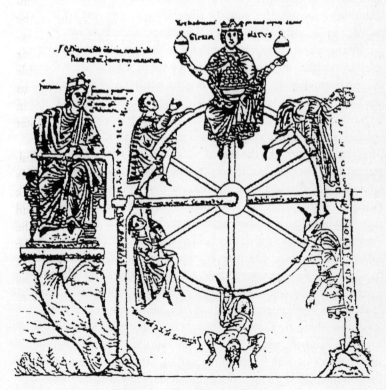

Figure 2-1: The "Wheel of Life"

order of the universe, and change always incorporates loss. But this image also conveys much about the process of how change affects our lives.

At the top of the wheel stands a beautiful, smiling person usually seen as a king or queen, suggesting that no one, regardless of his or her position in life, is exempt from the turning wheel of life. This top position is labeled *Happiness*, though in some versions it's called *regno*—"I reign." This, I think, is the Latin equivalent of our modern expression "I rule!" In this state, the image shows what life is like when things are "normal": everything is going great. Job's children are alive and well, his animals healthy, and his land fertile. Boethius hasn't been downsized and is in line for a big raise. Mark O'Brien is a healthy six-year-old. And my father and Deanne have arrived safely home from their West Virginia trip. Naturally, this is where we would like to stay. But that's impossible because the wheel always turns, just as life always turns, and is constantly in motion. Happiness never lasts.

As the wheel turns, the character at the top moves to the three-o'clock position on the wheel. What we see here is the same character falling through space. His smile is gone, replaced by a look of worry and fear. Fortune has moved the wheel, created change, and the character is challenged to relinquish his previous position. Pure terror is probably a better description of this guy's expression. We can imagine that the character, like the rest of us, would like nothing more than to return to the status quo, to stay in Pleasantville by shoving the wheel counterclockwise and once again know the happiness and safety of a familiar position. But that's not possible. The character here is plunging downward into a "dark night of the soul." It is here that we are stripped bare of our previously held illusions and our insistence on seeing life as we would like it to be rather than as it is. This image of a descent and passage over a dark, frightening threshold where one is snatched from a secure and happy position and tossed into the abyss abounds in mythological literature from all human cultures. To name just a few, there are Dante's visitations through the cycles of hell, Jonah in the belly of the whale, Kore-Persephone's visit with Hades, Sumerian Inanna's descent to the underworld, Celtic hero Finn MacCool's being swallowed by a monster, the Inuit story of Raven darting into the gullet of a whale-cow, and medieval knights of Western Europe in shining armor entering the lairs of dragons. This universally recognized plunge into the unknown can be horrifying. We often feel deserted by God and the comforts of the familiar. We may feel frighteningly alone in spite of the fact that every human being in the world has had similar experiences. This position on the wheel is simply called *Loss*, or sometimes *regnavi*, meaning "I *have* reigned."

The next position at the bottom of the wheel is named *Suffering*— *sum sine regno*, or "I have no kingdom." Here the character is naked and being dragged through hell. Look at him. He's hanging upside down and his expression is one of pure despair. This symbolizes raw vulnerability in the face of the ravages of unplanned sorrows, loss of normality, and the natural emotional consequences unleashed by the destruction of life as we knew it. At this point on the wheel, the character feels anxiety, sadness, grief, tension, anger, and conflict.

When we are immersed in periods of suffering, most of us feel it will never end. At those times, it helps to remember that the Latin root of the word *suffering* itself means "to allow" or "to experience." In the midst of turmoil brought about by an unexpected loss or change, very often we have no answers that ease our anguish; we simply must "be" and experience the full pain of our loss. This is a particularly difficult notion in our culture, where we have learned to look for simple solutions, magic pills, or quick fixes to short-circuit the pain of suffering. It can be helpful to remember that even in the midst of our anguish, the wheel continues to turn. We can be certain that even in the blackest night our situation will change again.

Emerging out of suffering, the character on the "Wheel of Life" moves to the fourth placement on the wheel. This nine-o'clock position is simply called *Hope—regnabo*, "I shall reign"—and here we begin to see that there is a vision of a return to "normality." Once again, there is a thought, however fleeting, that we might once again be happy. The notion that our suffering might end comes into view. For some who suffer, hope never seems to appear on the horizon. They may remain stuck in their suffering, grieving until they die. This is the worst of all possible fates.

If we are wise and strong and willing to entertain the notion of hope, we can emerge psychologically and spiritually transformed by our experiences on the wheel of change we all ride. Change and loss—and how we respond to them—can be doors to higher levels of consciousness. You'll remember that it is said that the gods have ordained a solemn vow, and that it is through suffering that we achieve wisdom.

As the wheel turns, we once again return to the position of "Happiness" at the top of the wheel. But it is a mistake to think that this is the same position from whence we started. This will not be the "old" normal. This will be a new state of equilibrium. We might like to think "I rule!" but the cycle inevitably begins again.

⌒

About six months after my mother died in 1992, my father came to visit and, as was his custom, invited several of my close friends and Nancy and me to go out to dinner. Both my parents always enjoyed meeting and getting to know my friends and looked forward to visiting with them when they would stay with us. Going out to dinner together was something we did regularly. My parents had been married for forty-seven years, and then my father had nursed my mom through two brutal years of leukemia before she died. But because my parents had been so close and did almost everything together, every activity for my dad was filled with memories of days gone by. Even this dinner with friends harked back to the many times my parents would visit and my friends would gather with them for cookouts or dinners at O'Sullivans—a local seafood restaurant and our favorite hangout. I could see that Dad was making progress in his grief, but I knew, as did he, that his healing would take a long time. Even this dinner would present its sad moments—memories called up by simple things like familiar faces, laughter, and music, even by the mouthwatering aroma of the steamed shrimp and hush puppies we always ordered. During dinner, my good friend Kathryn, who has known my father for twenty years, leaned over and gently asked how he was doing. "Are you getting back to normal yet, Jim?" she said. My dad paused for a long time as he considered the question. Finally he said, "I'm doing better, Kathryn. But I don't think I know yet what normal is going to be."

My father intuitively understood what the Wheel of Life was designed to teach and take us to new places. We can never go back to the "old normal." Once having seen, we can't unsee. Once having known, we can't unknow. And no matter how deep our suffering, the wheel will turn. Hope will appear on a distant horizon, and we will find a new equilibrium: A new normal. And we'll rejoice in this moment until the wheel once again begins its inescapable turn.

After dinner with my dad and friends I thought about the "Wheel of Fortune" and where he was on it. I realized that this medieval meta-phor held many important insights into change in my life and in those of the people I knew and worked with as a therapist. It was very clear to me that this was not just an image for folks in the Middle Ages. It had real power to explain the psychological reactions to change in our modern-day lives.

Like Boethius, Tom seemed to be leading a charmed life. He had a great job, a healthy, happy family, and wonderful prospects for the future. He's at the top of the wheel. But just two weeks after he was given a significant raise and promotion, he was "downsized" in a cor-porate restructuring that eliminated both his new, as well as his old, position. "We're sorry to see you leave, Tom," his supervisor told him. "You've been a great asset to the company." Unprotected by the "golden parachutes" of benefits, stock options, and severance pay that insulate the upper-level management of the company, Tom found him-self middle-aged and out of work with no income, a hefty mortgage, a family to support, and tuition payments due for his college-bound daughter. Fortune has turned the wheel, and Tom has plunged into the abyss. He wonders what he did wrong but can come up with nothing. He earned regular raises and promotions. His boss constantly told him what a great job he did. "Why did this have to happen to me?" "Why now?" he asks himself. He keeps looking for reasons why this has hap-pened, but like Job, he finds none. Of course, Tom can look to the big-ger picture to see that his company's merger with another meant that there were too many midlevel managers for the new organization. Downsizing and outsourcing are ways that companies say that they stay lean, productive, and able to offer larger dividends to stockholders. But Tom doesn't really care about all that. He's suffering, stressed about money, ashamed to tell his successful friends about his present plight, and feels like a large part of what defined him as a person is now gone. If you were to show Tom the "Wheel of Fortune" and ask him to point out where he is, I'm sure he'd select the bottom of the wheel.

Karen wishes she had Tom's problem to deal with. "I can always find another job," she says. "Right now, I'm battling for my life." Karen has been diagnosed with Stage IV cervical cancer. She has no family history of this disease and is only thirty-three years old. She has none of the risk factors and has had yearly PAP smears from her doctor. She's a semi-vegetarian, has very little fat in her diet, exercises regularly, and rarely uses alcohol. In short, she's doing everything right to avoid this disease and many others. And yet, she, too, has plunged into the despair of loss and suffering with the diagnosis of this life-threatening disease. She's started chemotherapy and will then take radiation treatments, but her prognosis is very poor. There's a very strong chance that Karen will die in the next year. The form of cancer she has is particularly virulent and aggressive; it has already invaded her lymph system. Karen feels depressed and hopeless but continues to fight on. "I have a six-year-old and a three-year-old to think about. I don't want them to have to grow up without a mother," she says.

Whatever form it comes in, change always implies loss. As a psychotherapist, I have accompanied many people on the journeys that change initiates. In most cases, it's easy to understand why a person suffers: She's been diagnosed with a serious disease; he lost his longtime career as a result of organizational downsizing; her husband has left her for another woman; he cannot stop grieving over the death of his father; they have to declare bankruptcy as a result of a business loss. What can truly blindside someone is when change ushers in loss as a result of good things happening. I suppose that's why there are support groups for lottery winners throughout the country. Even what we might consider "good" changes demand that we must leave something behind. Something that has defined us or brought meaning or pleasure to our lives will be replaced by something else.

Mary came to my office in tears. She couldn't quite understand why she was depressed because everything in her life seemed to be going so well. She has a happy marriage, plenty of money, excellent health, and many friends. But since her youngest son graduated from high school, she has found it hard to get out of bed in the morning. She can't sleep, lacks energy, can't focus on anything, and says that life has lost its zest. Her family physician prescribed an antidepressant that she's been taking for more than six months, but it doesn't appear to be helping. After a lot of soul-searching, Mary realized that she was experiencing a powerful emotional reaction—the "empty nest" syndrome—when her son left for college. Mary is a good mother. She understands that her whole life has been focused on raising her child to become a healthy, strong, and independent adult. She and her husband set out to raise their son to become a young man with confidence and compassion. They succeeded. Their son is all those things. And yet, Mary was not prepared for him to leave. On the day when she and her husband left her son in the dorm room of an excellent state university, her whole life changed. This change brought the loss of a role in her life that had defined her for eighteen years. She understands what she is experiencing but doesn't know how to accept this loss in her life. She doesn't yet know what her "new normal" will be. During her visits we talk about the new activities she finds beckoning or old interests that she may want to explore with the new time she has. We discuss how she feels and, as the months pass, the depression eases as new doors open and Mary comes to terms with her unfolding, changing role in life.

Like Mary, Angela came to my office suffering from a change that many people would view as positive and good. She was suffering because she received a big promotion at work. Angela is one of the hardest-working people I've ever known. Her natural intelligence, uncompromising devotion and loyalty to her company, and her ability to get along with people propelled her into a management position in a computer software development firm. Nothing was ever handed to her; she worked hard for all her promotions. She and her friends justifiably broke out the champagne when Angela was appointed to a high-level management position. She was paid a great deal more money and moved to the executive offices in a tony building across the street from the main office. But the changes in her job responsibilities and the stress she experienced as a result of her new position caused her to suffer. She began to have constant headaches and felt guilty about the lack of time she had to spend with her two young children, and she was not keeping up with her new work obligations. She says she feels like "an impostor" and doesn't feel prepared for disciplining her staff or delegating responsibilities to them. She feels out of touch with the people she's now supposed to be supervising. She explains that her anticipation of getting up and going to work in the morning has turned to dread. She longs for the creative, technical challenges that she loved in her previous position as a computer programmer. She feels lonely. She misses her old friends on the job and the spontaneity of taking a quick coffee break together and catching up on the news of each other's families.

Angela and I worked together exploring options. She was miserable in her new position but felt that she now needed the additional income it provided. At first, it seemed as if there were only these two choices: keep her present position and continue to suffer or ask for her old job back and learn to live on a reduced paycheck. But as we talked, we decided to brainstorm some ideas and allow our creativity to pursue any and all options that would solve her problem no matter how incomprehensible or far-out they were. By freeing our imaginations and refusing to accept that there were only these two possibilities, we discovered a third, perfectly reasonable, solution. Angela said that the management structure of the company kept her too far removed from the technical development department. In fact, that was one of the causes for her high stress level; she felt she was being asked to take responsibility for things over which she had no control. She proposed a change in management structure and arrived at a solution that not only solved that organizational problem but also required that she move back to her old building and colleagues. There she could be more involved in the day-to-day workings of that department. In this newly created position—which her boss thought was "a brilliant idea"—she now divides her time between technical computer programming and managing other programmers. She kept her manager's salary and is now doing the work she loves in an environment that nurtures her. She's back at the top of the wheel—she rules! At least for now.

For both Mary and Angela, good changes—a son's departure to the new adventure of college and a big promotion at work—still created a sense of loss and sadness. Though not everyone experiences pain at these kinds of life events, I've been surprised at how many who do. Most of these people seem to have problems talking about the suffering that comes with changes that others would view as positive. "You'd win the lottery and complain about the taxes you have to pay on it," they expect to hear. But the truth is that even positive changes are accompanied by the loss of something. And loss, as we know, is often experienced as suffering.

When Fortune turns the wheel, we descend into a dark pit of pain. Happiness, it seems, is merely transitory, brief, and unpredictable in its length. Boethius was right about staying close to the center, to embrace larger, more transpersonal values and self-knowledge, the things that don't change when the wheel spins. It seems to me that the answer to suffering is to find meaning in it and to realize that while we may not always control the events of our lives, we do have the power to determine how we will respond to them and grow through them.

We Determine Our Responses to the Events of Our Lives

Life sometimes feels like a trip in a sailboat on the open sea that is being driven by the tides and winds that change daily and which cannot be seen except by their effects. Given these powerful forces beyond our control, don't we have license to sit in the bottom of our boat eating bonbons as we are driven here and there by prevailing winds and tides? After all, how can our small efforts direct our little boat against the jet stream and other prevailing currents? Bonbons and basking in the sun sound great, but allowing the forces of fate to entirely control our destiny is not a good idea. We do have some other alternatives that will serve us much better in our water journey. We can learn about our boat, its strengths and weaknesses, where it does well and when we have to work harder to hold the rudder. We can learn how to navigate these larger forces, knowing when to raise the sail, ways to tack, and how best to move in concert with the wind and waves. Jungian analyst and writer June Singer writes, "In learning to sail you do not change the current of the water nor do you have any effect on the wind, but you learn to hoist your sail and turn it this way and that to utilize the greater forces which surround you. By understanding them, you become one with them, and in doing so are able to find your own direction—so long as it is in harmony with, and does not try to oppose, the greater forces in being."[7] In other words, we can learn some things that can help us.

My father once gave me a small gift of a rock with the following words inscribed on it: "If there is no wind . . . row." I love it and live by this bit of good advice. The truth is that all our lives will be buffeted by many of the realities and losses of human existence. Even the most enlightened beings in the world have endured physical pain and suffering. There will always be mysteries, the workings of Fortune that we can only struggle to accept and be humbled by. Ask Job, or Boethius, or (as Kisagotami learned), ask your next-door neighbor. But suffering offers opportunities for new wisdom, an awakened consciousness, and the development of courage and compassion. In fact, suffering may be the only route to these blessings. The early-fourteenth-century Christian mystic Meister Eckhart wrote: "Suffering is the swiftest steed that brings us to perfection."

My Aunt Teresa always told me to live with the understanding that "what doesn't kill you, makes you stronger." I had quoted her so often to my psychotherapy clients that one talented woman made a calligraphy banner of this wise saying—attributed to "Aunt Teresa," of course—which now hangs over my desk. It was only years later that I read that Nietzsche was the original source of these words (actually he said, "What does not destroy me, makes me stronger"—a minor point). As you can see, I like this thought so much that I used it for the first epigraph in this book. Teresa lived by that motto, and her life was one filled with great inner courage and the ability to withstand serious financial downturns and many painful losses including the deaths of her mother, father, brother, and sister. In spite of those losses, and even during the long and tortuous process of dying from non-Hodgkins lymphoma, Teresa met the world every day with grace, humor, and grit. She would come home from a grueling session of chemotherapy or a blood transfusion and hold court with our big extended family, sip a glass of good merlot, rock the infants just born into our clan, and ask about my book projects and screenplays. Even at its very end, she savored every second of her life. Not once did I hear her complain about physical pain or bemoan her fate. In fact, only hours before she died, she held my hand, comforted me, and said, "Kathy, I love life so much that I'd never make the decision to leave it on my own. God had to make this choice for me and at this time. Knowing that I'm dying has made me even more grateful for all the living I've done. In fact, I don't plan to miss one single second of the time I've got left. I'm going to live and love just as I always have."

I've thought about Teresa's words every day since. She gets it, I thought. Teresa understood completely how to live with a warrior's courage and grab the joy in every moment of life as if it were your last one. Teresa's courage in the face of enormous suffering—during her final hours—touched my soul. I feel such admiration for her and people like her who go through life's most difficult tests and keep their eyes and hearts open throughout their ordeals. What powerful models we have in those with the courage to bear their suffering and transform through their pain. These people are our greatest teachers.

I felt this same admiration—the same sense of being in the presence of a great teacher—when I happened to see an interview with actor Robert Urich conducted by Diane Sawyer on television. Robert and his wife, Heather, had just completed building their dream house in Utah. In fact, that's where this interview took place. He was starring in a new series that was getting great reviews and seemed sure to be renewed. Their teenage kids—Ryan and Emily—were healthy and thriving. Just as life was delivering all its blessings, Robert was diagnosed with synovial sarcoma—a very serious and rare form of soft-tissue cancer—that threatened to take his life. When the producers of his successful television show—coincidentally titled *The Lazarus Man*—learned of his illness, they were so scared that he would die midseason that they canceled the series. Robert's responses to Diane Sawyer's questions were so down-to-earth, so genuine, and so filled with both pain and courage that I was moved to tears.

My first book, *Awakening at Midlife*, had just been published, and it was about loss and opportunity during this developmental period of life. It has been my belief that people either "get" this book or "don't get it." I was convinced that Robert would be one of the people who would get it. I happened to be at my friend Kyle's house and mentioned that I had been very touched by this interview with Robert and said that I was going to try to find an agency address to send him a copy of my book. Kyle had just returned from Los Angeles and pointed to a photocopied list on his dining room table. "Maybe his address is in this thing," he said. During his trip to L.A., Kyle had purchased *Richard's Guide to Celebrity Addresses* for reasons he couldn't explain. We looked up Robert Urich and there was an address. I've always felt that this bit of synchronicity was the universe's way of saying, "Yeah, send Robert the book."

In book marketing, publicists send hundreds of copies of new books to reviewers, producers, and anyone who can give the book national media attention. I am an involved author in marketing my work and can be a shameless self-promoter; but sending this book to Robert was an act of love and from the heart. My only hope was that it would help him.

About three weeks later I received a call from Robert. He told me that the book was important to him and had helped him through some of his struggle. Since then, we've had a long-distance friendship and are working on several projects together. I'm honored to have the opportunity to continue to learn from his insights and courage.

Recently I hosted a radio show about surviving cancer, and Robert graciously agreed to participate by phone from his vacation cottage in Canada. "Life is filled with defining moments that test our character," he told me. "Cancer was one of mine." Robert endured three surgeries and many rounds of chemotherapy and radiation treatment. He lost his hair but reclaimed a powerful love of life and profoundly energized spiritual beliefs. These developments helped him live in the moment in a way he never had before, Robert said. His struggles came with gifts.

Robert recovered. When he was cancer-free for a year, he and Heather adopted a beautiful baby girl, Allison, something they had planned to do before Robert's cancer. During the radio interview Robert said that he had spent the morning rocking his infant daughter on a porch swing for over three hours. "Before the cancer, I would never have done that. I would have missed this most remarkable experience," he says. "I would have felt the need to be 'doing something'—making phone calls, mowing the lawn, or washing the car." Like many people who have suffered serious health threats and felt the presence of death nearby, Robert experienced spiritual and psychological growth, an invigorated passion for life, and newfound joy in simple moments by recognizing and responding to his illness with courage and wisdom.

What is it about people like Robert Urich and my Aunt Teresa who respond to suffering as an opportunity for change and growth while others would simply say, "Why me?" Where does this resilience, this ability to live with grace in spite of life's difficult blows, come from? At the end of the last century, American writer Christian Bovee made the case for the idea that it is our *relationship* to the circumstances and the events of our lives rather than the events themselves that determines how we will see them. "The same wind that carries one vessel into port may blow another offshore," he observed.

Why is it that some individuals understand, almost intuitively, that even in life's darkest moments there is the promise of blessings yet to come? Why do some people act with courage in the face of suffering, even grow psychologically and spiritually through their experiences of loss, while others become embittered and closed hearted? Perhaps the answers lie in our basic perceptions about life and what to expect from it. Perhaps the answers lie in refusing to accept comfortable but false illusions. Yaqui sorcerer Don Juan described the path of a man of knowledge as that of a warrior to anthropologist Carlos Castañeda. His words offer an interesting alternative to seeing the events of our lives as either good or bad; through his eyes, our position on the Wheel of Life is of little consequence. "A warrior cannot complain or regret anything," he says. "His life is an endless challenge and challenges cannot possibly be good or bad. Challenges are simply challenges. The basic difference between an ordinary man and a warrior is that a warrior takes everything as a challenge, while an ordinary man takes everything as a blessing or a curse."

Each of our lives is unique but has the most important circumstances in common with every single other human life. We will all find ourselves at different places on the Wheel of Life in a never-ending cycle of happiness, loss, suffering, and rediscovering hope. But, we are all born, we will lose important things along the way, we will all suffer, and we will all die. We can deny these truths and live with fear, holding everything close in, refusing to risk or to learn with the hope of keeping the boat steady and not losing what we have. Or we can embrace reality as a series of changes and live with passion, meaning, and joy. We can focus on taking our blessings where we find them, often in simple moments. If we can acknowledge and accept the fact that we share the same ultimate destiny with every other living being, we can allow our hearts to open to the world. In so doing, we often discover an end to our loneliness. Embracing the truth of our existence can lead us to a deeply felt connection to all others. This is the beginning of true spirituality and love. This is an awakening of consciousness. With this understanding, we can recognize that everyone's life is a balance of blessings and letting go.

Gifts Hidden in Suffering

For many years, I have loved to walk on the beaches of the Outer Banks of North Carolina with my yellow Labrador retriever, Dorothy. We like to get up early in the morning, before daybreak. We sit on the beach and watch as the sky turns pink, then orange, and the sun pops up over the horizon. It's a quiet time of day; usually there are no sounds at all except the pounding of the waves and the chattering of the gulls and sandpipers.

True to her breed, Dorothy has always been a great lover of sand and water. She adores racing down the dunes and leaping into the waves the second I release her from her leash. When she was younger, Dorothy would splash in the ocean and tumble in the waves—sometimes fetching a tennis ball, but more often waiting for me to wade in to find it—for hours and hours. In those days, the beaches were wider and the dunes were higher and more durable, offering better protection to the salt-worn wooden cottages along the shore. But time has passed since Dorothy and I first began our morning walks. Many nor'easters and hurricanes have battered this fragile beach, and it's not as wide now. The dunes have eroded and a number of cottages have been moved back. Other, less lucky ones have been swept out to sea. I notice that each year this landscape changes—sometimes just a little and sometimes dramatically, depending upon the weather of the season. Although this constantly changing shoreline is a bane to the cottage owners of this small coastal town, erosion is to be expected. After all, this is a barrier island, whose whole nature is to move.

Dorothy is now ten years old (about seventy in people years?), has been through two knee surgeries, and, although she walks without limping, she can no longer run in wet sand the way she used to. Her veterinarian tells me that it's not a good idea for her to "dart" on the beach given her repaired "Joe Namath" knees. I feel sad that Dorothy will never be able to play with the sweet abandon that she once did, but I realize that physical limitations often come with age for all of us. This is how life is. Given the different life expectancies for humans and dogs and playing those odds, I even accept that there will come a day when Dorothy will no longer be with me on these morning treks and I will grieve deeply for her. But until then, and perhaps especially because I understand what the future is likely to bring, I'll hold my tears and we'll take every morning as it comes. I often wonder if I would experience each of these mornings as the precious gifts they are if I didn't know that someday they will end.

I look as Dorothy stands in a tidal pool of rushing water, vigilantly watching the movements of seagulls, hoping that one will come within closing distance. But I can't let her bolt and hurt her knees, so she's on a leash now. Dorothy will have to be content to walk the beach instead of chasing the birds or crashing through the waves. Still, as the sky turns pink, heralding the rising sun, we walk down the beach toward the pier, a bit slower, perhaps, but I sense that we carry the same joy with us this morning as we have always had.

If we accept that life is transient and that we will lose everything of importance in time, then perhaps we can learn to really live in the present, in the reality of what is happening here and now. We can be vibrantly alive and greet each moment with passion, gusto, and a soul open to whatever it may hold. We can learn to love more easily, experience pure compassion, and create more freely. In short, we can live large. Suffering often is the key that opens the door to a full realization of what we were born to do and the urge to embrace it. It sets a course for our destiny.

Deborah Cook knows something about suffering and destiny. She also understands pain's transforming power and has experienced, first-hand, how her life has changed as a result of how she chose to respond to the challenges that confronted her. In the late fall of 1995, Deborah's insurance was changing and she selected a new primary care physician. She was forty-one and enjoyed robust health but decided to have a complete physical so that she would know her doctor before she ever really needed him in an emergency or sudden illness. She asked that the examination include a mammogram despite the fact that she had already had a baseline one done about five years previously and had no risk factors that would suggest she needed one now. "Something inside pushed me to ask for this," she tells me. Fortunately, her new doctor listened and ordered the test. The mammogram revealed a mass. A subsequent biopsy confirmed that it was cancer. Deborah had a mastectomy and reconstructive surgery immediately and recovered quickly. Because of the kind of cancer Deborah had and its early diagnosis, she did not have to undergo chemotherapy or radiation.

Deborah returned to her job as a nurse, where she was responsible for working with patients who were scheduled for surgery. She made certain that necessary lab work was completed, performed physical exams, and talked with each person about his or her upcoming surgery, explaining what to expect and how best to participate in one's own healing process. On one of her first days back at work, Deborah was scheduled to see a woman in her sixties. Several peers offered to take this particular patient. "Why?" Deborah asked them. "Because she has breast cancer and isn't coping very well. It might be hard for you." Deborah acknowledged that this might be unsettling but wanted to go ahead anyway. "If I tear up, I tear up," she said. What Deborah discovered was that her own personal experiences as a breast cancer survivor along with her medical knowledge and skills as a nurse enabled her to offer enormous help to this frightened patient. "For the next six weeks, it seemed as if every pre-op exam I did was with a woman with breast cancer."

Two years later, Deborah says she was living in Pleasantville. She and her husband, David, had moved to a comfortable suburban neighborhood in northern Virginia. Deborah's children from a previous marriage, Graham, eleven, and Edlyn, ten, were making new friends and the family was living the good life in a beautiful four-bedroom house on a cul-de-sac. To complete their consummate suburban American life, they got a great big malamute dog and named him Sam.

Deborah's life was perfect when she detected a lump in her other breast. Though a mammogram failed to spot it, a sonogram and biopsy showed that Deborah, once again, had cancer. But this time it was a very aggressive strain that would require surgery, chemotherapy, and radiation.

Just after Labor Day in 1997, Deborah was recovering from her surgery, beginning her chemotherapy, and getting the kids ready to start school. She was still weak, but her mother had come from Connecticut to help out and David and the kids were busy shopping for new clothes, book bags, and other necessities for the upcoming academic year. On the fourth day of school, ten-year-old Edlyn came home deathly ill. She was clutching her chest in pain and she was shockingly pale. Her heart was pounding at 186 beats a minute. Still in pain from her surgery, Deborah rushed Edlyn to the pediatrician. The next day, results of tests showed that Edlyn was anemic and the source of her condition was lymphocytic leukemia (ALL). In a terrible, catastrophic act of fate, both mother and daughter now had to fight cancer at the same time. "I went to pieces," David told a reporter. "It seemed like getting sucker-punched. Here's this little girl who twenty-four hours before was running around. Now there's a doctor telling me she has cancer." But even at that moment, Deborah was preparing for a new battle. "It was pretty simple: I had to get well so I could take care of my daughter."

Together mother and daughter fought the good fight, taking chemotherapy, and getting sick together. After Edlyn's hair began to fall out from the chemo, they sheared off their hair together in a wild two-woman head-shaving party. David and Graham did chores. Neighbors and friends pitched in to help as well. They walked Sam, delivered meals, donated a computer, and helped Deborah and David with financial contributions. Although insurance covered Deborah's and Edlyn's medical treatments, Deborah had to take a leave from her

$40,000-a-year nursing position. David picked up a second job as a security guard, but their bills were mounting.

Deborah stayed with her daughter for more than three weeks in the pediatric oncology ward of Fairfax Hospital. As long as she was busy taking care of Edlyn, meeting with doctors, or researching information about her treatments, Deborah said that she could stave off the great despair that threatened to overwhelm her. But in the dark hours of night, she had no other course than to think about her life and that of her beloved daughter. "At three o'clock in the morning, I would sit next to Edlyn's bed, listening to her purring in her sleep, and cry. I was afraid of the unknown and so I would try to grab on to every little bit of hope. And it was uncanny the way hope would reveal itself, even from strangers who would just happen onto my path. I prayed that if God would let us live, He could put me to some important use. I prayed that I could find some way to use all this pain to some good purpose."

Today, both Edlyn and Deborah are in remission and there is an 85 percent chance they'll both remain cancer-free. Each must continue to take oral chemotherapy, but their lives are filled with hope and happiness. Deborah now works at a large hospital in Virginia with women who are suffering from and surviving breast cancer. She feels as if everything in her life—from her interest in science and anatomy as a child, her education as a nurse, and her own survival of cancer—has led up to this work that she loves and has such a passion for. In addition, Deborah says that her suffering opened up her heart. She feels greater compassion for and connection to other people these days. She describes herself as infinitely more patient and tolerant than she was before her illness. "I ask myself, Why get stressed out in traffic or because someone is annoying you? Having cancer," she says, "can be the beginning, not the end, of life."

During our conversation, Edlyn runs into the kitchen. Her hair has grown back in curly, something she's not so sure she likes. Her father has arrived to drive her to one of her weekly blood tests. She's twelve now, full of life, racing to get the blood test over with before heading to a rehearsal dinner on this eve of a big family wedding. "You took your pill, yes?" Deborah asks her. Edlyn nods and then is on her way out the door, more excited about the wedding than anything else at the moment.

"Since all this happened, I see things differently. I even look at the clover on my lawn not as a weed but as a wonderful, miraculous thing," Deborah says. "Life is different, more gracious, more wonderful when you know that you might not be here tomorrow. I understand now how important it is to enjoy every minute of it. I'm the luckiest person alive."[8]

· 2 ·

Lead into Gold,
or
the Alchemical Process of
Making the Best from the Worst

We are born to be awake, not to be asleep!

—Paracelsus, sixteenth-century Swiss alchemist

✐ Once we accept the universal nature of suffering, we have to learn what to do with our pain.

An Alchemical Story

Can suffering open pathways to new awareness? Can we trust that anguish will lead us on a path to greater self-realization and wisdom about life? I think the answer to both of these questions is an unequivocal "yes." In fact, there are many analogies and metaphors that speak to this truth. One of my all-time favorite stories is about the alchemist Nicholas Flamel, a man who learned how to turn lead into gold and discovered the secret to immortality. Or so they say. Nicholas Flamel, a struggling bookseller and copyist, is not a fictional character; he did indeed live in fourteenth-century Paris. As for his discoveries, much speculation and mystery still surround them. But this, at least, is certain: The story of Nicholas Flamel is fascinating, and a rich metaphor for life's greatest challenge: finding the gifts in suffering.

It was said that Nicholas had always been interested in the Hermetic arts, the occult, and the search for the philosophers' stone—a substance rumored to hold the power of transmuting lead into gold and proffering the blessings of eternal life. Throughout Europe in the Middle Ages, there was a great renaissance of interest in the original alchemical teachings of the ancient Egyptians and the Greeks. Like most of his contemporaries, Nicholas had something of a passing interest in this esoteric wisdom, but he only became truly passionate about it after a dream and a bizarre synchronous event aroused his curiosity further.

One night Nicholas dreamed that a radiant angel came before him holding a book in his hands and saying: "Look well at this book, Nicholas. At first you will understand nothing in it, neither you nor any other man. But one day you will see in it that which no other man will be able to see." The angel extended the book toward him, and Nicholas reached out his hand to take it. It was then that the angel dissolved into a splash of golden light and he woke up.

Nicholas didn't give much more thought to the dream until one day a stranger appeared in his tiny two-foot-square stall in the Paris marketplace. The man needed money and offered to sell him a manuscript. Nicholas wasn't particularly interested in this unusual document held together with an old binding of worked copper and engraved with curious diagrams and ciphers. Some of the symbols he knew to be Greek letters; the others were unintelligible to him. Nicholas started to wave off this unknown man, but in a moment of blinding insight he recognized the book to be the same one the angel had held out to him in his dream. Nicholas called the man back, paid a mere two florins for the manuscript, and sat down to read.

He noticed that the leaves of the book were crafted from the bark of young trees, not parchment, as was typical of the time. Each page was edged in gold and covered with precise writing made with an iron-pointed pen. The book was written, or so it said, by Abraham the Jew "Prince, Priest, Levite, Astrologer, and Philosopher." The first page also contained a series of threats and curses against anyone reading it who was neither a priest nor a scribe. Nicholas was frightened by that but then, realizing that he was, after all, a copyist and a professional letter-writer, which was sort of like a scribe, he continued to read on. But he understood little of what the pages held. After studying the book for more than twenty-one years he still couldn't decipher its contents.

Finally, Nicholas started asking the learned men of his day for some help. But they offered little assistance and actually were even more confused than he was by the book. Of course, Nicholas had a twenty-one-year head start. What he did know was that the book had been written by a Jew and at least part of the text was written in ancient Hebrew. Perhaps a rabbi or Hebrew-reading Jew could help me, he thought. The problem was that there were no Jews in Paris who could translate for him. The Jews had been persecuted and driven out of the country. Nicholas knew that many Jewish people had migrated to Spain, which was under the more enlightened dominion of the Moors. Disguised as a Christian on pilgrimage for St. James of Compostela, the patron saint of his parish, he set off for Galacia. Terrified that he might be robbed of his precious book, Nicholas prudently carried with him only a few carefully copied pages, which he hid in his bag.

He wandered around Spain looking for a Jew or a Cabalist who could help him but, quite understandably, most were suspicious of a Christian Frenchman, since they had just been viciously exiled from France. No one seemed particularly eager to help. Disappointed, he began the long journey home to Paris when he stopped for the night at an inn in Leon. There he met a French merchant from Boulogne. For some reason, Nicholas trusted the man and explained to him the real purpose of his journey. The merchant introduced Nicholas to Maestro Canches, a Jewish scholar and physician who offered to look at the material. Nicholas spoke hesitantly to the Jewish scholar at first but when he mentioned "Abraham the Jew," Maestro Canches became ecstatic. "Of course, I have heard of the book," he said. He told Nicholas that Abraham was a master of the wandering race, a venerable sage who studied all the intricacies of the Cabala, and was the highest initiate of wisdom and knowledge. Maestro Canches went on to say that the book disappeared from sight centuries ago, but tradition held that it had never been destroyed and that it passes from hand to hand, always reaching the man whose destiny it is to receive it. That's when Nicholas says something like "Well, guess what? I've got the book at home and some samples right here to prove it."

As the lights go out in the village, Nicholas and Maestro Canches sit huddled over the strange pages Nicholas has produced. In the yellow glow of a sputtering oil lamp, the two of them examine the words and symbols Nicholas has copied from the original manuscript. Maestro Canches translates the Hebrew and teaches Nicholas in the process. Maestro Canches tells Nicholas that he believes the writing is a variant of the Hebrew language dating back to the time of Moses. But Nicholas has brought only a few pages, just a minor portion of the work, and there is not enough information to reveal the secrets the tome was said to carry. Maestro Canches agrees to accompany Nicholas back to Paris. Unfortunately, the elderly Maestro Canches falls ill before they even reach Orléans. Seven days later, despite Nicholas's tender care, he dies.

Nicholas returns home heartbroken at the loss of his new friend and frustrated that the book will forever remain a mystery to him. But as he continues to study the manuscript, he realizes that Maestro Canches has taught him enough Hebrew to translate the rest of the book. It takes him three more years to make his way through the text. Finally, Nicholas interprets all the esoteric wisdom contained in the book of Abraham the Jew. He strictly follows the instructions given in its pages, and, the story goes, on January 13, 1382, Nicholas changed a half pound of mercury first into silver, and then into gold. The great secret at last was his.

According to historical records from several different churches and hospitals in France, it is at this point that the bookseller and his wife become rich beyond imagination. Though they continued to live simply, Nicholas and his wife, Pernelle, donated huge sums of money to many worthwhile causes. Nicholas dedicated the rest of his life to study and charity. That he was deeply immersed in the practice of alchemy is certain as he wrote several books and treatises on this subject, which still survive today. Several years later, Pernelle died and was buried in the small cemetery near the nave of the church of St. Jacques de la Boucherie. Nicholas was now about eighty years old, and some say that he died at that age, a year after losing his faithful and loving wife, and was buried beside her. But his friends say that shortly after Pernelle's death Nicholas discovered the *Elixir Vitae*, a substance that grants eternal life, and lived to be one hundred and sixteen. For hundreds of years, adepts and initiates into the study of alchemy insisted that Nicholas was still alive and that he would live for more than six hundred years.

The house on the corner of the rue de Marivaux where Nicholas and Pernelle lived most of their lives has been sold and resold many times by speculators who hope to find gold or clues to the alchemical mystery. In 1816 it was reported that some lodgers found several jars filled with an unidentifiable and mysterious dark-colored liquid. Was this the magical philosophers' stone? Spurred on by the rumor, one man bought the house and tore it to pieces, ransacking the cellar and pulling apart every wall and timber looking for the secret. Nothing was ever found.

Some people say that alchemy was the foundation for chemistry and for much of what is now modern-day medicine and pharmacology; however, alchemy, as it was practiced, is much more intimately related to "mystical" spiritual traditions than to the empirical or natural sciences. The alchemist was looking to transmute base metals into gold and find a substance that gives eternal life. The influence of this esoteric body of thought is abundantly clear in ancient texts of Taoism in China, Yoga in India, Gnosis in Greece and Hellenistic Egypt, the Hermetic traditions of Islamic countries, and the Qabbalah, Hermeticism, and both Christian and secular mysticism in the West, particularly during the Middle Ages and the Renaissance.

What are we to think of the story of Nicholas Flamel? Alchemy, to our modern minds, conjures up images of sinister medieval laboratories in which Merlin-like wizards labor over steaming cauldrons of sulfur and salt waiting for gold to appear after a pinch of magic elixir is tossed into the pot. Yet the alchemists themselves always spoke of their art as being one of "sacrifice" and "spirituality." If transmuting lead into gold is not the real truth of alchemy, then what wisdom is hidden beneath its symbols and archaic images?

The Alchemical Metaphor

We discover the truth of alchemy when we accept it as metaphor—*an intricate allegory—for consciousness and as a clearly defined path for both spiritual and psychological development in which suffering and loss are seen as initiating events.* This is what is meant about turning lead into gold: It's the Buddha waking up. It is coming to new and expanded consciousness. It is realizing your ultimate potential and fully becoming the person you can be. Every true alchemist, including Nicholas Flamel, fully understood this. Artephius, a twelfth-century alchemist, wrote: "Is it not recognized that ours is a cabbalistic art? By this I mean that it is passed on orally and is full of secrets . . . I assure you in good faith that whoever would take literally what the alchemists have written will lose himself in the recesses of a labyrinth from which he will never escape." Sixteenth-century Swiss physician and alchemist Paracelsus makes clear that he is not really writing about changing physical metals like lead into gold, but about something else altogether, when he says, *aurum nostrum non est aurum vulgi*: "Our gold is not the gold of the common herd."

In describing the transformative process that emerges through suffering and a melting down of the self we think we are, Paracelsus wrote that alchemy is "nothing but the art which makes the impure into the pure through fire." Twentieth-century psychiatrist Carl Jung found alchemy a natural and exquisite metaphor. To Jung, the alchemical transformation of lead into gold perfectly describes the process of *individuation*. What is the gold the alchemist in all of us seeks? Jung put forth—the Self. Jung's description of the process of individuation illustrates the alchemical powers we all possess, to wake up as Buddha did, and become our most authentic Self. It is only in the process of every human being realizing his or her potential and becoming everything that he or she is capable of becoming that each of us can begin to see life as it really is and live it fully and with joy. Jung believed that the purpose of life was the unfolding of the unique, individual inner core or "Self" that is inherent in every person.

Jung described the Self as the archetype of wholeness, the regulating center of the psyche that transcends the ego or the "small self." The person you present to the world is the "small self" and is what we often think comprises everything about us. But, the most central, authentic aspect of ourselves is the Self (usually written with a capital *S* to differentiate it from the lowercase *s* of self, or ego). Just as the sun is the center of our solar system, the Self is the center of our psyche. It is the divine spark within us. It is our soul, the place where both spirit and the knowledge that we are part of a larger, transpersonal reality dwell. It is the Self that knows that we are more than just this insignificant person in a time-limited body who will cease to be upon our physical death. The Self is our essence, that which we would most want to carry through, in some form, in our children or in life beyond our own. It is the Self that shows us how to soar among the heavens, knowing ourselves to be just a little less than angels and destined for eternity. The Self is who we truly are; it is our life's gold.

The Self to Jung was far more than just a construct of personality theory. Self, according to his theory, incorporates soul, mystery, God-image within, and the ultimately unknowable essence that infuses every cell of our being. Symbols for the Self—the ideal of completion, integration, and perfection—abound in religious and wisdom traditions throughout time. The perfected Self is seen in the images of Christ, Buddha, Adam, the Cabalistic Tree of Life, the diamond in the lotus, mandalas, yantras, and the gods of pantheons too numerous to list. In all spiritual teachings to find the Self is to become enlightened. Buddhism teaches the importance of knowing *anatma*—the "not self"— that comprises our true nature and has nothing to do with what we typically call "myself." In Buddhist philosophy, as in Jung's, what we generally call "myself" is nothing more than the ego complex, a tiny part of our consciousness which usually holds such self-importance that it thinks it's all there is to us. In fact, the ego revolves around the Self—the true center of our being. *Atman* in Hinduism is the "Supreme Self" that cannot be comprehended by the mind. Instead it must be felt, experienced directly. To know this vital principle is to know everything and to realize that *Atman* is identical with the Absolute. Twentieth-century Hindu spiritual guide Anandamayi ma, called by her devotees Blissful Mother, is succinct in instructing this truth: "When one finds one's Self, one has found God; and finding God one has found one's Self." In the Gospel of Thomas, Jesus clearly points to the power of the Self and our inner Divinity when he reminds us that "the Kingdom is inside you."

Our Western rational minds often have trouble with these kinds of concepts, ones that dive deeply down into numinous waters. The experience of the Self is better described in the language of art, poetry, imagination, myth, and religion than by logical discourse. The *Katha Upanishad*, a sacred Indian text written prior to 400 B.C.E., says, "Soundless, formless, intangible, underlying, tasteless, odorless, eternal, immutable, beyond Nature is the Self." In spite of the difficulties in comprehending the idea of the Self, those who do encounter this most authentic part of ourselves find it an awe-inspiring and unforgettable mystical experience. If you have ever felt—however briefly—truly at one with yourself, deeply connected to a larger reality, and totally at peace, then you have met your Self. In his autobiography, Jung described the power of the Self in knowing both one's unique personality and one's connection to all that is: "The greatest limitation for man is the 'self' [lower case *s*]; it is manifested in the experience: 'I am *only* that!' Only consciousness of our narrow confinement in the self forms the link to the limitlessness of the unconscious. In such awareness we experience ourselves concurrently as limited and eternal, as both the one and the other. In knowing ourselves to be unique in our personal combination—that is, ultimately limited—we possess also the capacity for becoming conscious of the infinite."[1] In Jungian psychology the Self is the "God within us." And it is toward the experience of this spiritual and psychological wisdom that the path of individuation guides us. Suffering is often the door to individuation, and this Self *is* the gold the alchemist seeks.

It is the journey—the process of individuation—that brings us to fulfillment and new self-definition. We don't just wake up one day and know the Self. What characterizes this journey to Self-knowledge? The individuated person has accomplished the inner work of bringing dark, unconscious aspects of his or her personality into the light of awareness. Through such a journey, polarities like masculine/feminine, dark/light, positive/negative, good/bad, divine/human, alienation/inflation are reconciled and brought into new harmony and balance. We evolve a wiser, deeper understanding of the true nature of reality. In short, the individuated person—like Buddha—has awakened. The result is the expansion of consciousness.

A life well lived is a life of expanding consciousness and deep inner knowing. That, of course, is the opus, the Great Work, the goal. I could live my life, fearful of what each day may bring, always trying to keep my blinds drawn to sorrow and loss. Of course, I could not share myself with any living being (sorry, Dorothy), for fear of losing him or her, and I dare not look around and see how I am like others. Or I can embrace the dangerous beauty of life, opening my heart and expanding my consciousness to know my true Self, and to feel my connection to the universe.

Most of us will never truly reach the goal of individuation. Some sages even say that if you accomplish this great work, then you have about three days left to live because you've done what you were here to do. But to be in the process of knowing oneself, on the path of individuation, is enough because the value of this process lies in what happens along the way. On this path the important thing is what we learn about ourselves, about the experience of being human, about our relationship to ourselves, to all of life, and to the cosmos. It is the journey itself that is the destination. When we are on the path, we are at the goal. The psychological and spiritual process of individuation is the source of discovering meaning in one's life and the supplier of energy that allows us to live in truly creative, symbolic, and individual ways. With this newfound awareness, we are naturally happier, more mature, kinder, more compassionate, and we feel more connected to all of life.

If you think about how an oak tree is already contained in a tiny acorn or how a bloom is present though not yet visible within a seed, you'll have a good sense of Jung's process of individuation. Other thinkers and writers have used different words and images to describe the same process. Abraham Maslow, for example, called this journey of growth and self-awareness *self-actualization*. Others have referred to it as *self-realization*. On the cave wall at the Temple to Apollo at Delphi from whence the oracle spoke, ancient Greeks carved these plain words, "Know thyself." The *Tao te Ching* teaches that "knowing others is intelligence; knowing yourself is true wisdom."

Twentieth-century psychologists, like Jung, Maslow, Carl Rogers, Fritz Perls, and Alfred Adler, were not the first to see the process of "coming home to the Self" or fulfilling one's destiny by following one's unique path of development. This is an idea that has resonated in all cultures throughout history. The core of this philosophy of the development of personality is found in Western philosophy since the time of Aristotle and was discussed by Schopenhauer, Aquinas, Leibniz, Spinoza, and Locke, among others. The ancient world is filled with images, myths, music, fairy tales, poetry, and prayers that outline this spiraling pathway to the Self. The Navajo called the journey the *Pollen Path*, the

Sioux named it the *Good Red Road*, and the Chinese simply refer to it as the *Tao* or *the Way*. All these belief systems touch the dimension of divine mystery. But the common theme in all of them is that life is a journey and the goal is the discovery of one's true nature, a transformation of one's view of the world, an enhanced wisdom, and an authentic, loving connection to all of life and to some transcendent, universal power. It is this objective of the fully realized Self that is clearly implied in the alchemical process. It is the gold in lead, the light in matter, the *philosophers' stone* that represents the goal of the individuation process.

The "secret hidden in plain sight" of alchemy and Jungian psychology is that the goal, the sought after, is always there to be found. Both posit that the process of bringing forth gold from lead is not achieved by adding anything at all. In fact, both assume that the core of what is searched for is already present though hidden. That is, the gold is already there in lead and with enough time it would, by itself, transform into this splendid metal. After twenty odd years of looking at the same book, Nicholas Flamel discovers he can read it. Gautama Buddha when wracked with questions, doubts, and sorrows about life explores the world for wisdom without luck. He finally found the answers he sought when he sat glued to one spot, searching within. Deborah Cook looked within for the strength to go on when she faced a serious illness in herself and her child. Now she looks out at the same lawn and sees wonder where she once saw weeds.

The alchemists' task is simply to help the knowledge Nature provides by speeding up the process through boundless amplification. A frequently used axiom of alchemical writings is "Nothing from nothing comes." Scholar Manley P. Hall sums up this philosophy nicely when he observes that "alchemy is not the process of making something from nothing; it is the process of increasing and improving that which already exists."[2]

The wise of all ages acknowledge this tenet as it applies to many materials and situations. Michelangelo was once asked how he created such magnificent sculptures from a slab of hard, cold marble: "How did you create such beauty, such divinity that is the *Pietà*? How did you carve such magnificence into *David*?" Michelangelo reportedly was surprised at the question and simply replied, "I didn't do anything. God put them in the marble; they were already there. I only had to carve away the parts that kept you from seeing them." Just as Michelangelo believed his sculptures to be inherently contained in the marble, Jung believed that the whole, authentic person is already there underneath the neuroses, self-doubts, and unconscious blockages of our personalities. Viktor Frankl, in the midst of the hell of a concentration camp, realized that he had nothing to lose but his "ridiculously naked life." All the comfortable illusions that we hold dear, the constructs we patch up into the "ego" or "small self" that we show to the world, must be chipped away to reveal the true Self. This true Self is the acorn's promise of a tree, the pure, total potential we were at birth.

In fact, each of us was born whole with everything psychologically and spiritually intact. At the very beginning, we are one with our mothers and one with the universe. There is no consciousness, no ego; all is in the unconscious. We are one with everything. But as we grow and develop we begin to experience separation from all that is, from other people, and from objects in our environment. At about age two, we begin to hear this psychological process reflected in language, as we start to speak of ourselves in the first person. For the first time, there is an "I" or "me." As we go through life, we acquire a growing identification with the ego that acts as a barrier disconnecting us from our own Divine nature. In fact, as we struggle to adapt to our external environment and be accepted by the world around us, "I" becomes a heightening sense of who we are supposed to be rather than who we are. We become less like individuals and more and more like one another. We conform to social prescriptions, gender demands, family designs, and religious caveats. By the time we're adults, we begin to think that we are only the person we show to the rest of the world. Most of us have all but forgotten who we really are inside. We have forgotten the Self.

Most of us don't take the task of self-growth or individuation to heart. We're busy and sometimes lazy. I've yet to hear of someone who comes home after a hard week at work and looks at his or her spouse or partner and says, "You know what I'm going to do this weekend, honey? I'm going to grow." Daily life seems to take up most of our time and energy. Few people make space for meditation, reflection, or introspection about who they really are, what they are doing here, or, most important, what brings meaning to their life. To delve into ourselves is not always a pleasant journey or without risks. Facing the dark parts of our own personality can be terrifying. After all, who wants to discover that we are more than just the nice, acceptable persona we show to the world. Most of us want to cling to our comfortable sense of who we are or, rather, who we think we are. Most of us prefer our illusions—the status quo, our own versions of Pleasantville—to the cold and frightening truths about life. When things are going our way, we say to ourselves, "Don't let that wheel turn!" When we see before us the big train of suffering and loss that matches our ticket, most of us would just as soon stay home. Without a catalyst we would remain the same, would never grow, and never again know our Self. It is change and loss that create suffering, and it is suffering that propels us from the quiet shores of everyday life into the turbulent sea in which real growth occurs. Considering the emotional costs of the journey, we must take comfort in the assurance that a conscious life is golden.

Suffering is the alchemical fire that has the power to transport us from our ordinary, mostly unconscious lives into ones filled with meaning, purpose, and self-knowledge. It is the only way back and forward: back to who we always were and forward to who we can fully become. The unearthing of the gold of the Self in the lead of the ego is the gift of suffering. But this savage journey requires leaving what we know behind and becoming open, and truly vulnerable, to the truth about living a human life. We must bear the pain, endure the excruciating moments that declare with their arrival: "Life will never be the same." It's the price we pay, for new consciousness and the birth of the authentic Self can only be won through the refiner's fire. Because in spite of the promised benefits, the powerful ego usually resists. Most of us refuse to wake up, to let go of who we thought we were. We don't like to feel bad in this culture and so we grasp at straws, reaching for anything that will forestall the journey or offer the promise of a painless passage. Easy answers are offered by a wide variety of persuasive snake-oil salesmen, but none are true. The only way out is through.

If we allow ourselves to be laid open, in spite of our terror and trembling, it is possible to emerge, battered and bloody, but transformed. This journey is not for the timid or faint of heart; in fact, it requires enormous moral courage. Ordinarily, we do not choose the journey. Most often, it chooses us.

The Alchemical Process

Jeffrey Beaton had his life planned out. An honors student majoring in government and foreign affairs at the University of Virginia in 1977, he was about to wrap up his junior year. He'd been nominated for a Rhodes Scholarship and was going to spend an academic term at Oxford before returning to the States and law school. He describes himself, in those days, as ambitious: a career in trial law for certain, possibly elected positions beyond that—senator, maybe even president. Six foot three, handsome, athletic, and bright, Jeff Beaton was the model of the gentleman scholar and athlete at Mr. Jefferson's university.

Jeff was the captain of the UVA gymnastics team when good luck presented itself. The team was invited to help train the cheerleaders in exchange for the opportunity to perform with them the during half-time at one of the Cavaliers' legendary football games. Imagine. The gymnastics team right there strutting their stuff on the fifty-yard line in front of thousands of screaming UVA fans. It was too good a deal to pass up.

Jeff was working with the cheerleaders demonstrating a trick when suddenly the trampoline gave way beneath him. To this day, no one is completely sure exactly what happened. The trampoline was defective in some way. It moved or changed position. Jeff fell on his head and snapped his neck at the fourth vertebra. His spinal cord was severed. The swelling was quite severe at first, and so there was damage as high as the third vertebra (C3). When he landed, Jeff couldn't feel his arms or legs, and couldn't breathe. It was April 21, 1977. It was the last day Jeff was able to move any part of his body below his neck. "I immediately knew it was severe," he tells me. "It was pretty scary, but I didn't know that I'd never regain the use of my arms. I had known enough people who had been in accidents. I knew then that I might lose the use of my legs. I knew about paraplegia. I knew that there was death and there was paraplegia from these kinds of accidents. I didn't know about quadraplegia."

In spite of his devastating injury and his limited physical abilities, Jeff returned to classes in September. He dictated answers to exam questions and learned to turn the pages of his textbooks with a mouth stick. His stepfather's military insurance paid the doctor bills and he made his own luck. He earned scholarships and took out loans. He finished his undergraduate degree and UVA's challenging law school just five years after the accident.

Today, Jeff is forty-three, and a partner in a law firm he founded in Virginia Beach, Virginia, where he specializes in cases related to disability issues. It's a typical lawyers' office, lots of identical fat brown books on shelves, paralegals and secretaries streaming through with paperwork, jangling phones, and the hum of a copy machine whirring in the next room. But the waiting area is graced with several remarkable paintings. As I wait to meet with Jeff, I'm particularly taken with one that shows a peaceful beach scene. The color of the water is remarkable and I'm not ready to stop looking at it when his assistant calls to me. When I am ushered into Jeff's office I expect that the first thing I'll notice is that Jeff is in a wheelchair and that he can only move his head. I've wondered if his hands will look younger than those of a forty-something-year-old since they haven't moved in twenty-two years, haven't been hammered, scarred, or scraped as most of ours have. But, instead, the first thing I become aware of is his eyes. They are blue, the color of the ocean on clear fall days. There's a depth behind them and a wise, somewhat ironic, humor.

I learn something about his practice. In one of his landmark cases, he initiated a class action lawsuit against the City of Virginia Beach, which resulted in greater accessibility at the newly built Virginia Beach Amphitheater in 1996. I had been there not long ago to see a Tina Turner concert. I wondered how many Tina fans with disabilities might never have made it there were it not for his efforts. He sued the same city that had recognized him for his civic contributions and, in fact, just three years earlier named a day in his honor. He was an inaugural member of the Virginia Beach Human Rights Commission, a chairman of a training and advocacy center for people with disabilities, and an officer in the local Democratic party. He teaches as an adjunct faculty member at a local college and publishes widely on disability issues. He paints with acrylics on the weekends, holding the brush in his teeth and instructing his aide on the colors he'd like to mix. He reads every day and tends to like biographies, history, and books on the chaos theory of matter. He dictates journal entries and plans to write a novel. He was recently certified as a mediator, to help his clients find ways to solve conflicts without going to court.

To relax, Jeff tells me he loves to cook. It's his way of decompressing after a tough day at the office. "My way of cooking is telling someone else how to make a dish," he tells me. He loves cooking fish, fresh vegetables, and grilling outdoors. He makes everything from Southwest to Italian. "It's a chemistry thing for me," he says. "I don't use recipes as really good cooks might; I just use them as a point of departure. I'm that kind of cook." After dinner, Jeff and his wife, Sally, spend time reading, chatting, and having conversations about and with their Golden retreiver puppy, Cisco.

Jeff's dream of becoming a trial lawyer is unrealized. With a three-hour routine of physical therapy, dressing, and breakfast every morning, he'd never make the early-morning docket calls that trial lawyers must endure. Instead he specializes in cases that allow him to control his own schedule: estate planning, employment law, and disability cases.

When we talk, I raise the questions I am curious about. Does he regret what has happened in his life? Does he mourn for the paths not taken—the loss of a career as a trial lawyer or a stint as senator? "Sure," Jeff says, but then quickly adds that there are doors that open and doors that close. "I probably would be playing touch football on the beach and trying cases with the rest of them. I wouldn't get satisfaction out of teaching. I wouldn't paint. I wouldn't write. I think I'm a better person because I'm not just worried about beating someone's brains out in court."[3]

"We shouldn't expect that things will always be easy or fair. I kind of like the Buddhist ideas about life sometimes being a reign of shit and so when you are experiencing a good time you should notice it. If you have a day when the sun shines, you can be really happy and thankful because it will end at some point," Jeff tells me when I ask what his life has taught him.

This son of a Navy chief quite naturally turns to a military metaphor when he thinks about how he has chosen to live his life. "I think often about the World War II generation and what they did without ever asking 'should I go and fight?' The men who went to fight and the women who went to do their part as nurses or aides knew that it was a duty that was required of them and that it was part of their life. It was just a thing that had to be done. In the same way, I feel that life is a gift that's been given; our duty is to live it. I have a little credo and I don't expect anyone to adopt it but I just believe that if you feel simply, care deeply, and act passionately your life isn't going to go terribly wrong. Figure out what you care about and go and do it. That's it. After all, it's a life, not a lifestyle."

I wish that lead would simply turn into gold—"Poof!" If there were some instantaneous magic potion, we might all take a crowbar to Nicholas Flamel's old floorboards. But that's not how it happens. Alchemists describe a three-part process of transformation. The lead faces an arduous series of stages before it becomes changed into a precious metal. Alchemists called the first stage of the process of transformation the *nigredo*, or the "blackening." And it is here that everything is broken down into its primary elements, also known as the *prima material*, or the essence. Whatever was has ceased to exist. What we knew to be true can no longer be trusted. Like the caterpillar entering into the chrysalis and dissolving into a prebutterfly stew, it's total meltdown—everything is reduced to its constituent parts. This is the "fall" from our sense of normality, or the familiar.

Things come apart, the center cannot hold as we sacrifice our safe and predictable existence to embark on a journey that will take us who-knows-where. Old hurts, irrational assumptions about ourselves, and life itself are revealed as the imposters they are. Ways in which we've built our life upon the rickety foundation of erroneous preconceptions show themselves as shams. We may discover that we've elaborated a whole worldview—a comprehensive philosophy based on spurious dogma or a willful blindness to life's more painful truths. Perhaps we believed we would never have to suffer. Wrong. Perhaps we believed that we deserve our suffering because we're not good enough. Wrong. Perhaps we believed that somehow we're different, separate from every other human being in the world. Wrong. One by one these falsehoods die in the smelting of the *nigredo*, the terrible descent from where we were to where we are going.

At this time, unconscious material and long-ignored complexes simmer to the surface from deep below like bubbles oozing up from some primeval tar pit. We start to see things about ourselves that we'd rather not. We may see how we've used past hurts to live in a state of seething pain. Perhaps for the first time, there is lucid and indisputable evidence that there is more to us than simply the acceptable self we show to the world. As agonizing as this can be, a certain kind of freedom is granted: freedom to extend our views and develop a more flexible, expanded, and accurate take on the world. We may also begin to know other more positive things about ourselves. We may see courage, love, creativity, and passions long ignored. Just as there are no magic potions that instantly change lead into gold, a shift in consciousness cannot be scheduled in between appointments. This stage may take time to unfold, and the pain and knowledge that come about may take years to reveal themselves. This process is the ultimate testament to the old adage "Nothing worth doing is easy." A new consciousness percolates only through the pain of the descent.

The worst part of the journey is not knowing, sometimes not even being able to imagine, where we might emerge. It's no wonder we feel betrayed, disoriented, depressed, anxious, maybe even scared to death during this time. Marion Woodman speaks to the panic of initiation by simply observing that "life as we have known it is over."[4] Emily Dickinson, with her typical economy of language, gets right to the point: "There is a pain," she says, "so utter."

The *nigredo* stage was announced at the moment when Jeff Beaton fell from that trampoline. It's Deborah Cook sitting anxiously in her doctor's office as he clears his throat and delivers the bad news that her daughter has leukemia. It's Tom watching his boss fumbling through paperwork, smiling apologetically, and telling him that in spite of his outstanding performance, his job is gone. It's Deanne and my dad watching helplessly as nanoseconds move in slow motion and a Buick sedan plows head-on into their car. It's a phone call in the middle of the night announcing the death of a loved one, the whirling gray blur of a tornado streaking across the landscape headed toward your house. It's lipstick on his collar or a lump in your breast. It's chaos revealed, the dark night of the soul, the night sea journey, the descent into hell, and the belly of the whale. Alchemists in a genuine "department of redundancy department" moment, referred to this stage of the journey as a "black, blacker than black." The *nigredo* begins with a million different moments but with a single common theme—life as we have known it is now over.

Amid the sheer fright of initiation it's hard to hold on to hope for life after the fall. In the daze of such astonishing pain, it's almost impossible to imagine that this is but the first phase of a process that holds the potential to transmute lead into gold. In this violent coming together of the conscious and unconscious parts of our personality there can be the thrill of discovery, as Jeff Beaton found in his paintings and Deborah Cook sees in the wonder of clover on her front lawn. It is here that we can learn to love ourselves as we are and work at self-improvement with compassion rather than through guilty, mean-spirited reproach. In the midst of all of it, it's important to remember that there will be better days ahead. At one point, we will awaken to a bright new morning with eyes that are clear and see the world anew.

Michael Maier, an alchemist working in the early seventeenth century, confirmed the metamorphosis that is inherent in the alchemical process. He elaborated the chemical model into one that is singularly psychological: "There is in our chemistry a certain noble substance, in the beginning whereof is wretchedness with vinegar, but in its ending joy with gladness," he wrote in *Atalanta Fugiens*. "Therefore I have supposed that the same will happen to me, namely that I shall suffer difficulty, grief, and weariness at first, but in the end shall come to glimpse pleasanter and easier things."[5]

Initiation demands a sacrifice, to be sure, but even the word *sacrifice* itself predicts light at the end of the tunnel. From the Latin *sacrificium*, it means the forfeiting of something of importance in the service of receiving something of even greater value. The word literally means "to make holy." In the psychological and spiritual sense, it means giving up the daydreams and dependencies of childhood to reenter the world as an adult who can understand the realities of the human experience. It is waking up and the emergence of the light of consciousness from the dark prison of illusion. It is the splendor of gold from simple lead.

The stage called the *albedo*, "the whitening," follows the *nigredo*. This is a purification of all the constituent elements mixed together in the alchemical process. Matter becomes transparent. Chaos begins to settle into some kind of order. Hints about the true potentialities of the *prima materia* can be ever so slightly glimpsed by those who dare to keep their eyes open. It is here that we come to really know ourselves. We have begun to realize at this point that we have been given a remarkable opportunity to work through conflicts and issues that have been repressed in the service of daily life. Unconscious aspects of the Self tentatively thrust their way to the surface of our awareness in the way the first green shoots, tiny and barely seen tendrils, push their way through the scorched earth following a raging forest fire. This work of whitening is that of bringing silver from lead—pure, subtle, luminous, clear, like water from a pure spring. It's a washing clean, a baptism. It is spiritual and psychological awakening. We begin to see ourselves and the world, quite literally, in a new light.

Jung knew the alchemical process to be an accurate metaphor for individuation and consciousness. Yet, much of his writing on this subject is ethereal. This may be because to attempt to catch a clear meaning of this process is like trying to hold smoke in your hands. He does, however, recount correspondence from a former patient whose simple and trenchant words illuminate this process of transformation most clearly. Sometime prior to 1968, she wrote to Jung the following letter:

"Out of evil, much good has come to me. By keeping quiet, repressing nothing, remaining attentive, and by accepting reality—taking things as they are, and not as I wanted them to be—by doing all this, unusual knowledge has come to me, and unusual powers as well, such as I could never have imagined before. I always thought that when we accepted things they overpowered us in some way or other. This turns out to not be true at all, and it is only by accepting them that one can assume an attitude toward them. So now I intend to play the game of life, being receptive to whatever comes to me, good and bad, sun and shadow forever alternating, and, in this way, also accepting my own nature with its positive and negative sides. Thus everything becomes more alive to me. What a fool I was! How I tried to force everything to go according to the way I thought it ought to!"[6]

Like Jung's patient, Jeff Beaton also intends to play the game of life. With all his numerous accomplishments and in spite of his great losses, Jeff thinks often of his art. He is drawn to many subjects: buildings because they have their own way of expressing things and water because it reflects so many colors, creating its own at the same time. "When the sun is low in the sky and it's shining through a tree onto water, the light can be like gold coins, no longer blue or green," he tells me. "It's not a reflection but a dark, deep inviting color with this gold on top. That's what I see; it's one of the most beautiful images that water effects."

Jeff's voice lowers a bit when he talks about painting and his work as an artist. There's a reverence that shines through his words, and I sit speculating about whether or not an aggressive trial lawyer would ever have noticed the way water reflects light and creates gold coins shimmering across the surface.

The *albedo* stage begins when we have mourned long enough to see new possibilities. It's the crack of dawn but not yet sunrise. We are more aware of our complexes and, therefore, less likely to project our hurt and anger on other people. We've established a new relationship and a dynamic inner dialogue between the unconscious and conscious parts of our personality. We've accepted the reality that life includes suffering and there's no reason to think that we'll be exempt. With a newfound consciousness that is both alert and adaptable, we're far less likely to get blindsided by dissociated feelings and beliefs. We're becoming free from our conditioned responses, our habitual, often quite inaccurate, view as to what to expect from life or from ourselves. We're moving toward what the Greeks described as the true meaning of life. We're beginning to know ourselves.

If we can hang in there and not attempt to avoid our reality, we enter the final stage of the alchemical process called the "reddening," the *rubedo*. In it, we experience a reclamation of passion, an aliveness that we may have never known before. Our personality has changed. Our spirit is renewed. Through suffering, we've moved light-years ahead in our development. Abraham Maslow outlined the characteristics of a fully actualized human being who embraces both psychological maturity and spiritual enlightenment. In researching great numbers of diverse individuals, he says that over and over again, he found the same common features. These are the ones that he says are shared by all individuated people: aspects of people who have "awakened," and turned lead into gold. These are the rewards for the painful journey. As you read these, think about how they apply to you:

1. Realistic orientation
2. Acceptance of self, others, and the natural world
3. Spontaneity
4. Task orientation, rather than self-preoccupation
5. Sense of privacy
6. Independence
7. Vivid appreciativeness
8. Spirituality that is not necessarily religious in a formal sense
9. Sense of identity with mankind
10. Feelings of intimacy with a few loved ones
11. Democratic values
12. Recognition of the difference between means and ends
13. Humor that is philosophical rather than hostile
14. Creativeness
15. Nonconformism

Maslow's ideas about the self-actualized personality describe a psychologically mature individual who is self-knowing, is able to experience meaningful, intimate relationships with others, has a deep understanding of the human experience, and is capable of great joy and a sense of connectedness to the powers of the universe.

After the soul's journey of individuation, and the pain of suffering that propels us, are we apt to waste a God-given day fuming about the guy who cut us off on the freeway? Will we plot our revenge, while recounting the tale to everyone who has the misfortune to see us that day, carrying and feeding our slight with a constant infusion of unconscious negative emotions tied to every small injustice we ever experienced? I think not.

The outcome of individuation, the *rubedo*, is the gold that alchemists searched for with such insatiable hunger. This stage of the process is often described as feeling as if we've connected with some deep, wise, healing part of the unconscious psyche. Jung would call this "a meeting with the Self" and a chemical marriage between the conscious and unconscious. Deborah Cook would say, "I see things differently." Viktor Frankl would announce that he had found his meaning. Robert Urich would talk about his "defining moment." The alchemists would declare a completion of the opus, the Great Work. Like the butterfly emerging from the long isolation and despair of the chrysalis, like the Phoenix powerfully rising from the smoky ashes, we spread our wings and fly. The *rubedo* makes known the deeper meaning of our existence. Here is the substantial self-knowing that is, at once, deeply spiritual as well as psychologically and philosophically enlightened. This is wholeness, completeness, the goal of the individuation process. Here is the sunrise. Rebirth. Resurrection. Here are gold coins on the surface of water.

Brick Houses and Straw Houses: How Prepared Are We for Hard Times?

A deep distress hath humanized my soul.

—William Wordsworth

In *Animal Farm*, author George Orwell describes the emergence of a totalitarian state. This political allegory still makes me tremble many years after having first read it. In the beginning, all the farm animals create rules to live by that they hope will result in an enlightened society. They develop a list of seven commandments, the most important of which is their ultimate doctrine of fairness: "All animals are created equal." Throughout the course of the novel (as so often in life), power and greed corrupt the piggish farm leaders and, in the end, their utopian ideal of justice is wickedly debased. In the end, there is only one commandment left: "All animals are equal, but some animals are more equal than others."

That rings true, doesn't it? Some animals are more equal than others. Among us human animals, although we are all created equal in a deep, spiritual sense, not all of us are equally blessed with benefits, love, safety, inclusion, or even bare necessities. In meeting the challenges of suffering that life brings, not everyone is equally well prepared or well equipped. This may not be fair, but it is true. Adults who were loved and cherished as children, who felt safe and protected by their parents, who learned that they were truly a part of a family or tribe and even given some opportunities for optimal frustration are *generally* more resilient. They are often better able to bounce back, after experiencing difficult and painful losses. Those who came from only moderately dysfunctional families (in my experience, there is no such thing as a "perfect" family or one without a few twists and turns of dysfunction) and were taught to draw on and respect their own inner courage will usually have an easier time rolling with life's punches than those who were not granted those blessings. In fact, this disparity is shown very clearly in another familiar parable that, once again, uses barnyard animals to make a point.

The fairy tale of *The Three Little Pigs* shows us that we don't all construct equally durable shelters that can protect us in difficult, painful times. As adults, most people who have had a trauma-free history have personalities that are figuratively like the brick house of the resourceful little pig. These structures are better able to withstand the huffing and puffing of the big bad wolf. On the other hand, children who are raised with violence, abuse, neglect, addicted caretakers, or a lack of love by wounded parents often find themselves as adults living in stick houses, some in even less stable straw houses. These adequate shelters offer little protection from the blowing of the wolf. And, as we've seen, the wolf will blow into everyone's life eventually. Challenging times will visit us all and shake our foundations, but some of us will come through relatively intact while others will be shattered.

It would seem that we might be able to predict accurately who will fall apart when painful times present themselves simply by knowing a person's history. Conventional wisdom holds that someone who endured a difficult childhood should be carrying deep psychological wounds and would, understandably, not be as resilient as someone who did not. These unfortunate people, "less equal than others," should not be as capable of extracting gold from the lead of suffering as those who grew up in less challenging families. But conventional wisdom does not always hold true. Not everyone who was raised with difficult childhood circumstances has psychological problems as adults. Not everyone who suffered abuse or great pain as a child becomes a criminal, mentally ill, or unable to cope with life's suffering. In fact, I'm often amazed at the ways in which many people who suffered great hardships as children rise to courageously meet difficult circumstances, translate suffering into self-growth, become compassionate through their own losses, and discover spiritual wisdom by way of pain. As a therapist, I've met many, many people whose backgrounds fill me with sorrow for the child they were, while they sit before me now as competent, caring adults.

It appears that history alone is not enough to explain who will become bitter versus better as a result of life's battering. I've always been intrigued by the notion that some people are born as "old souls," building on multiple reincarnations to learn the tricks about how to be resilient, coping, compassionate human beings. But there are less mystical explanations. There are some attenuating circumstances, some variables that are not yet fully understood, that inoculate a child against carrying the pain of the past into the adult present and, ultimately, the future.

Psychoanalyst Alice Miller's breakthrough work on children and abuse shows clearly both the profound difficulties and tendencies toward violence as well as the unbelievable creativity of adults who were victims of inadequate—even abusive and cruel—child rearers. In analyzing the life histories of famous people, Miller explores the question of what makes one child channel her suffering into art while another expresses that same kind of anger and pain through deadly acts of revenge or self-hatred. What makes one victimized, suffering person reach out for paints, musical instruments, or notebooks as tools for healthy self-expression, while another grabs for a gun or an overdose, turning his torment back out against the world or himself? The answers are not entirely clear, but some thinkers have put forth some interesting and plausible ideas. For example, by comparing the life histories of Picasso, Buster Keaton, Hitler, and Stalin (among many others), Alice Miller concluded that it is the presence of an enlightened witness—a counteragent to the cruelty that surrounds a child—that makes the difference between constructive and destructive expressions of trauma and anguish. If Miller is right, and I believe she is, her evidence speaks mightily to the power that we adults have in our roles as teachers, relatives, and neighbors to diminish the suffering of children and build foundations for a healthy, violence-free society.[1] Longitudinal studies have demonstrated that at least one in ten adults who grew up surrounded by loss, parental illness, divorce, poverty, or turmoil is an exceptionally capable person.[2] Based on my experience, I would argue that the percentage is higher than that.

By the same token, those who grew up in "good-enough" families, without abuse or disaster, do not inevitably grow up to become competent, healthy adults. There is not a one-to-one correlation between having a relatively painless childhood and becoming a psychologically and spiritually healthy adult. Uneven playing fields for children don't always explain adult scores.

Regardless of statistics, almost everyone who has experienced great suffering in childhood knows in their hearts that they didn't start on a level playing field. Because they were victims of an emotionally impoverished, traumatic, or terrifying childhood—many people in this group, unfortunately, believe that they are destined to fall apart when the demands of life become hard, or when they are again confronted with the suffering that is an intrinsic part of life.

Uneven Playing Fields

Stacy was one of those people whose challenges in life started very early. She was twenty-eight and looked like a young Diana Ross. Stacy was one of the most physically beautiful women I had ever seen. Tall, even statuesque, with stunningly fine features, she carried herself with the grace of a dancer. In addition to her exceptional beauty, Stacy was very bright, kind, well-read, and motivated enough to be putting herself through college while she worked at a full-time job. I met Stacy after she had been admitted to a psychiatric hospital following a near-fatal suicide attempt. She had tried to take her life in response to her boyfriend's leaving. Stacy never said much about her own experience or feelings during the group therapy sessions. Her body language suggested profound shyness and, although she seemed interested in and concerned about the other group members, she rarely offered a comment and never made direct eye contact.

During an early-morning session, a middle-aged woman named Lynn was telling the group how unprepared she was to deal with her recent divorce. "I never saw it coming," she said. "After almost thirty years of marriage, he just walked out the door as if he didn't feel a thing about it."

Stacy cleared her throat and in a genuine moment of empathy said, "That must have broken your heart wide open. I feel that, too." Lynn nodded and told her it felt good that somebody else knew exactly how she felt. She thanked Stacy for her support. With that comment, that wee bit of affirmation and thanks, Stacy's floodgates opened wide. It was as if she had waited for this very moment, safe and encircled by caring people, to unleash a lifetime of unspoken pain. She told us about the night her boyfriend came home and said that their relationship was over, he was moving out. This shouldn't have come as a surprise to Stacy, because his announcement followed numerous affairs with other women during their four-year relationship. But Stacy's world exploded. She described the chill that descended on her, the pure sense of loss and abandonment that she could barely put into words. She told us about being sexually abused when she was seven and the physical violence that filled her childhood. Without a hint of self-pity, she related a story that still sends shivers up my spine.

There was one time, Stacy said, when she snatched her six-year-old brother out of their father's vein-popping stranglehold on his throat and ran, dragging him with her, into the woods. Stacy scrambled over thistles and dead trees, scraping her legs until they bled, but didn't stop. She hid both of them from her father who raged and screamed while wildly firing his shotgun into the trees after them. She remembers that it was a still night and the ground was damp. The air smelled of burnt leaves and the earthy scent of horses and newly cut hay from the meadow nearby. At first, the sounds of squirrels and rabbits moving through the underbrush unnerved her—she thought her father had found their hiding place. But soon the night became quiet and the rustling leaves and the small creatures making the sounds became somehow comforting to her, Stacy explained. Her brother shivered all night, and so she covered him with her own body and hummed an old song that her grandmother had taught her to keep him quiet. They stayed there until well past dawn, watching for their father to leave the house; only then did they return home. Without taking a breath, Stacy then told us that she always knew she would never amount to anything. The group was shocked at Stacy's conclusion.

"How can you say that? Look at how brave you were, and you were only a child yourself. You protected your little brother, maybe saved his life," one woman said.

Stacy looked completely bewildered. The idea that she could be brave seemed never to have occurred to her. "My father always told me

I'd never amount to anything. He called me a whore because I walked home from school with a boy in third grade. He said I'd never be able to take care of myself." Stacy's childhood was an unending torrent of abuse and condemnation. She was told that she was "weak," "ugly," and "spoiled" and could never learn to cope with life's problems. Her parents and siblings nicknamed her Wimpy and mocked her when this sensitive little girl cried normal tears for the disappointments in her life. The therapy group listened quietly, offering unspoken support and compassion, but everyone became slack jawed when this beautiful woman added, "Besides, I'm so ugly, no wonder I can't keep a boyfriend." One older man in the group looked carefully at her for a moment, then timidly and not a bit unkindly said, "You *must* be nuts!"

It might be hard for some people to identify with Stacy. After all, most people don't attempt suicide and end up in a psychiatric hospital. But until that moment of complete despair, Stacy was a coping adult. She held a responsible job, had friends, and was an active member of her church. She was able to hold herself together until life delivered one of its inevitable losses, and then she blew apart. Plunged into the *nigredo* and believing that she lacked the tools to painstakingly find her way back, Stacy gave up on life itself. When the rug was snatched out from under Stacy by her boyfriend's rejection, her ideas about how life should be stopped working. Stacy's unconscious defenses, which were her repression of her childhood hurts, denial of her past pain, and rationalizations for staying in an unhealthy, one-sided relationship, fell apart. It was as if all the suffering of her past had just been sitting there, patiently waiting to plunge her into darkness when her heart broke open and her psychological defenses were unable to withstand the strain.

We've been conditioned to think that suffering only comes from major losses in our lives: the death of a loved one, loss of relationship or security, diagnosis of a fatal illness. But suffering comes in lots of flavors, and a great deal of our pain arises from day-to-day experiences that challenge our courage and erode our sense of well-being. B. J. appears to be a very successful, happy man. He's never attempted suicide and never been hospitalized for psychiatric problems. But when I met him, he was in very different straits.

B. J. grew up on the wrong side of the tracks in a dirt-poor, little town in western Virginia. The only major employer in the area was a paper mill. B. J. recalls that the stink rising from that plant made newcomers gag three miles away. The town was settled in a bowl-like valley where nothing could escape; foul brown air hung like a dirty canopy, and even on nearly clear days it was impossible to see the Blue Ridge Mountains that surrounded it. A filthy river flowed behind the factory and carried off its chemicals and collapsed boxes beyond the valley. The people's hopes and dreams seemed to follow that brown river right out of town. Most families lived in old wooden houses that were sad and gray, their paint worn away from a thousand rainstorms and never replaced for lack of money and caring. Porches and front steps sagged and rotted; most were propped up with cinder blocks halfheartedly shoved underneath. Poverty and despair shadowed this place.

The whole town was hard up, but B. J.'s family was among the poorest because his father couldn't keep a job and was always bouncing around in neighboring towns looking for work. In fact, B. J.'s father was never able to hold down a job for more than a week at a time. He'd make it to the job for a few days, then come home from work, go on a drinking binge, and wouldn't show up again for the rest of the week. Of course, he'd get fired and warned that he should never come back. But, then, the plant would have some rush job, need more help, and hire him on again. B. J. reports that his father did have a temper and sometimes when he came home smelling of beer and bourbon, he'd get nasty. However, B. J. is quick to point out that his father's parents were also abusive alcoholics. "My father never beat me like he was beaten. For that, I'm grateful," he says. When B. J.'s father was drunk and not at home, you could count on the fact that he'd be thrown in jail for fighting in the bar. In a little town like this one, everyone knew everyone else's business and, so it was no secret when B. J.'s father was in jail. B. J. recalls the shame he felt when he'd get on the school bus and the other kids would tease him about his father. They made up singsongy rhymes that made fun of him and his younger siblings. As the oldest son, B. J. felt a strong responsibility to the younger kids in his family and he often found himself in detention hall for punching the kids on the bus who were taunting the little ones.

"It was like living on a merry-go-round," B. J. told me. "Some days my father would resolve to straighten up. He'd hit work hard for a few days and he'd come home, cheerful, acting real responsible, telling us to clean our rooms and help with the dishes. Sometimes he'd come home and bring me a present even though it wasn't my birthday or Christmas."

One afternoon, B. J.'s father came home with a silver bike sporting red, white, and blue streamers on the ends of the handlebars. B. J. loved this bike, and he told me about the thrill he felt riding out past the edge of town. Here, he says, he could see the tops of the mountains and the country road that led to the interstate. It was in this spot that B. J. realized that he would never live in this town once he was grown. He could almost see the way to Richmond or Washington. From there, B. J. looked out and knew he could go anywhere. Sadly, B. J. had the bike for less than two weeks. His father was fired again, money got tight, and the bike vanished. Its disappearance was never discussed. It was just gone.

But B. J. had the bike long enough to see his way out and make a decision about his future. "I was in the fourth grade, I remember exactly the moment when I decided I was getting out of there as soon as I could," he told me. "I was going to show them that I wasn't going to be made fun of anymore."

When he was seventeen, B. J. left home and joined the Navy. He felt guilty about leaving his mother and his younger brothers and sisters at home. He wrote them often, and sent money home to help with the bills. B. J. was naturally smart, motivated, and a quick study. He did very well in the Navy and used the G.I. Bill to get a college education. Today, he makes good money as an engineer, and it seems as though he's really gotten his life together. B. J. should be proud of his many accomplishments, but he doesn't see them. He could feel good about himself if he could only acknowledge how far he's come from his humble and difficult beginnings. But he doesn't.

Instead, B. J. is constantly in debt because he spends far more money than he earns. He feels driven to prove to other people that he is good enough. I think B. J. unconsciously believes that if he can surround himself with enough of the trappings of success, then no one can make fun of him. When I point this out, he doesn't necessarily believe me and says that he's "just not good with money." But I sense that he's on a mission. B. J. consistently buys more and more expensive clothes even though his closets are already overflowing and his charge cards are maxed out. He drives a $75,000 automobile despite the fact that he struggles monthly to make the payments. Recently, B. J. bought a house that costs far more than he can afford and joined an expensive country club that he rarely visits. B. J. is not enjoying spending money or the things he purchases with it. In fact, his habits are ruining his life and making him ill. He is always stressed out about his debts, becomes despondent when he sits down to pay bills, and has declared bankruptcy twice in the last fourteen years. B. J.'s been diagnosed with hypertension and serious ulcers that his doctors say are obviously made worse by stress.

Because a great deal of his stress is created by dunning letters from creditors and his inability to meet his monthly financial obligations, you would think B. J. would have a great incentive to make changes in the way he spends money. But he doesn't change a thing. In the middle of his second bankruptcy, even as the paperwork was being recorded at city hall, he borrowed money to buy a classic 1920 automobile. When B. J. explains his purchase to me, he says it is a showpiece that he "had to have." When I met him, B. J. was well on his way to a moment of true suffering in the loss of his health or all of his beloved material possessions or both.

Both Stacy and B. J. would agree that the playing field of their childhoods was uneven. But it took each of them time to see how they continue to suffer greatly because they carry their pasts with them as part of their self-image. Because both experienced difficult choldhoods, their self-definitions were set earlier and more narrowly. Stacy believed that she was ugly, would never amount to anything, and couldn't be expected to endure suffering with courage or grace because she had always been told that. Her parents and those around her shone that distorted image of herself back on her like some grotesque reflection from a funhouse mirror. She was told that she was worthless, inadequate, and weak. How could such a person be competent to take care of herself as an adult or be capable of learning from life's difficulties? This was the conclusion Stacy reached at a young age and kept with her into adulthood. This negative message was the truth she saw when her life came apart. With it firmly rooted within her, Stacy had no foundation, no basis, to believe that she could handle it. In spite of all her successes, her self-image has never changed from the brutalized little girl who was told she was worthless. That is what surfaced when Stacy faced the challenge of her boyfriend's rejection and the prospect of life alone.

A great deal of B. J.'s suffering—his daily stress about money, the health problems resulting from his chronic anxiety, his feelings that he's never good enough unless he drives the right car and wears the best clothes—is self-imposed and, like Stacy's, emerges from an inaccurate self-image based on faulty reasoning. He has internalized images of taunting children and his feelings of profound shame about the poverty he lived in as a child. He lives with these mental pictures every day, although he has not experienced their reality for more than twenty-five years. By keeping those images alive in his mind's eye, B. J. unconsciously creates his own suffering. So does Stacy. Her beliefs that she is worthless and unable to cope allowed her to accept a relationship with a self-centered and philandering boyfriend. Then, when he left her, she was ready to die. It's easy to see how both B. J. and Stacy are creating their own cycle of suffering by holding on to their childhood pain and self-images that don't reflect the truth about their own abilities and realities as adults.

Self-Images and Suffering

B. J. and Stacy deserve our compassion and should not be blamed because they are unconsciously replaying a cycle of suffering. But we can learn from their examples and perhaps reduce our own self-inflicted suffering. When we understand how our self-image is contributing to our pain, we can begin to make changes that put us on a different course. We can look at our lives and explore how we see ourselves, setting off with a more balanced and truthful self-image and view of the world that will enable us to confront life's challenges NOT as self-fulfilling prophecies, but as opportunities for growth.

Take a moment now to think about how you see yourself. Do you hold a self-image that causes you unnecessary suffering? How does your self-image come into play when you've suffered a great loss? Do you understand how your personal self-image was formed and, most important, do you think you can change the parts of it that are self-defeating or inadequate to the task of living that is destined to include loss and grief? These are probably not questions that you can answer fully right now. But if you keep them in mind as you move through life, you may be surprised at what you uncover.

What we're told about ourselves, especially at critical developmental periods, informs our conscious and unconscious self-image. There are positive and negative messages we receive. But, there is strong evidence that traumatic experience is more deeply encoded in our minds and more easily recalled in our memories. That is why people can remember extraordinary sense-filled details—the merest particulars like the smell of burnt leaves or the faces of taunting children—of tragic or terrifying moments that happened twenty years ago, as Stacy and B. J. both did, while at the same time they can't tell you what they had for lunch yesterday. Recent psychoneurological research has revealed how emotions and memories are processed in the brain and confirm that traumatic experiences in childhood are stored and processed by early-developing, nonverbal parts of the brain such as the amygdala. This goes far in explaining why we may experience strong emotions that seem illogical in our present circumstances as adults. Now we know how and why they may stem from the responses we had as children. For example, as children we may have felt panic when our mother screamed at us. Now, as adults, we may have that same automatic anxiety-filled reaction when our spouse raises his or her voice.

We're hard-wired, it seems, to remember our suffering. The details of it are shuffled into both conscious and unconscious places in our psyche. The parts of ourselves that are conscious are the least problematic, for self-awareness allows us to look at our histories and see where and why we learned some of the things we have. When something is conscious, we can look at our experiences with understanding. B. J., for example, was able to describe his father with a real understanding of the factors that contributed to his alcoholism and faulty parenting. Consciousness has a way of seeing into the truth and that is essential to knowing one's Self. Acknowledging the truth about ourselves, our experiences, and the nature of the world is the goal toward which suffering propels us. It is the way of individuation. I know that it's not easy facing these dark places where truth resides because it requires revisiting painful experiences. It's a walk through a dark forest, an encounter with the dragon. Thoreau was right when he observed that both "truth and roses have thorns about them"—yet perceiving what is true is the only path to enlightened consciousness. Our unconscious, however, makes this journey one that is much more challenging. It is a puzzle that can take a lifetime even to begin to solve.

I like to think of the relationship between what is conscious, what we know, and what is unconscious, what we don't know, as being like an iceberg. Consciousness is the small amount (maybe less than 10 percent) that we know about ourselves, and that's just the tip of the iceberg—the part that shows above the water. The greatest amount of the iceberg's mass, which is submerged beneath the waves, is the unconscious. The unconscious is what we *don't know* about ourselves. That chunk of cold, blue ice *above* the surface of the water isn't what sinks the ships. What we can see, we can navigate around. It's the part that we can't see that rips the ship wide open and sends it spiraling to the bottom of the sea.

Underneath the surface, the unconscious draws all of its conclusions by way of deductive logic. That's a form of reasoning by which a specific conclusion is accepted based on one or more premises. If deductive reasoning is valid, the conclusions must be true if the premises are true. Here's an example of accurate deductive reasoning: If it is true that all normal dogs are born with four legs and one head, and it is true that Dorothy is a normal dog, then therefore it must logically be concluded that Dorothy has one head and four legs. (This is true, by the way.) Much deductive reasoning is phrased in syllogisms, which are arguments in which two premises are given and a logical conclusion is deduced from them. Over and over, with every life experience, the unconscious sits there and says, "If A is true and B is true, therefore, the conclusion C must be also true." Stacy's unconscious—like all of ours—used this form of logic. Had it not been for an unexpected visit from a concerned neighbor who found Stacy (quite literally) unconscious after overdosing, this faulty reasoning would have killed her. One can almost hear Stacy's inner thoughts, her unconscious grinding away day after day, night after night: "All children who are weak, ugly, and unable to cope become weak, ugly, and noncoping adults. I was a weak and ugly child who couldn't be strong, therefore I am a weak and ugly adult. I can't cope." With this only conclusion to guide her, Stacy felt hopeless and quite easily swallowed a handful of barbiturates when the man she loved left her for another woman.

There is a secret about the unconscious that few people know, but it explains Stacy's and B. J.'s erroneous beliefs about themselves and, perhaps, many of our own misconceptions: *The unconscious draws conclusions from false premises just as effortlessly as it does from those that are true.* False premises—based on one's history, experience, belief system, or worldview—are not seen by our unconscious minds as the lies that they are. This is bad news because these lies are grist for the deductive logic mill in exactly the same way that truth is. The bottom line is that the unconscious is simply not very good at sorting out premises that are true versus those that are not true. Both serve equally well as the foundations upon which many conclusions will be built. When the same conclusions are repeated often enough, even though they might very well be false, they begin to solidify into our self-image. While most people don't think about what kind of reasoning process is going on under the surface, they reveal its effects with statements like "That's just the way I am," "I could never do that well," and "People like me can't _____ (be successful, change, overcome obstacles, learn to tap dance, or fill in your own 'can't'). Human beings seem to have an innate need to hang onto self-definitions that are solidly in place no matter how painful or off base they are.

I think it's easy to see how one of the most powerful causes of everyday suffering is the way we get trapped in false images of ourselves. Many people who've been wounded and humiliated as children—like B. J. and Stacy—continue to carry those injuries into adult life. As long as these wounds sustained in youth are unconscious and bleeding, they will continue to create suffering. I have a friend who was physically and sexually abused as a child. She calls herself a "survivor" and, of course, she is. She should feel proud of herself for living through those terrible times and retaining her strength and spirit. She will never forget those experiences—nor should she. But while her past abuse is a part of who she is today, she sometimes seems to think that it comprises her whole identity. Lots of people seem to use past pain as their primary and exclusive self-definition instead of just a part of who they are: "I'm an adult child of an alcoholic," "I can't have a good relationship because my parents didn't," and "I've always been depressed because depression runs in my family." I like to remind those folks that families also pass down native languages, like French, but that doesn't mean you can't learn a new language. There is great danger and enormous suffering that comes from allowing ourselves to remain trapped in the familiar, though painful, role of downtrodden victims heading down a road that is always self-destructive and quite often deadly. This unhealthy and habitual attachment to our negative histories is what my friend Ruth calls "ancient shit."

It's also very clear to me that the self-images we hold with our minds, hearts, and souls determine our reality. What we imagine, we will manifest. For example, if I believe that I'm a worthless person, then my decisions and actions will remain consistent with that idea and even prove it to be true. The human psyche seems to set up these self-fulfilling prohecies quite easily.

I once had a client named Anna who had been down the aisle eight times. I remember thinking: "Wow! She has the same number of ex-husbands as Elizabeth Taylor Hilton-Wilding-Todd-Fisher-Burton-Burton-Warner-Fortensky." But here's the really fascinating part: Every time—without a single exception—Anna married an abusive, alcoholic man. The fact that her father was an abusive, alcoholic who treated her badly and often acted as if she didn't exist was well known to her, but it took her a long time to see how she was reinstating her negative self-image by her choice of husbands. Every time she said "I do" to one of these guys, she reinforced her belief that she is insignificant and doesn't deserve to have a healthy, nonabusive relationship. I remember the first question she asked me after reciting a litany of her failed and miserable marriages. "Kathy, don't you think I just have the worst luck with men?" she said. "Honey, luck has nothing to do with this," I replied. "You're like a heat-seeking missile." I told her I was pretty sure that if she walked into a room filled with one hundred men and ninety-nine of them were good, loving, decent people, she'd find her way—unconsciously, of course—to the one abusive, alcoholic man there and make a play for him. There was a long silence before she broke into tears. She realized that this was true. She'd probably known it for some time, but the opportunity to have that truth reflected back to her broke through her unconscious denial.

The power of our internal images to determine our reality has been well known for centuries. The sixteenth-century alchemist and physician Heinrich Agrippa understood the incredible power of mental images to drive our actions and reactions to life events. He summed up this force very neatly when he wrote, "So great a power is there of the soul upon the body, that whichever way the soul imagines and dreams, thither doth it lead the body."

There are certainly enough distressing, debilitating, demoralizing losses in anyone's life to confirm the worst expectations of ourselves. For example, let's say your self-image includes the idea that you will never be successful. Perhaps that's what you heard as a child, or in some other way have come to believe. That's an easy assumption to "prove" because there will be hundreds of disappointments in anyone's life that can reinforce that belief. These can come in the form of the job you didn't get, the rejection by the popular hunk who never asked you out for a date, or your failure on a test or board exam. The list can be infinitely long and painfully specific. It's not necessary to look very far for evidence to confirm our negative self-image. Disappointment, failure, defeat, and bombing out are resplendently common experiences. In the midst of our suffering, it's easy to lose sight of the fact that lots of people didn't get hired for a job they wanted or failed important tests or went through a divorce or were diagnosed with a serious illness. Whether we meet those losses and painful experiences with renewed determination or give up easily depends in large measure upon our self-image and the behaviors that emerge from those conscious and, mostly, unconscious beliefs we carry around about ourselves.

Learned Helplessness

Now it's hard to imagine that cats, dogs, or fish have beliefs or self-images, but they do behave and they learn from their experience just as all creatures do. Psychologists have learned a great deal about how we learn and behavior in general from animal studies that experimentally create testing environments that are analogous to human situations. For example, we've learned how both behavior and beliefs are reinforced by repeated experience and quickly become the immediate response in similar future situations.

In the 1970s, an experimental psychologist named Martin Seligman investigated ways in which experiences of helplessness, during which we suffer pain or loss of control, became conditioned responses. Conditioned responses refer to our conscious and automatic reactions to certain kinds of stimuli or situations. When something is "conditioned," it will be our first and immediate response, like a reflex. Think about your high-school psychology class and how Pavlov's dogs learned to salivate at the sound of a buzzer because every time they'd been fed, their meal was accompanied by the sound of that buzzer. With sufficient training by way of enough pairings of buzzer and dog chow their little mouths begin to water just at the sound of the buzzer alone.

I don't think it's surprising to discover that Seligman had experiences in his own life that set the direction for his quest. When he was a teenager, his father suffered a severe stroke, leaving him permanently paralyzed for the rest of his life. Seligman watched his father become helpless and therefore began to attempt to explain why a person or an animal would stop trying to make positive changes. Why would they become stuck and accept painful situations without making any attempt to get out of them? In one of his early experiments, Seligman and his colleagues took a group of twenty-four dogs and placed them into one of two groups. In the first group, the dogs were exposed to shock that they could terminate by pressing a panel. The second group of dogs were exposed to the same level of shock, for the same amount of time as the first group, but pressing their panel did nothing to stop the shock. In other words, they had no control over the duration of the shock. I find this to be nothing less than an experimental analogy of pain and suffering that we face. We find ourselves in painful situations and have no idea how long they will last or what will end them.

Because all the animals in this study were raised in similar environments and exposed to the same amount and kind of shock, it was believed that any differences in their behavior had to be due to the fact that one group had some control over the painful stimuli in their lives while the others did not. Results of this experiment and many others over the past twenty years showed startling results. After just a few trials of inescapable shock, those dogs without control over the shock completely stopped trying to avoid the shock by pressing the panel. And more important, they didn't even try to press the panel when it *was* set to terminate the shock. They just stopped trying to get out of this painful situation. What's more, their behavior—even outside of the experimental situation—looked a lot like human depression to the experimenters. These animals didn't eat, copulate, or socialize in ways normal for their species. They appeared to be passive, withdrawn, lethargic, and uninterested in their environment. Their behavior suggested that they had come to understand that "no matter what I do, I can't change anything." It seems to me that their self-image became one of pure surrender. I think if they could talk, they'd say, "I feel like I'm damned if I do, damned if I don't." Those are my anthropomorphic projections, and any good experimental psychologist worth her salt would chastise me for making those assumptions. But that's what it looks like to me when I see the result with these animals. As a therapist I've seen the same behaviors so often in my clients that it's easy for me to script what those dogs might say.

This same effect has been shown in monkeys and rats, and in hungry cats who refuse to eat in an environment in which they've been shocked. Walleyed pike won't even pursue lip-smacking minnows after bumping into a Plexiglas divider that separates the tank from them enough times. Even after the barrier is removed, these fish make no effort to go after the minnows. In fact, by the end of this experiment the minnows can swim right by the pike—practically fin to fin—and the pike just ignore them. The same phenomenon—giving up after enough difficulty and pain that seems uncontrollable—has been revealed in human beings. Seligman referred to the phenomenon as "learned helplessness" and it's most often described as "the failure to avoid or escape from an unpleasant or aversive stimulus that occurs as a result of previous exposure to unavoidable painful stimuli." When humans or animals are thwarted in reaching some goal (for example, getting rid of aversive shock) they conclude that they'll never be able to accomplish what they want to and stop trying.

It seems to me that learned helplessness is a special form of hopelessness. Hope is an expectation of something good, a confidence and trust that our wishes will be fulfilled. Hopefulness is a passion for the positive and a way of making what is future and potential into something actual and brilliantly present. In addition to accepting false evidence that reinforces our self-image and engaging in behaviors that support it as Seligman's animals did, some people who live in straw houses also tend to negate any input that is hopeful, affirmative, or optimistic. They, like the fish who refuse to see that the barrier that separates them from lunch is gone, rule out the positives and focus on the negatives. For example, I might bemoan the fact that I didn't get the job I wanted while at the same time ignore the fact that I was offered several other very good ones. Sometimes we just can't see what's right in front of us. In situations like these, it is as if we are staring at the stereogram before we can see the imbedded three-dimensional image. Stacy couldn't imagine herself as brave and coping, though she had, in fact, demonstrated those behaviors many times in her life. B. J. didn't see himself as successful and worthy of respect from others in spite of all his accomplishments. It's as if we toss out the evidence that refutes the deeply held beliefs we have about ourselves with the garbage.

Psychological research has demonstrated that people with poor self-images tend to think differently and attribute different reasons to what happens to them. Their way of thinking maintains pain and suffering and reinforces their negative self-image. Other research by Seligman shows that some people—he calls them pessimists—make their experience fit into thought patterns that are permanent, pervasive, and personal. Here's an example of how that kind of thinking expresses itself: Let's say I didn't get the promotion I hoped for. If I'm a pessimist, I think, "I'll never get a promotion" (permanent), "I can't do anything right" (pervasive), and "I didn't get the promotion because I'm a total loser" (personal). Patterns of thinking among optimists, on the other hand, find difficult times to be temporary, specific, and external: "There will be other promotions that I can earn," "Maybe I don't yet have all the skills needed for that promotion, but I can learn them," "This company rarely promotes anyone until they've been here for at least two years."[3]

These different ways of making attributions are not rationalizations for why we are disappointed, why we suffer, but are automatic and accepted at face value. American psychologist and theorist George Kelly described the construction of personality by noting that each person looks at the world through "transparent templates," which we create and then attempt to fit over our realities. We use these personal constructs to predict the things to come. The world then rolls on and reveals these predictions to be true or false. Thus, someone who was unloved as a child meets the world with the belief that she is not worthy of good things happening to her. Since there are enough experiences of bad things happening as an inevitable part of living a human life, each downturn confirms this person's general feeling of "unworthiness." Kelly had a way of describing what many people cognitively do with their history and experience: "You are not the victim of your autobiography," he said. "But you may become the victim of the *way you interpret* your autobiography" (emphasis is mine). This tendency can really get in the way of our growth and development. But, how do we change our templates and end our negative interpretation?

We can listen to our inner dialogue and pay attention to the messages we send ourselves every day. Our self-image is constantly being reinforced and solidified not only by our behavior and our interpretation of our experiences but also by our inner dialogues, our negative self-talk. Many of us repeat critical statements like "You are so stupid, I can't believe you did this again" or "You're never going to get ahead" endlessly to ourselves. In fact, most of us talk to ourselves in ways that we would never, ever speak to another human being. This kind of destructive self-evaluation is a major cause of day-to-day suffering for lots of people. It's proof positive that suffering results not only from the great losses of life but from the quiet moments of everyday existence in which we fail to love and respect ourselves. If you doubt that this is a common occurrence, I challenge you to listen carefully to the way you talk to yourself. Write down the regularly occurring phrases and statements. The chances are good that you'll begin to see an obvious pattern. You can also observe other people being so self-critical that the joy of being alive in any given moment is sharply snatched away.

If you are observant, you will be able to listen in to these presumably private conversations more often than you would think. I was playing tennis with a friend. During a short break, I watched two men playing on the next court. Both were very good and had a hard-hitting, lively match going. Though he was playing quite well, the man nearest me became increasingly disturbed every time he missed a shot. I could hear him talking out loud to himself. After each missed shot, he'd smack the racquet against his knee and mutter, "Mike, you idiot. Why did you try that overhead then?" "You don't deserve to get to the net with a lousy passing shot like that." "Great, Mike. Give the f****** game away with your double faults." With every lost point, he became louder and more agitated. Not once did I hear him tell himself one positive thing like "Nice shot," even when he made one. In spite of his verbal self-abuse, he was most gracious to his opponent even when he lost a point. Many times I heard him say, "Nice try, Al. You almost had it."

I started to think about how I would react if this constant criticism were being directed toward me as I played tennis. It would not be major suffering on the scope of Kisagotami, but I'm certain that I would lose confidence and stop having fun. I could see the same thing happening to Mike. He began to miss easy shots that I had seen him return effortlessly earlier in the match. As the match went on he clearly became more angry and upset. Fun was no longer part of his experience as far as I could see. Because of his unrelenting self-nagging and faultfinding, I knew he was destined to lose that game. In short order, he did just that.

It's clear that negative self-images, especially ones that include the beliefs that we are incapable of coping with life's losses, are reinforced and strengthened by the things we say to ourselves. Why do we talk to ourselves in such vicious, negative ways? We know that the powerful effects of "self-talk" are not limited to athletic competitions. We determine a great deal of our reality by the things we think and say to ourselves. Psychological research has consistently demonstrated that our inner dialogue profoundly influences our emotional states, behavior, and expectations. If we tell ourselves we aren't any good and are bound to fail, we most surely will. If we say that we can't cope with life's losses with grit and courage, then we certainly won't. A rapidly building body of evidence in psychology, medicine, and physics is demonstrating the remarkable power of thoughts and self-talk as a form of energy that can be channeled in positive, healthy directions. More traditional research by cognitive psychologists has clearly shown that our thoughts dramatically affect *all* aspects of our behavior and emotions. But long before modern science offered its results, great thinkers understood these ideas: Aristotle noted, "The actuality of life is thought." Emerson believed that nothing less than "thoughts rule the world."

Although the examples of Stacy and B. J. are somewhat extreme—thankfully, most people don't experience the kind of terrible beginnings that they did—we would all be wise to look at the way our beliefs about ourselves create suffering in our lives. Maybe you don't believe that you are worthless, but do you believe that you must be perfect? This is one of the most prominent self-defeating beliefs that many successful people hold. If you believe that you must be perfect and never fail or make a mistake, you are setting yourself up to suffer. Why? That's easy. No human ever has been or ever will be perfect, and if you think you should be you're destined to fall short of that unachievable goal. That is not to say that you shouldn't strive to do a good job or improve your skills, but those are reasonable and attainable objectives. The sense of failure, sometimes even shame, that arises from our inability to achieve irrational goals causes us a great deal of everyday pain and suffering. Think about the irrational, self-defeating beliefs that you hold. Do you feel that you must be liked, or approved of, by everyone? Do you think that things should always be the way you want them to be and it's a terrible day when they're not? Do you believe that you can't change because your present and future behavior is irreversibly dependent upon past events? This is what Viktor Frankl referred to as the "expectation of dysfunction" and what psychologist George Kelly called "being prisoners of our biographies." It is an extremely self-limiting point of view.

Illusions

Our interior self-image includes two important and interrelated areas: how we see ourselves and what we believe about life. On the one hand, Stacy and B. J. suffered from very negative self-images about themselves that arose from their experiences and now manifest in their everyday decisions and actions. It's easy to see why they continue to suffer. On the other hand, I was luckier than both of them. I was fortunate enough to be born into a family that didn't experience the kinds of problems that theirs did. I'm in no way suggesting that my family of origin is or was perfect, but it was certainly "good enough." I like to say that my family put the "fun" in dysfunction. I was loved and taken good care of and developed an image of myself that is, for the most part, positive. But even my reasonably healthy sense of self didn't protect me from internalizing some pretty irrational beliefs about life.

Perhaps I was always too lucky; maybe things came too easily for me. It could be I didn't get enough "optimal frustration" to develop wisdom about the truth of life. But somehow I felt "golden," protected, and almost impervious to suffering. It's not that I never suffered—no human being can honestly say that. In fact, I had some very significant losses in the early part of my life. My beloved Uncle Jim was killed in a helicopter accident when I was thirteen, and it was a devastating loss. Nana developed Alzheimer's disease, and visiting her in the nursing home each week when she could no longer recognize me or anyone else in the family broke my heart over and over again. By the time I was forty, I had lost all four of my grandparents and several other older relatives whom I loved dearly. In spite of those losses, I ambled along with the spurious belief that everything in my life would always be just great. There was nothing I couldn't handle is what I thought to myself time and again. This was how I was cruising along in my life, feeling particularly and inexplicably shielded from suffering. But in the spring of 1990 I began to be stripped of that arrogance.

It all started when my mother made an appointment with a dermatologist because she noticed that her hair was coming out when she brushed it. Mom had recently switched to a new shampoo and stopped using it thinking that might be the problem. But, she kept the appointment with the doctor anyway just to check things out. When my mother arrived at the office, this doctor gave her a physical and ordered a standard CBC (a complete blood test)—just routine procedure, like taking blood pressure and weight on an initial visit. When she left the examination, he could offer no reasons for her hair loss. But at seven-thirty the next morning he called her and said he had already made an appointment for her to visit her internist later that day. She asked him if there was a problem. He replied, "There could be, Mary." Many months later, she told me that she could tell by the tone in his voice when he said "hello" that something was terribly wrong.

Her internist's blood test revealed the same problems as the dermatologist's did—her white cells were way too high and her platelets and red cells were dangerously low. Some of her blood cells had a characteristic shape and form that indicated even more serious problems. Her internist referred her to a hematologist, and there it was confirmed: My mother had leukemia and a particularly dangerous and mostly untreatable form of the disease known as chronic myelogenous leukemia, or CML.

I was home working in the yard when the phone rang. Before I picked up the receiver, I was suddenly, and for no logical reason, filled with an odd feeling of dread. My mom and I always had a witchy thing with each other; we knew immediately when something was wrong with the other. She confirmed my unexplained reaction when she told me that she had been to the doctor's office. When I picked up the phone, I had no idea that she had suspected any kind of health problem. I wasn't aware of hair falling out or the first trip to the dermatologist or the visit to her internist or her doctor's referral to a cancer specialist. She told me that she hadn't told anyone about the blood tests except my father. She didn't want anyone in the family to worry until there was a reason to. Now there was a reason. That's when Mom told me that she had had CML.

I don't recall crying during that conversation with my mother. But I do remember that I had to sit down. It felt like the air had been squeezed out of my lungs and my head felt suddenly foggy, my thoughts vague and unfocused. I told Mom I was coming to her house immediately, and she tried to talk me out of it. Actually, she told me not to come. "No. It's almost dark and it's too far," she said. "I don't like you girls driving on interstates at night. I worry, you know." "Really?" I said. "You worry?" We both laughed. My mother's overprotection of my brother and me was legendary in our family. She told me that there was no point in driving up now because I had many things to do. She was meeting with the hematologist the next day, and she'd know more then. She'd call me tomorrow, she said, and then we'd decide what to do. Then, I remember, she changed the subject abruptly and told me some cute anecdote about my niece and nephew, Matthew and Katelyn, that I can't remember now. We chatted about other things for a few minutes. "You're not going to drive up now, are you? Promise me you won't drive up," she said. "I won't drive," I promised. After we hung up, Nancy and Dorothy and I left immediately for my parents' home in Fairfax County. I didn't quite lie to my mother: I didn't drive; Nancy did. We were there in less than four hours. She didn't have to worry.

At first it was hard to believe Mom was sick. She was taking chemotherapy and getting regular blood tests to determine how well the interventions were working, but she looked great and had plenty of energy for the challenge ahead. Our whole family was filled with great determination. We were certain that she was going to beat this thing. We did all we could to help. We learned everything we could about this disease. My father insisted that he be sent copies of my mother's biweekly blood tests and then bought each of us fax machines so he could transmit the charts and data on her blood work to us as soon as he received them from the lab. We bought textbooks about leukemia and medical dictionaries to help us translate them. Through reading those textbooks and hundreds of journal articles, we identified the world's medical expert in CML research. My parents went to Thomas Jefferson University Hospital in Philadelphia to see him for a second opinion to confirm or, we hoped, refute her hematologist's diagnosis. But the news was not good. My mother had CML, and it was progressing rapidly. We made fresh juice from carrots and beets—good sources of beta-carotene that studies said had healthful effects in general and on cancer in particular. We demanded information from her oncologists and presented them with ongoing graphs of her blood cell counts that my father made on his computer. Mom registered and participated in clinical trials for a new type of Interferon that seemed to hold promise in curing her particular disease. We did everything that reason told us to, until there was nothing left to do. Throughout it all, we prayed and we made our deals with God.

In spite of everything that good medical care, an optimistic attitude, and a supportive family could offer, my mom continued to grow weaker and weaker. She had the best doctors who were on top of all the latest research and genuinely cared about her. Our own family had become experts about platelet development, but nothing could stop the cancer that was producing more and more immature and useless blood cells. Nancy and I drove to Fairfax County every weekend to spend time with my family. At first our visits there were the same as they had ever been. We would go out to dinner, have lunch at Fuddruckers, or rent a movie and laugh or cry as the film demanded. We spent lots of time on the deck, sipping wine and talking about all the things that we normally did. We'd discuss my cousins, our extended family, Matthew and Katelyn, the fact that my brother worked too hard, and how my mom was never terribly fond of dogs, but that Dorothy had changed her opinion about the whole species. My aunts, uncles, and cousins were making lots of extra trips from New Jersey to visit with her and lend support. Often, we'd have a big crew on that deck and sing Irish songs and James Taylor tunes to my brother's guitar.

During the two years that my mother was sick, the tenor of visits slowly changed. She was getting weaker and thinner. The immature blood cells were proliferating at an alarming rate and clogging up her veins and arteries like a logjam on a slow-moving stream. Her healthy cells couldn't work their way through the others to carry vital oxygen and nutrients to her starving organs. Mom was getting so much worse from weekend to weekend that I would find myself anxious and scared to walk into my parents' house—not knowing what new symptom or loss she would be experiencing. When my mother no longer had the energy to go out to dinner, we'd barbecue at home and eat on TV tables in the den. When she couldn't eat at all, we'd make milk shakes spiked with nutritional supplements and urge her to finish them. By the end of the first year of her illness, she had absolutely no appetite and was losing weight quickly. After a year and a half, at the end of August, the doctors finally told us that there was nothing more they could do.

My mother knew she was dying but wanted to live until Christmas. That holiday was always a wonderful occasion in our family, and my mother especially loved watching Matthew and Katelyn find their gifts under the tree early on Christmas morning. She was a great cook and totally in her element while she was preparing a huge turkey dinner. The year before, my mother had had enough energy to sit on a stool in the kitchen and direct us in cooking the traditional Christmas fare. Nancy's a great cook, but the rest of us are quite lame in the culinary arts. We were, I'm certain, a challenge to instruct. We had great fun then, but this year I realized would not be a repeat of that scene since Mom was too weak to leave her bed. The doctors told us that it was impossible to predict such things but that based on what they knew from her blood work, it was unlikely that my mother would live until

Christmas. With each passing week she needed more frequent blood and platelet transfusions. At this point, she was already getting transfused three times a week and her tiny arms were black and blue from the needles. I watched my mother, this vibrant woman I loved beyond words, endure pain and become increasingly helpless and I was humbled by the extraordinary anguish that life had delivered so routinely.

One Sunday afternoon in mid-September, I sat on the edge of the couch while my mother nodded in and out of sleep. The TV droned in the corner and I had a book on my lap, though I couldn't tell you what I was reading or what program was on. Everyone else was running errands, and it was just the two of us in the house. She asked me if I was okay, and I said yes. She took this as a go-ahead to share her wishes for her funeral with me. Mom told me that she wanted two particular songs played at her memorial service but that there was to be no Irish music. With the name Mary Catherine Bernadette Kelly Brehony you can see that my mother honestly came by her love of all things Celtic. "Irish music will be way too hard for your father to hear at the funeral," she said. "Please don't play it and don't let him talk you into it." I listened. I told her I would do just what she wanted. She asked that I find recordings of "Somewhere Out There" and "Here, There, and Everywhere"—a song written by the Beatles—but the version she most loved, she said, was the instrumental done by the Boston Pops Orchestra.

I had accompanied dying people before, and so I knew how important it is to be where they are—not to try to convince them that things will be fine when they want to talk about their own death or to make them think about what is to come when they'd rather talk about the past or the wonderful things they're going to do in the future. I told her that I'd take care of the music for her and, without another word, we reached for each other and wept. I had never felt tears like those before. They came jagged and wrenching from some deep place that I could not fathom. But in that moment, the truth about life became clear to me. While holding my mother and feeling her tears running down my neck and mingling with my own, I awakened. It was in that moment that my arrogance left. My comfortable image, my innocence, my need to convince myself that life should be what I want it to be instead of what it is vanished into the air. I realized just how inadequate were my illusions that somehow I would never have to suffer like this. I didn't need to go looking for a mustard seed. The pain of every suffering human being was right there surrounding us in that room.

My mother died on November 6, 1992—less than six weeks after our conversation. She didn't make it to Christmas.

Our view of ourselves and the beliefs we hold about life determine how we will live our lives and how we respond to our own inevitable suffering. Most of us will survive whatever life throws at us. Most of us are unlikely to kill ourselves, although 30,000 Americans do so every year, or experience depression for the rest of our lives after we've been through a devastating loss. We'll grieve, time will pass, and we will get back to some semblance of "normal." But I made a decision that afternoon while I was holding my dying mother to reach beyond that cycle. I decided then and there to squeeze every drop of meaning and self-growth from moments like that one when my heart was broken so wide open that it seemed to travel out beyond the stars until it was no longer beating in my own chest. I'm determined to be greedy—extracting every bit of wisdom my pain can teach me. I'm going for the gold and I'm being pragmatic, not noble. I believe that these losses in our lives simply hurt too much. They are a pain "so utter" not to take the payoff that has been so fully earned. We can use them as opportunities to change our unhealthy self-images and update our tired old, sorrow-filled scripts about who we think we are. We can relinquish the false impressions and irrational beliefs that keep us locked in narrow prisons of self-pity or fear or the illusions of invulnerability. We can let go of who we thought we were in order to become who we have the potential to be. We can welcome pain as our teacher. Psychologists often speak of the importance of resilience, the ability to spring back from suffering, disappointment, and loss. This is a great place to start our journey. But I want more. I want to go beyond resilience to a warrior's courage, to pure compassion, and to advance—even just a little—down the path toward enlightenment.

· 4 ·

Beyond Resilience

Deep, unspeakable suffering may well be called a baptism,
a regeneration, the initiation into a new state.

—George Eliot, *Adam Bede*

✐ Last winter the unrelenting winds of back-to-back nor'easters brutally twisted a stand of saplings in my neighborhood. During the hurricanelike gusts and drenching downpours of January and February they were bent almost parallel to the ground. Leafless and brown, they appeared to be dead, lifeless sticks barely attached to the earth by their immature roots. Dorothy and I passed by them every day during our walks by the river. I can't speak for her, but I felt sad that these young trees had been destroyed by the wind before they had a chance to grow and plant their roots firm and deep in the dirt. But, as spring approached, I realized that I was too hasty in my judgment about the power and determination of these saplings. Ever so slowly, they began to rebound. By the beginning of April these little trees were sporting tiny green buds and by mid-May they were standing upright, small leaves adorning every branch.

They were down, but not out, these young trees. Just as we try to ignore the universal nature of suffering, at least as it relates to us, we often miss something equally as strong and pervasive: the power of resilience. We cannot speak about suffering without also noting the innate ability of living things to recover from devastation. A good place to start understanding resilience is simply to look at its definition. The word *resilience* comes from the Latin *resilire* and means "spring back; to resume a prior position or form after being stretched or pressed."

When I think of this word, I see again these strong saplings reach for the sky after being driven nearly horizontal by winds just months before. Resilience implies a kind of toughness and flexibility that harbors the power to recover. It is elasticity in the face of pain and suffering. To me the word also conjures up optimism, perseverance, and resourcefulness.

Resilience

Although psychologists have only recently been interested in learning more about resilience, observant athletes, both professional and amateur, seem always to have understood it. When you watch almost any sporting event, you will often see examples of dramatic resilience. If you're a fan of tennis, think about Andre Agassi's 1999 comeback from the nether world of "has-beens." Watch the Washington Redskins—or your favorite football team—bash it out on any autumn Sunday afternoon as the quarterback slings a breathtaking "Hail Mary" pass ninety yards to an open receiver in the end zone. What appeared to be a certain loss suddenly becomes a ticket to the playoffs, and it all happened in an instant. You can see victory snatched from the gnashing jaws of defeat on your own basketball court, the greens of the U.S. Open, and on playing fields large and small around the world.

One of my favorite stories about the power of resilience is the comment made by athlete Lance Armstrong as he stepped from the podium after winning the 1999 Tour de France, the most prestigious and grueling bicycle race in the world. In 1996, Lance Armstrong was battling a deadly case of testicular cancer that had spread to his brain and lungs. Given less than a 50 percent chance of survival, he fiercely beat the deadly disease and came back to his sport better than ever. Just three short years after having been given what amounted to a death sentence, Lance showed us the extraordinary power of resilience and more. The world watched as he raced for more than two thousand miles in twenty-three days across mountains and flatlands, always ahead of the pack and easily recognized by the distinctive yellow jersey or *le maillot jaune*—reserved for the leader. The predominantly French crowd chanted his name over and over as he stepped from the podium on the Champs Élysées and told a reporter, "I hope this sends out a fantastic message to all the cancer patients and survivors around the world. We can return to what we were before—and be even better."

That's resilience—the springing back from defeat or loss. Quite often resilience wins the game, and sometimes it emerges to shake off the loss and become even more triumphant in the second round.

In his book, *Values of the Game*, former senator Bill Bradley uses his experiences as an NBA player to describe what he's learned about handling adversity and defeat. He says that hard times offer a richness of experience and that even victory has its pitfalls. One night in his early years as a basketball player, Bradley was devastated over a loss and his own on-court mistakes. A teammate told him that he would never survive in professional sports with that kind of attitude. "Even a great team will lose twenty games a year," his friend pointed out. At that very moment, Bradley realized the importance of letting things go, of refusing to carry the past around with him, and of allowing himself to spring back after loss and failure. He also thought about what victory really meant. "When you begin to expect it as a continuum instead of seeing it as a reward that has to be fought for, you're in trouble," he says. He sums up this philosophy with the words of Rudyard Kipling who said, "Meet with triumph and disaster and treat those two impostors just the same."

Instead of heeding those wise words, many people ride dangerously high on victory and allow defeat to crush them. People who live best are those who celebrate winning moments but know that suffering and loss will visit everyone's life, even their own. They understand the importance of flexibility, of springing back when life has thrown a curve. They also recognize that suffering offers defining moments for those brave and alive and awake enough to squeeze meaning and wisdom from each encounter with darkness. Some psychologists have looked at the characteristics of people who seem to be particularly resilient for clues about how they got that way. Studying men and women who have bounced back from extreme suffering—like the saplings bent by the storms and resurrected in the spring—can teach us something about our own inner strength.

Sybil Wolin, a clinical psychologist, and her husband, Steven, a psychiatrist, interviewed a number of people who had suffered greatly as children and survived their horrific experiences to become healthy, functioning adults. In the beginning of their book, they rightly criticize our modern emphasis on pathology and problems rather than the natural human ability to recover from suffering. They say, "Unfortunately, the professions of psychiatry and psychology, as well as a growing self-help movement in this country, have done a lot to alarm you about your vulnerability but not nearly enough to inform you about your resilience. Everywhere you hear news of your damage, but reports of your competence are sparse."[1]

In synthesizing what they learned, the Wolins identified seven distinctive traits of people they found to be extremely resilient. They say that these are the characteristics of resilient people:

1. **Insight** is the mental habit of asking searching questions and giving honest answers, which includes *Sensing* (reading signals from other people); *Knowing* (identifying the source of the problem); and *Understanding* (trying to figure out how things work for oneself and others).

2. **Independence** is recognizing the right to place safe boundaries between oneself and significant others. This includes the abilities to *Distance* (being able to emotionally distance from people who jerk you around) and *Separating* (knowing when to separate from bad relationships).

3. **Relationships** is the capacity to develop and maintain intimate and fulfilling ties to other people. Relationships include: *Recruiting* (the ability to select healthy partners and to start new relationships) and *Attaching* (the ability to maintain healthy relationships).

4. **Initiative** is the determination to master oneself and one's environment, including *Problem Solving* (creative problem solving/enjoyment of figuring out how things work) and *Generating* (generating constructive activities).

5. **Creativity and Humor** are safe harbors of the imagination where one can take refuge and rearrange the details of one's life. These include *Creative Thinking* (creative/divergent thinking) and *Creating to Express Feelings* (being able to use creativity to forget pain and to express emotions) and *Humor* (using humor to reduce tension or make a bad situation better).

6. **Morality** is knowing what is right and wrong and being willing to stand up for those beliefs. It includes *Valuing* (knowing what is right

and wrong and being willing to take risks for those beliefs) and *Helping Others* (liking to help other people and feeling blessed by the opportunity to do so).

7. **General Resilience** includes *Persistence* (persistent efforts at working through difficulties) and *Flexibility* (confidence that one can make the most of bad situations).

I agree with the Wolins that our culture has a fascination with vulnerability, and often a corresponding blindness to resiliency or human potential.[2] We would be doing ourselves a favor to take note of the strengths we have to lean on in challenging situations. Think about the people you know who've demonstrated resilience in the face of disaster and suffering. Do these characteristics describe them? Think about your heroes and how they've rebounded after unbelievable losses. Consider the lives of Mark O'Brien and Jeff Beaton. Think about Viktor Frankl and other survivors of atrocities so horrific that they can barely be conveyed with words. Even the scratchy black-and-white films of the concentration camps being liberated or the full-color news photos of murders in Vietnam or Sierra Leone do not express the degree and duration of suffering that some human beings have endured. Yet, for most, even those who have suffered unbelievable horrors, there is resilience, a springing back to some kind of "new normal" state.

This new normal state is very different from the normality that preceded suffering. When the "Wheel of Life" turns full circle, we never return to the same place from which we started. Some people emerge from their trials and spring back not to their former shape but fundamentally changed and enriched: spiritually enlightened, wiser, more compassionate, and confident in their abilities to withstand whatever hardships and heartbreaks life will deliver. These people have gone beyond resilience. They've wrung every bit of meaning and growth from their tragedies and emerged transformed. They've embraced the hard work of individuation, done battle with the unconscious, and risen as a Phoenix from the flames. They've taken the hero's journey.[3]

The Hero's Journey

Whether you are familiar with the term *hero's journey* or not, you've most likely seen evidence of it in many places in your life. Most films and novels follow the specific course of this adventure. From *Star Wars* to *A League of Their Own* to *Troop Beverly Hills*, we see in these films the transformation of character that results from a willingness to let go of what is, discover what can be, and become a hero in the process. Fairy tales, myths, and epic poetry from every culture retell this very same tale of human development embellished only with their own characters and cultural perspectives. The tales of the Greek Ulysses or Prometheus, the Sumerian Inanna, the Celtic Finn McCool, the Inuit Raven, and the postmodern Luke Skywalker mirror and explain this central story of human existence in uniquely dramatic ways. But in spite of the many different flavors, the essence of the hero's journey always remains the same. Writer Willa Cather explains this truth in *O Pioneers!* "There are only two or three human stories," she wrote, "and they go on repeating themselves as fiercely as if they had never happened before." Philosopher Joseph Campbell, who has done more to explore and popularize the concept of the hero's journey than anyone else, says that the story of the hero is so important that it is "the only one worth telling" and with the examples of it that surround us we don't even have to risk the adventure alone. "For the heroes of all time have gone before us," he says. "The labyrinth is thoroughly known."[4]

The hero's journey is about a departure, an adventure, and a return. I read once where a screenwriting teacher summed up this process in a way that made me laugh. He described the hero's journey in three acts as: "Get the protagonist up a tree (act I), throw rocks at him (act II), get him down (act III)."

In every case, the hero's journey requires leaving what is known, encountering hardship and danger, and returning home as a changed person. These are the critical plot points, but the valuable message for us lies in the way in which the hero within is awakened by this experience and the main character creates a meaningful life from the dullness and unconsciousness of ordinary existence. The journey of the hero gives us comfort, providing hope for resurrection in the wake of anguish and loss. This timeless, mythic journey is the way of the Self, individuation, and transformation. It represents a rite of passage in the midst of unbearable pain. When we're suffering, it helps to understand that the journey to which we are summoned grounds our personal experience, our own tragedy, in the larger story of humankind.

The mythological hero's journey begins with a *call to adventure*. Somehow the hero is drawn out of her ordinary life where she has some measure of control. Occasionally she may make this decision to venture out voluntarily, but most often she is carried off or plunged onto the threshold of adventure by an experience that rocks her world. Usually, she is in a situation in which she can no longer refuse the call. This reluctant hero must then leave the safety and security of everyday life and set out to battle dragons, enter a dark forest, or embark on a night sea journey. In doing so, she suffers a *separation* from all that has been known. This is the moment when the hero innately understands that life as she has known it is now over. As she travels through foreign terrain, she must confront many dangers and bear many sorrows. This loss of control and lack of the familiar is the descent into hell, the lair of the dragon, or the belly of the whale. It's darkness fully experienced. She has been snatched and dropped into the Underworld where she struggles to survive in this strange and, often, terrifying new land. The challenges and ordeals are beyond what she has ever known before or ever thought that she could endure.

During this *initiation* or *adventure* the hero's courage will be tested in ways that demand both heart and wisdom. During this terrifying part of the journey imagining that she will survive these trials, much less be transformed through their pain, seems almost impossible. The German poet Friedrich Hölderlin offers insight into this stage when we most likely feel hopeless, stripped of our soul, and abandoned by the divine. He wrote, "the god is near, but difficult to grasp; where danger is, there Deliverance gathers."[5] But, by staying the course with courage in spite of her trembling knees, our hero looks inside and discovers who she is, and finally *returns* home triumphant.

Now here is the most important point in understanding this mythological structure—*the hero returns changed*. No longer the innocent, immature village girl, she is now transformed, enlightened, and wise. It has been the battles themselves and what she has learned about herself and life along the way that are the true gifts of the journey. Whether she returns with a magical elixir, the dragon's head, the Holy Grail, a pot of gold, or some other symbol of victory and hope, the primary treasure she now offers is her authentic Self. She has been resurrected, reformed, and enlivened. It's true that life as she has known it is now over, but our hero now has the consciousness of a mature adult and holds the power to restore the world and share her findings with others.

In his PBS interview with journalist Bill Moyers, Joseph Campbell described the psychological and spiritual power of the hero's journey in these words: "We have only to follow the thread of the hero path, and where we had thought to find an abomination, we shall find a god. And where we had thought to slay another, we shall slay ourselves. Where we thought to travel outward, we will come to the center of our own existence. And where we had thought to be alone, we will be with all the world."[6]

There are thousands of tales that tell the hero's story, but my favorite is one that is most likely quite familiar to you. I love this story so much that my dog, Dorothy, is named after Dorothy Gale, the heroine in *The Wizard of Oz*. *The Wizard of Oz* is a hero's journey, and from the moment I saw Dorothy as a scrambling puppy, I knew that she would be my good friend and faithful companion on my life's journey. I also correctly surmised that when she was fully grown she'd be way too big and athletic to be named Toto, so I gave her star billing on our travels together.

At the beginning of *The Wizard of Oz*, Dorothy Gale laments the boring life she lives on the Kansas farm of her Auntie Em and Uncle Henry. She yearns for wider horizons, more interesting people, and exciting surroundings. She is given the *call to adventure* with the sudden arrival of a tornado. Unable to reach the family storm shelter with the others, she, her little dog, Toto, and her house are all sucked into the spiraling winds of the twister and dropped down in a land that is both magical and frightening. *Separated* from all that was familiar, safe, and reassuring, Dorothy first appeals to the strangers she meets to help her find a way home again.

As in most myths, as in life, there is help along the way. Glinda, the good witch, arrives, gives her some new walking shoes—a fabulous pair of sparkling Ruby Slippers—and points her in the right direction. "Follow the Yellow Brick Road," she tells the trembling and frightened girl. Dorothy really has no choice but to follow this curious advice, so she sets out for Emerald City where she believes the all-powerful, all-good Wizard will help her return to Kansas. Lord knows, we are always looking for that wizard.

As she travels, Dorothy makes new friends who are also looking for important things in their lives. She meets up with the Scarecrow, who agrees to accompany her and ask the Wizard for a brain for his little straw head. She meets a Tin Woodsman who wants a heart and a Cowardly Lion who wishes only for courage. Interestingly, these characters want the same things that most of us searching for meaning are after: brains (wisdom), heart (compassion), courage, and a map to show us the way back home again (finding our true Self, our center).

In Oz, Dorothy suffers greatly. Let's not underestimate her pain. She's scared to death. She's set adrift among strangers and yearns for the safety of home and the companionship of her family. She doesn't just face unknown surroundings, the Wicked Witch terrorizes her. I don't just mean getting ripe fruit thrown at you from nasty apple trees either. The Wicked Witch wants nothing less than to kill Dorothy and her little dog, too, since Dorothy's house dropped on the Witch's sister. Making their way down a long and dangerous road, Dorothy and her pals finally arrive for an audience with the Wizard. They are thrilled and informed by him that their wishes will be granted after they complete one single task. It's no big deal, really, the Wizard assures them. He tells them they must return with the broomstick of the Wicked Witch of the West. But Dorothy and her companions understand the real meaning of this assignment: in order to get the broomstick, they're going to have to kill the witch.

Dorothy and her friends are sick with fear at the idea of confronting this most powerful and evil witch. But there's no other way to get brains, or heart, or courage, or home again. So, frightened to death, they head out on their mission. In the course of their *adventure*, they learn important things about themselves and one another. First of all, they discover that they have a true relationship with one another. They learn to care deeply. In fact, as they travel along together, their absorption with their own desires becomes less important than helping the others get what they need. Second, they begin to find that they already had what they were looking for inside themselves. Though in search of a brain, the Scarecrow makes many wise decisions. The Tin Woods-man, looking for a heart, acts always out of loyalty and love; and the Cowardly Lion responds with courage in spite of his fears. Dorothy learns that she always had the power to go back to Kansas through the Ruby Slippers. All she ever had to do was click her heels together three times and say, "There's no place like home."

Like all true hero's myths, this story reflects the call to adventure, the separation from the familiar, the adventure itself, and the return. As in all classic myths, Dorothy remains forever changed by her experience. She wakes up, literally and figuratively. Upon returning home, she now understands just how much she is loved. She knows that there really is no place like home and that everything she every really wanted was there all along. This post-Oz Dorothy is no longer the little girl who wishes her life away. She's matured and individuated with a new-found appreciation for the people and reality of her life.

Myths and stories that aim to teach us have to hold up in real life or they lose their importance and value. The story of Dorothy Gale is fictional, but the structure and outcome of her journey are not. Ordinary people who have found themselves being called to the adventure must bear the darkness of suffering and loss, to have the opportunity to emerge transformed. Dan Maslowski's hero's journey is one of mythic proportions. It began when, like the Greek Icarus, he fell from the sky.

When I first began writing this book, I knew that I wanted to talk with Dan and include his story. He's a good friend of my brother, J. P., who has talked admiringly about Dan for many years. J. P. told me that Dan was the most positive person he'd ever met and that even during downturns in his life, he was always upbeat and determined, never losing his remarkable sense of humor or optimism. "Any day they're not shooting at you is a good day," he would tell my brother when things were tough for either of them.

I meet Dan at his beautiful home in Fairfax, Virginia. Like others in his neighborhood, Dan's house is neat, the yard is well tended, children ride bikes around cul-de-sacs, and neighbors wave as you ride by. As I walk from his driveway to his house, the only material evidence I see of Dan's hero's journey is the black-and-white POW banner that flies on the front porch next to the American flag.

Dan greets me at the door with a firm handshake. He's tall with a broad smile and laugh lines that tell me he smiles often. I sense an immediate and strong connection to him. I like him right off and I don't know whether it's because I feel as if I already know him through my brother's stories or because he is so present, warm, and informal. It's a balmy day for late September but it's not hot and Dan is shuffling around barefooted, wearing shorts and a sweatshirt. His hair is still wet. "I just jumped out of the shower, but I timed it just right! I'm so happy to meet you," he says. He ushers me into a small den that is crowded with a desk, computer, bookcases, and two comfortable chairs. Large windows look out over his front porch, and every other wall is cluttered with framed photographs, service awards, and memorabilia. Dan offers me a beverage, I choose water, and he brings in the largest glass I have ever seen. Seriously, I had to pick it up with two hands. "We drink a lot of water around here," he says.

Dan is remarkably friendly and extroverted. "If I go on too long, stop me," he says, laughing. "I love people. I love stories. I love to talk to people."

Dan and I have spoken a few times by phone to arrange this interview, and so he knows the subject of this book. He's quick to point out that he is in no way special. He's not a hero. He's just a guy who did what he had to do. I tell him that there are many things I want to know about his story, but mostly I want to understand why he believes that any day they're not shooting at you is a good day. "To understand that philosophy," Dan says as he leans toward me, "I'll have to start at the beginning."

Dan tells me he joined the U.S. Army and left home in 1969 because he was bored with college and felt that he had to discover his own way in the world. His father owned a machine shop in Chicago and expected that Dan would take over the business someday. "I didn't like that idea. I wanted to do something on my own terms," Dan says. "How would I ever know that any success I had was because of my own efforts? I'd always wonder if I could have made something of myself without my father's business." This decision—to find his own destiny and way in the world—demanded that he separate from life as he knew it. Dan says he was determined to set his own course in spite of his parents' protests against his decision. Who can blame them for their concern? It was 1969, after all, and the United States was in the middle of the bloody Vietnam War. They didn't want to lose their son.

After joining up, Dan trained to be a pilot, and a little more than a year later he was at the controls of a Huey (UH-1) cargo-carrying helicopter flying over the jungles of Southeast Asia. The main job of the Huey helicopters, Dan explains, was to transport supplies, ammunition, and sometimes personnel from one place to another. "We moved parts for machinery, bullets, pots and pans, mail, money, people, anything, it didn't matter." With his typical understatement, Dan says what he was living wasn't a glamorous pilot's life, it was more like being a "taxi driver."

On May 2, 1970, the day after President Richard Nixon ordered U.S. troops to invade Cambodia, Dan was serving as copilot as he and his three crew members were flying a routine mission to move tank parts, ammunition, and four passengers from a base camp in South Vietnam into one in Cambodia. "We had a crew of four and the aircraft was packed. Our four passengers were sitting on top of stuff with their feet hanging out. It was raining. Hard. When it rains in Vietnam, honest to God, you can't see your hand in front of your face," Dan says. The pilot was unable to follow the road. In Vietnam, pilots flew by referring to visual landmarks like roads, trees, or small buildings. They literally looked down and followed roads to determine their routes. "It was raining so hard, we couldn't get a good visual," Dan says. "We knew that we had to go north where there was a main road, but we couldn't tell where we were. We made a ninety-degree turn eastward to try to get out of the rainsquall and see if we could find the road." Suddenly they were fired on. The pilot made another ninety-degree turn to avoid the enemy fire, and then they realized that this was not small arms. They were being shot at with fifty-one-caliber radar-controlled ammunition. "My helicopter had been shot before, but by small arms," Dan says. "With those you would just hear things. This fifty-one-caliber doesn't care about storms or rain. It hits the mark. Every sixth round is a 'tracer' that lets a stream of red, iridescent light out behind, like fireworks. The purpose of a tracer is to help them aim the next shots because when you're shooting from the ground up into the air you can't see where your bullets are going. I looked out the window and saw lines of red coming straight at us. We could see them coming through the rain. They were huge, the size of basketballs," Dan says. "When you see that, you don't think they're firing at the helicopter. You think they're aiming right for *you*."

Several rounds hit the helicopter. The back of the Huey shattered with concussive force and burst into flames. Dan explained that this was especially dangerous because they had just loaded 1,600 pounds of JP4—jet fuel that flashes, explodes, and burns incredibly hot. The hit set the hydraulic fluid on fire. When that burns, it releases a poisonous gas that can kill you after a few breaths. "I'm sending Mayday calls. We're in a dive. We can smell the jet fuel burning and feel the heat. The four passengers and two crewmen in the back are yelling and crawling all over everything to get away from the smoke. This stuff is toxic. Now there are six people scrambling to get into the two front seats. Then I hear the pilot say, 'Oh, shit.' He looks down at the chin bubble (a Plexiglas bottom that allows pilots to see the ground beneath them), and it's filling up with hydraulic fluid," Dan says. "We know in seconds this will go on fire and burn. The pilot has got to get out of that seat. He's got to move. He backs off the controls and gives them to me."

The Huey spun down to five hundred feet over a triple-canopy jungle. Dan explains that it would be certain death to land it here, but what were the choices? The bird was on fire and toxic fumes were sizzling and smoking through the sheeting rain. The only question seemed to be whether these men would die from crashing to the ground or from the inevitable explosion of the burning aircraft itself. Miraculously, the shuddering helicopter cleared the trees, then all of a sudden a rice paddy appeared beneath them. "We're on fire. People were jumping out, choking and gasping for breath, before we even hit the ground," Dan says. He landed the aircraft and as the skids touched down, he tried to get out his door but it was jammed. He crawled across the pilot's seat and bailed out the right window. As the men stood away from the burning helicopter, they were suddenly fired on by enemy ground troops. They had landed in the middle of a major Viet Cong base camp in Cambodia.

Dan tells me this story in an urgent, though not emotional, stream of consciousness. Throughout it, he's taken time to explain things to me like what happens to jet fuel when it burns and how Hueys are constructed with chin bubbles and what they're for. As he described where the helicopter landed, he went over to the bookshelf and took down a mock-up that a friend had made for him years ago. "This will help you see this scene in the movie," Dan says smiling. That's what he calls this part of his life, "the movie." He brings the model over and places it on the desk. This replica is like a model train setup with painted grass and miniature trees. In the middle of it is a toy metal Huey helicopter. Orange-and-red paper flames are fire. Blackened cotton—depicting smoke—pours out from the side doors and the roof of the chopper. Eight plastic soldiers represent each of the men who had been on board this fateful flight. Six of them are running toward the jungle on the east side of the helicopter. At the edge of the green rice paddy toward the west, two small figures lie head-to-head in mud that is shown with brown paint. The green rice paddy is covered with model grass and is encircled by a jungle. Hundreds of enemy troops surround the paddy and swarm through the shrubby model trees.

My heart is pounding as Dan continues to tell me his story. He points to one of the figures in the mud at the edge of the rice paddy. "This one is me," he says quietly.

The eight Americans raced for the trees to get out of the middle of that open rice paddy where they were easy targets for enemy guns. Dan and one of the passengers, Bob Young, ran in the same direction. They dived for cover behind a small earthen dike that bordered the open field and lay head-to-head, less than a foot apart, in the mud and water. They were terrified and shivering. Bob was unarmed since there was no time to grab his weapon from the burning chopper. Dan had only a small gun, a .38-caliber pistol that had been strapped to his leg. When the enemy began shooting at them, Dan had shot back. He thought he hit one of them. He knew if he were to be captured that he might instantly be killed for shooting, perhaps killing, one of their own. Dan had no idea what had happened to the other six men aboard the aircraft, but he did know the enemy was very close by the way bullets were flying overhead, grenades were exploding around them, and by the sounds of automatic gunfire that echoed through the jungle. Less than a hundred yards away, the Huey was burning out of control and the rounds of ammunition inside it were beginning to go off.

"There was no doubt in my mind that we were going to die there," Dan says. "I was shaking like this," he says as he held out his hand and shook it rapidly. "It was still pouring rain and now it was starting to get dark. The bad guys were really close. When the gunfire stopped, we could overhear them talking in Vietnamese. Several bullets went right between Bob's and my head." Dan says he was so scared that he's never been exactly sure how long it was before three enemy soldiers jumped over the small dike and shoved their bayonets in his face. Then one said—in English—"Surrender or die." Dan dropped his gun. The enemy soldiers took the Americans' boots and used the laces to tie their elbows behind them. Within ten minutes, another party of enemy soldiers carried in Dan's crew chief, Fred Crowson. Dan and Bob thought he had been shot because blood was gushing from his neck, but it turned out to be a leech. The Viet Cong blindfolded all three of them with scraps of material and marched them through the jungle toward the prison camp. When they got there, Dan was slammed into a wooden tiger cage built halfway into the ground. It was May 2, 1970. He had been in Vietnam for only thirty-one days and was just three days short of his twenty-first birthday.

For the next three years, Dan was chained in a tiger cage, brutally beaten, and psychologically tortured. Dan said that as each night fell, he never knew whether he would be alive to see another day pass. Dan says he watched other POWs in his camp die from wounds, from malaria, and from the devastating loss of hope. His good friend Bob Young died in his arms. Dan's eyes hold a deep sadness as he explains that his friend passed away just four months before Operation Homecoming, when the United States and Vietnam made a deal to mutually release their prisoners of war. Dan explained that Bob never saw his baby daughter, who was born during his Vietnam tour.

"No one would ever choose to go through something like that. You would never think you could," Dan says. "But sometimes in life you don't have a choice. The power can come through. When this happened to me, about two days into it, I said to myself, 'You know what? It's all up to me now.'"

Though he doesn't dwell on it, Dan says he never wants to forget his experience. He wears a bracelet on his left wrist that is made from the chain that held him to the tiger cage. This is not a fine gold or silver representation made by a jeweler to remind him of his past; it is the chain itself. Rusted and bent, it is anything but beautiful but Dan says it serves as a way to remember that "any day they're not shooting you is a good day."

Dan is not certain whether his hero's journey changed him or to what extent it fueled his optimism about life, his determination in rising to meet life's challenges, or his compassion for other people who suffer. After all, he was very young when he embarked on the path of the hero. "I went from being under the control of my parents to the control of the Army. I don't really know who I would have been without those experiences," he says. Still, he recognizes that many POWs did come home from the war bitter and angry. He thinks that maybe tough experiences, the suffering that life gives to everyone, amplifies and intensifies the personality that's already there. "If you were a bitter person before, then maybe now you have more justification to be even more bitter after bad things happen to you," he offers.

Dan himself seems to have no time for nor inclination toward bitterness. "Look, everybody suffers hardship. Think about people who lose children or whose kids are born with terrible problems. They're the ones that really suffer, I think," he says. "I'm blessed. I came back with two arms and two legs and, even though there are a few medical problems from it, I'm doing great. I've had a chance to raise a family, have a career, and a great marriage."

In 1989, Dan retired, after twenty-one years' service in the U.S. Army, as a lieutenant colonel. He's thankful for the opportunity to engage in his "second careers" in mortgage banking and real estate investment. He says he will never forget the three years he spent in a tiger cage but doesn't want it to define him or the life he's made for himself.

When Dan goes to look for a videotape of one of his speeches and gather some other material to complete our interview, I look around his little den. He told me earlier that while he enjoys his nice house and having good things in his life, he knows that he simply prefers to have them and doesn't need them. He believes there's got to be some reason that he survived and that gives meaning and purpose to every day he's alive. "Everything I have right now is gravy," he tells me. "If I had to live in a room this size for the rest of my life, I would be just fine. I'd still go out every day and enjoy my life. I need people, not things, in my life to make me happy."

In the middle of one wall is a framed black-and-white photo of the guys from his POW camp. There's a young Dan Maslowski, thirty years younger but with the same slightly irreverent smile, standing next to other young men, shirtless and wearing Army fatigue pants. Next to Dan is his friend Bob Young, who never came home from the war. In fact, his remains weren't even returned until 1989 and not categorically identified until DNA analysis had sufficiently progressed to the point of being able to do so in 1996. By then, his daughter was in her mid-twenties.

Dan's awards, the Silver Star, Distinguished Flying Cross, Bronze Star, Purple Heart, the Air Medal, and the Legion of Honor are simply framed and hung next to a yellowed copy of the telegram sent by the Department of Defense to Dan's parents telling them he was missing in action and presumed dead. In the middle of all the framed documents is a small motto that I think sums up Dan's philosophy about meeting the challenges of pain and suffering. It says:

> *If you think you're beaten, you are.*
> *If you think you dare not, you don't . . .*
> *If you think you'll lose, you've lost*
> *For out in the world, you'll find success*
>   *begins with a fellow's will*
> *It's all in the state of mind.*

Dan's story is one of epic proportions, but one needn't literally fall from the sky to make a hero's journey. It's a journey that can beckon us from our own surroundings, announcing its presence quietly in the ordinariness of everyday life. Like Dorothy being hurled toward Oz by an unexpected tornado, we don't seek for or expect our world to change. Ernest Chapman certainly didn't foresee the path his life would take when he made a routine visit to the doctor's office.

Ernest simply had a cold that was taking a long time to clear up and decided he might need an antibiotic. So he made an appointment with his physician. A medical examination showed that his spleen was enlarged and his blood tests came back with confusing, but concerning, results. A subsequent bone marrow analysis showed that he had small-cell non-Hodgkins lymphoma. In fact, tests showed that the disease was so advanced that Ernest was not expected to live more than six weeks.

Singer-songwriter Beth Nielsen Chapman tells me about the sheer fright and pain of that moment of diagnosis. How does one assimilate the news that this healthy, beautiful man—her husband, Ernest—has less than two months to live? The diagnosis of Ernest's illness in 1993 came precisely at a time in their lives when Beth's career was flourishing and all the things they had worked so hard for and dreamed about seemed within easy reach. Beth had already written award-winning songs for Trisha Yearwood and Willie Nelson. And her new CD, *You Hold the Key*, in which she sings her own material, had just been released. She was ready for takeoff. Ernest's work as a counselor and creator of programs for troubled adolescents was moving in new and exciting directions. Their thirteen-year-old son, Ernest III, was thriving. It was at this high point that the Chapmans were called into the hero's journey without being asked and without a single warning sign to alert them to the treacherous path ahead.

On the day of the diagnosis, Beth and Ernest held each other and cried for hours. That night, she was scheduled to sing at an important banquet for the Anti-Defamation League at the Vanderbilt Plaza Hotel in Nashville. It was a big step in Beth's career—the president of Warner Brothers Records was going to listen to her perform. "I can't do this," she told Ernest. "I can't go for half an hour without crying. How can I possibly get up and sing?"

"You have to do it," Ernest said, and he helped her get there.

"Performing that night was surreal, shocky, like a bad dream," Beth tells me. "At that point, Ernest and I were the only ones who knew about his illness and the prognosis. I looked down at him, less than twenty feet away in the audience, and I couldn't believe it. He looked so healthy and handsome in his tuxedo." Beth got through that performance, though she admits she forgot the words to the second verse of one song and, to this day, doesn't have a clue as to what she actually sang. Still, nobody but Jim Ed Norman, her producer, noticed it. He quietly came up to her after the concert and said, "Nice second verse, Beth. Interesting."

As the reality of Ernest's illness set in, he made a proactive decision. "Nobody can tell me when I'm going to die," he said. That was the beginning of whole new attitudes for everyone. "It was at that moment," Beth says, "that we really began to live our lives differently." They turned their attention to each other, their son, and to living each day as fully as possible with whatever time would be left to them. "Knowing we only had so much more time together really intensified our lives," Beth told a reporter for a Michigan newspaper in 1997. "Even though it was difficult to go through, it created a lot of learning for me and instilled an appreciation for each moment because there's so much to be thankful for."[7]

I love Beth Nielsen Chapman. Her music comforts and inspires me. Even more than that, it gives me hope. I think of her, first, as a poet who also writes great songs and sings with a magnificent voice. It is the soul and passion of her lyrics that first attracted me to her work. During the two long years of waiting helplessly for a liver that could be transplanted into my dying father, my family listened over and over to her song called *Life Holds On*. We chanted it like a mantra:

> *I was swinging on the swings when I was a little girl*
> *Trying to get a handle on the big, wide world*
> *When I noticed all the grass in the cracks in the concrete*
> *I said, "Where there's a will, there's a way around anything."*[8]

Ernest fought a long, hard fight and defied the odds. He underwent chemotherapy and a bone marrow transplant. Throughout it all, he never lost his humor or his compassion. Bone marrow transplants are risky procedures, and a great many people do not survive them. Before Ernest went to Colorado, where the transplant was done, he wrote a letter to his son. In it he forgave the young man for "every mistake you will ever make" and told him that he'd be happy to see him "in six weeks or in eighty or ninety years."

Ernest died in August of 1994. He lived eighteen months from the time of his diagnosis, far longer than any of the medical experts predicted. Though at first she couldn't even imagine continuing her music career, after time passed Beth did start writing and recording songs again. She found her grief spilling over into her music. One by one she peeled back the emotions of mourning after her husband died. One day at a time, Beth explored layer upon layer of sadness. Ernest had always told her that her words and music could comfort others. He was right. From her song "Sand and Water," Beth sings:

> *All alone I came into this world*
> *All alone I will someday die*
> *Solid stone is just sand and water, baby*
> *Sand and water and a million years gone by.*[9]

If it's possible to wear out the tracks on a CD from overplaying it, then that is what I've done with Beth's "Sand and Water." After my Aunt Teresa died on New Year's Eve Day in 1998—coincidentally, from the same disease that Ernest Chapman valiantly battled—I came back to Norfolk. I had been with her in New Jersey for a week or more before she died and then stayed for a few more days safe, though filled with grief, in the loving containment of my Uncle George and all my cousins and aunts and uncles. After I got home, I felt the need to be near the water. Teresa particularly loved the ocean and I felt closer to her there, letting my tears spill out unashamedly with no one but Dorothy to witness them. I would sit and watch the ocean, my Discman spinning and thrumming Beth's words into my ears, my brain, and my heart as the winter waves crashed and plowed into the deserted shore at Virginia Beach. From "Sand and Water":

> *All alone I heal this heart of sorrow*
> *All alone I raise this child*
> *Flesh and bone, he's just*
> *Bursting towards tomorrow*
> *And his laughter fills my world and wears your smile.*[10]

Beth's music gives voice to the deepest grief that human beings can feel, but there is no self-pity, no mawkish sentiment, because within the music and the words lie a bright and illuminated sense of hope and healing. There is lightness in these depths. Beth has the gift of her vision to share and conducts Art and Loss workshops following many of her concerts. It's a place for people to talk about their grief and find ways in which art can contain, transform, and help heal the pain of loss. A woman named Amy wrote the following email to Beth's Web site: "Sand and water is such a blessing! . . . My dad died in 1995, and I swear, I had never heard such a clear, eloquent expression of what I had been feeling. Listening to those songs has been so healing for me." An English woman, Dorothy, wrote: "It is now fourteen months since my husband died and having heard 'Sand and Water' on the radio I felt as if Beth had written it just for me." These letters and others like them are evidence of the hero returning with a treasure for the rest of us. This is coming home with the elixir of life, the pot of gold, the Holy Grail. This is the magic that the hero quested for—knowingly or not— and has brought back for all of us to share. To return with the power of healing is to transform the journey from one that is only about pain for an individual to one of transcendence and growth for everyone.

Her journey and heartbreak over Ernest's death have intensified Beth spiritually, psychologically, and artistically, she says. "The loss of Ernest and all the suffering has deepened my feelings of trust that we're cared for. I can't tell you how or give you proof, but I know that we're loved by whoever your name for God is. Somehow through all of it, my faith in that has deepened."

It's impossible to go through the arduous passage of the Underworld and have it only affect the way you think about things because this is the Warrior's Path—the path with *heart*—in which we are split open, and changed forever in ways both profound and simple. Beth says her experience of loss makes her appreciate small things in her life and has gotten her out of her intellect and more down into her heart. Understanding that logic will never answer the questions, the most immediate and important questions about life, it makes no sense to her to ask, "Why did this happen to me?" "Why does it happen to anybody?" she says. "Why does anyone suffer? The answer is not between my ears. It's not in my brain. It's in my soul. My mind is a wonderful tool," she tells me. "It's a wonderful friend and should be taken along at all times, but my mind is not who I am. I've been learning to separate my thoughts from what I know deep in my soul, which is a lot more than my brain has been giving me." Beth describes being "cracked open" and, in spite of the heartache and sorrow, finding gifts amid the wreckage. Beth gets to the core of the hero's journey and the blessings and awakened consciousness that can be found through its pain in a remark she made to a reporter for a music industry magazine in 1998. She said, "There have been incredible gifts. I'm so thankful for things that I think I might not have even noticed before. I think that's one of the things tragedy can do for you, if you let it—if you can get your heart to open in hell."[11]

The hero's journey has opened Beth's heart to her own talents for music and words. She admits that Ernest used to be frustrated with her sometimes because she didn't believe in herself often enough and he did. Now she says that she lives more in the moment, is more appreciative of her gifts, and although she doesn't consider them to be any more or less important than anyone else's, she's able to love them more. Before Ernest died she told him that she didn't know if she would ever sing again, but that if she did decide to, she would "always come from joy." "Even if I'm singing a sad song," she says, "I'm going to come from my joy, my gratefulness that I can do this, and that I have a gift for doing it."

"Something came from the depth of this experience, of letting Ernest go, that woke me up," she tells me. "You know, the whole thing is a gift. Life is a gift. I'm not going to just let it sit in the corner and get dusty. I'm going to use it and bring what I can into the mix with it."

On a balmy spring night in L.A., my friend Kathryn and I went to see Beth's concert at the Troubadour. Although Beth and I have been email acquaintances for a few years now and she's agreed to let me interview her for this book, we've never met in person. This will be the first time. The place is packed with all kinds of people of diverse races and ages. There are families with kids and people obviously alone and couples young and old, gay and straight. Kathryn and I each buy a beer that's not very cold, and the lights go down. Beth starts with a tune called "Wrecking Ball," a high-spirited, bluesy beat that belies that the words are about hoping that things continue to go great in one's life but that it's not a bad idea to keep a "heads up for the wrecking ball." I watch the crowd singing along quietly, swaying with the music. When the song ends, the applause in this little club is thunderous. "This Kiss"—Beth's award-winning song recorded by Faith Hill—follows and is a big crowd-pleaser with lots of movement, foot tapping, and smiles, but when she sings "Sand and Water," there's a hush in the audience. I turn around and see tears on the cheeks of a man two rows behind me. The woman next to Kathryn takes her partner's hand and squeezes it. Are they listening to their heart's own inner sorrow, as I am? Or are the words and music so archetypal, so primary and basic, that we don't even need our own suffering to feel their meaning? I don't know. I do know that the room was filled with an energy that united us and called us to love one another with understanding and compassion as fellow travelers on life's journey. The sorrow, so artfully expressed in Beth's words and music, became our pain, all of our pain. In the song was the struggle and anguish of living as a human being. It was a warning of trials yet to come and a healing for those we've already traversed. Like all true heroes, Beth brought back a gift for the rest of us from her trials. In this dark music club, I'm reminded of what Joseph Campbell told us about the hero's journey: that we need only to follow the thread and where we had thought ourselves to be alone, we will be with the whole world.

· 5 ·

Rowing versus Flowing:
Luck, Destiny, and Free Will

I shall never believe that God plays dice with the world.

—Albert Einstein

Since the moment I knew the details of their car accident, I've wondered what might have happened if my dad and Deanne hadn't stopped at that Amish store to buy apple butter. Apparently, I wasn't the only one to consider the possible influences of destiny or luck on that afternoon. One of my friends said, "Your dad sure has had some bad luck lately, hasn't he?" Is that what this is, I thought, bad luck? I suppose that's one way of looking at the cause of his suffering. Looking at his life from that point of view, I can't help but speculate that maybe the whole terrible accident might have been avoided if it hadn't been for that damn apple butter. Think about it. If they hadn't stopped, they would have been down the road at least an hour before that Buick sedan flew out of control.

But, maybe not. Once we open the can of what-ifs, all kinds of paths present themselves. Would they have met up with that very same car at some other point along their route? Was it their destiny to come face-to-face with a wildly careening late-model sedan that day no matter what their itinerary? Would they have met a different fate—an even more serious accident, perhaps a fatal one, with an eighteen-wheeler— if they had kept driving instead of stopping at that little Amish store? No matter what the answer to these questions, it's clear that a great deal of suffering emerges from these unplanned and unpredictable upheavals.

Good Luck / Bad Luck

When life slings us out of our normal routine, tossing us along a painful course, it's hard to know whether something is good or bad luck. In a similar vein, can we surmise that bad luck for one individual can be good luck for another? This is surely true in some cases. Every recipient of an organ is given life by someone who has just lost his or hers. It is also the case in some larger-scale examples, such as the one that follows. In the early hours of the morning on August 9, 1945, an American B-29 airplane took off from Tinian Island near Saipan in the North Pacific bound for the Japanese city of Kokura. The plane carried deadly cargo in the form of a plutonium atomic bomb called Fat Man that had the explosive power of thirteen thousand tons of TNT. But clouds covered Kokura that morning and the mission could not go off as planned. So the plane proceeded southward toward Nagasaki—an old port city and the contingency target. Fat Man detonated over Nagasaki and created a ball of fire that was described as twenty times brighter than the sun and that killed every living thing for miles around the epicenter. Kokura was spared because of clouds. Good luck for the people there. Bad luck for those in Nagasaki.

Is good luck hidden within bad luck? Certainly the man who misses his plane only to learn that the plane later crashed, would think so. Do we control or influence the transformation of bad luck into good? The not-so-simple answer might be yes and no. The man who missed his plane had no control over the traffic jam that caused him to be late, nor the ultimate and unfortunate fate of that plane. On the other hand, we're all familiar with stories of friends who, having lost a job or gone through a divorce, later relate that it was "the best thing that ever happened" as time takes away the sting of loss and they become ensconced in a profitable new career or in love again. Did their luck transform from bad to good or did they simply put the pieces they were handed into motion, change their point of view through free will, and act with newfound determination to seek the kind of job or relationship they really wanted? As you can see and may have already concluded on your own, it is not so easy to define bad and good and their origins in these situations.

One of my favorite stories that teaches about the difficulty in defining life events as good or bad is an ancient Chinese folk tale that I'd like to share with you here. The story begins with an old farmer who was poor and had just a single ancient horse to till his fields. One day the horse ran off and escaped into the hills. A neighbor heard about this terrible incident and sympathized with the farmer.

"What bad luck," he said.

"Good luck? Bad luck? Who knows?" the farmer replied.

About a week later, the farmer heard the sound of many hooves. He turned toward the hills and saw his old horse running home followed by a herd of wild horses. They all ran into the corral and he closed the gate. Seeing all these strong wild horses, the neighbor congratulated the farmer.

"What good luck," he said.

"Good luck? Bad luck? Who knows?" said the farmer.

Early the next morning the farmer's son went to the corral to tame one of the wild horses. Suddenly the boy fell from the animal's back and broke his leg. The neighbor—indeed everyone in the village— thought this to be very bad luck.

"What bad luck," they said.

"Good luck? Bad luck? Who knows?" the farmer replied.

Two days later, the army marched into the village and conscripted all the young men, forcing them to leave home and go off to fight a bloody war. Of course, when they saw the farmer son's badly broken leg, they knew he couldn't fight and so they let him stay home. The neighbor was very happy for the farmer.

"What good luck!" he said.

"Good luck? Bad luck? Who knows?" the farmer said quietly.

This simple tale reveals important insights about the nature of luck and destiny and our deeply held beliefs about it. Like the neighbor, most of us make immediate judgments about whether something is good or bad luck. "Oh my God, this is terrible!" we swear instantly when fate delivers what appears to be a loss or a difficulty. We rush off to stop the bleeding and protect ourselves from "that" ever happening again. Refusing the pain and confusion of "not knowing what will happen next," we often make immediate decisions that we believe will set things right again or at least put an end to the uncomfortable, often painful, feelings we have when we feel that our life is out of our control.

The response of the neighbor is one that is abundantly familiar to most of us. But what about the farmer in the story? Why does he offer such a calm reaction in the face of what appear to be such catastrophic losses? Why has he reserved judgment about the goodness or badness of these events that visit him? Is he just wishy-washy or brain-dead? Some might think he is surely one or both, though others would argue that, in fact, the farmer has mastered the art of nonjudgment, a philosophy that refuses to dichotomize the world and the events of our good or bad or right or wrong. In this case, the farmer knows Eastern traditions teach: that reducing all things to dualities of black and white categories, or, in this case, "good" and "bad" luck, is one of the primary causes of human suffering and a roadblock to wisdom. According to Eastern philosophies and religions, good and bad are not the absolutes we tend to think they are. Instead, they are like flip sides of the same coin. "Where there is good, there must be bad; the transition from one to the other is truly like turning over one's hand," wrote the Chinese philosopher Lu Wang in the twelfth century. Our judgments, beliefs, and ideas about how life is supposed to be are at the heart of our labeling process, and a great deal of our suffering, when we immediately deem something to be good or bad.

The *Tao te Ching* asks, "Do you have the patience to wait till your mud settles and the water is clear? Can you remain unmoving till the right action arises by itself?" Does the farmer know this teaching and understand that the red-hot moment when our perceptions are clouded by strong emotion and fear may actually be the very worst time to make a value judgement about whether something is good or bad? Does he know that there are benefits in allowing fate to finish its work, in waiting for his mud to settle? The farmer may believe that the ultimate outcome and meaning of these events is revealed only through the passage of time. Like the farmer, we cannot always control the circumstances of our lives, but we do have the full power to determine our reactions to them. The farmer seems to believe, as Shakespeare did, that within every moment of hardship lies the seed of something positive, some hidden good luck amid the turmoil. "Sweet are the uses of adversity; which, like the toad, ugly and venomous, wears yet a precious jewel in his head," wrote the bard in *As You Like It*. Surely it takes great patience to wait for a big, ugly toad to show its jewel or for your horse to return from the hills with a herd of companions.

I watched a story unfold in my own life that was much like that of the Chinese farmer, having to do with the difficulty with which we can, or should, judge a life event as being good luck or bad luck. In the summer of 1999, my partner, Nancy, lost her job. She had worked for more than twenty years as a manager in the wholesale flower business. About a year earlier, she had been hired to fill a new job in which she was responsible for launching a wholesale flower operation within a large grocery store chain. There was great potential for professional advancement in the new position. Nancy was enthusiastic about the opportunities the job opened to her and worked very hard. The company liked what she was doing. In fact, she earned regular promotions and raises. Then on one ordinary day in early July, her supervisor called her into his office, shut the door, and informed her that her position had been eliminated. It seems that the company had been sold to an even-larger corporation and now they were swamped with managers and were restructuring the whole organization. "It's nothing personal. We really like you," her boss told her. Nancy understood that her company wasn't to blame and really no one was at fault; it was just the unfortunate way things sometimes work in the world of big business.

I went to help Nancy clear out her office, and I could tell by the "deer in the headlights" look on her face that she wasn't in the mood for talk about Chinese farmers or toads wearing jewels. She was scared. She was worried about the loss of a necessary income and concerned about finding a new job at fifty and in a competitive marketplace. In spite of the fact that she'd been a valuable employee and done an exceptionally good job, forces beyond her control were definitely affecting her life. Nancy's not alone. In chapter 1, I wrote about Tom, who was in the same boat. Perhaps you're reading this book now because you are suffering from a loss of job, income, status, or security. At the moment when you're clearing out your office and staring at your savings account ledger to see how long you can last without an infusion of cash, it's almost impossible to think that the devastating loss that just occurred in your life might turn out to be good luck. But given a bit of time, perhaps you will find that your loss has made way for a new path or opportunity in your life.

For many years, Nancy had talked about her dream of working for herself—perhaps as a broker in the flower business. The demands of her profession were hard. Wholesale florists start out early in the day. Most flowers are delivered to retailers well before noon, and so her alarm went off at four o'clock every morning and Nancy was out the door long before the sun came up. I have often said Nancy's job required living like Katie Couric, but without the money. In addition to early rising, her work required lots of overtime, which, as a salaried employee, didn't bring any extra income with it. Nancy had to work many weekends from Thanksgiving, through Christmas, and then pull long hours again as Valentine's Day approached. The florists refer to this as V-D Day because they are crazed getting ready for the biggest flower-giving holiday of the year. Easter, Mother's Day, and most of June (big wedding month) were equally demanding. There were many occasions when we couldn't join our families for Christmas dinner or some special event because of Nancy's work schedule. She made a decent living but knew that she was in a low-paying profession. In spite of her spectacular performance in sales and marketing, the dollars just weren't there in her job as they were for comparable positions in other industries. Nancy often mused about where she'd be if she'd pursued a different line of work.

I thought that the loss of Nancy's job could be very good luck for her, though I admit that it's much easier to latch onto this idea when it's not your income on the line. I knew that this dramatic change in circumstances would force her to consider other alternatives and other paths that were more in line with the things she claimed that she wanted in her life. To her credit, Nancy did take this time to reflect on what to do next. Not that life slowed down to help her. The day after Nancy lost her job, my fifteen-year-old niece, Katelyn, and four of her friends were scheduled to visit and attend an 'N SYNC concert at the Virginia Beach Amphitheater. Let's see, which is more stressful: losing your job or having five wired teenage girls rushing around your house getting ready for a limo to take them to an 'N SYNC concert? Nancy decided to enjoy the visit with Katelyn and her friends and put her anxieties away for the moment. In spite of her fear, she kept a level head and refused to feel beaten. She waited for her mud to settle and did not label the loss of her job as bad luck. Instead, she tried to focus on the opportunities that might be available. We had a great visit with these kids while Nancy waited for the right action to arise rather than trying to force herself to make an on-the-spot decision about her professional future. In a few days time, Nancy called an out-of-town colleague whom she liked and respected. She wanted his advice and counsel about what she might do next. He told her that she should work with him and immediately signed her on as an independent contractor for his company. She had done business with him in the past and admired his integrity and creativity. She was thrilled at the job he offered her. Today, she essentially works for herself as a flower broker representing a company she respects a great deal. She's earning excellent money, far more than the income that she had before, and has more freedom and opportunities for expressing herself creatively through her work. She invested in a digital phone and a laptop and can handle her accounts from anywhere, so now we have the freedom to join our families for holidays even during busy seasons. We both agree on the fact that the alarm isn't ringing through the house at four o'clock in the morning is definitely good luck.

Was the loss of her job good luck or bad luck for Nancy? At the moment of loss, it's pretty easy to think we know the answer to that question. "Of course losing your job is bad luck," we say. But in light of the outcome in her situation, couldn't we also make a good case for the loss of Nancy's job as being "good luck"? I think so. The events of Nancy's life forced her to pursue what she always said she wanted. My partner's situation reminded me of Deborah Cook (chapter 1), who told me that she believed her battle with cancer helped her to move in the direction of her destiny. Being a cancer survivor coupled with her training as a nurse added up to giving her exactly the skills and experiences she needed to work as a counselor to women fighting breast cancer. She told me, "Every event led up to discovering my passion and life's work."

Destiny or Free Will?

Sometimes I wake up during the night and think about just how many of the events in our lives are determined by free will and how many by destiny or the even more spurious influence of luck. German play-wright Friedrich von Schiller wrote, "There's no such thing as chance; and what to us seems merest accident, springs from the deepest source of destiny." Is this true? Do the events of our lives, even the most painful ones, have a purpose? Are these frightening, sometimes devastating, occurrences the universe's way of prodding and tweaking us toward our true path? Do they redirect us toward our most authentic self-expression in our work, relationships, philosophies, and spiritual passions? Are losses and the attendant suffering that surrounds them the way the process of individuation is put into gear? If so, this is a very different way of looking at things. With this point of view, "good" or "bad" no longer seem relevant labels.

So what is this thing we call destiny or fate? Does destiny follow any higher order, any spiritual or metaphysical "rules"? If so, what are they? Do they instruct us on whether the right response is to row against the current or to flow with it? Think about the Chinese story of the farmer. What does it cost the neighbor, or the farmer for that matter, to respond as they did? Most often our immediate reactions to bad luck are like those of the neighbor: we make a quick value judgment and "react" to stop the discomfort, the painful feelings of loss and insecurity. But consider how the farmer might have changed his ultimate fate if he had responded in kind. What might have happened had he made any decision other than one to wait and see what fate had in store for him? For example, he might have thrown up his hands in disgust at the loss of his only plowing horse, moved to town, and taken a job with a steady paycheck. "Way to go!" we can hear the neighbor saying. If the farmer had taken this path, he would have missed the return of his horse and the gift of the wild horses. Without the wild horses, his son's leg would have been intact and the boy would have been drafted by the army and, perhaps, been fatally injured in the war rather than home nursing a broken leg. But there are other outcomes that could have arisen from the farmer's actions. No wild horses, no broken leg, so the son goes off to the war. Because he's never had a broken bone, his legs are strong and true. He runs quickly across the battlefield, avoiding the enemy's swords. Rather than being mortally wounded, he distinguishes himself by his great bravery. When the war is over, he is honored by the king. There, in the royal palace to accept his hero's medal, he meets and falls in love with the king's daughter, a beautiful princess, marries her, and lives happily ever after. He, of course, invites his father, the farmer, to come and live in the royal compound where he now has many horses at his command. Do we have the power to change our destiny and our future luck by the seemingly small choices we make day-to-day? Or will the outcomes—our fate—be the same regardless of our decision? It's that apple butter question all over again. What power do we have over our own fate and the fates of others who are affected by our decisions—as was the son's by his father's choices? Was that farmer destined to have a bunch of horses—no matter how that was to happen—or what!? This can be a frustratingly circular line of reasoning to ponder.

Perhaps that is why philosophers and spiritual traditions throughout time have tried to unscramble the complex relationships among human choice, destiny, and luck. The early Greeks believed that destiny was determined by external forces. Existing even beyond the omnipotence of Zeus and the other gods, the three Fates—also called the *Moirae*—kept watch over every human being. At the outset a soul chooses its life and goes before *Lachesis* (the Lot Giver) who appoints a guardian, known as a *daimon*, to keep the soul on track and living out its destiny. The *daimon* then leads the soul to an audience with *Klotho* (the Spinner) who spins the life thread of that soul into its particular twists and turns. Finally, the soul meets the most fearsome of the three Fates, *Atropos* (the Inflexible), who irrevocably determines the moment of physical death and will cut the thread at its allotted time. She also makes the web of destiny irreversible.

The idea of the Fates and all the control they have over our lives strikes me as a kind of fatalism, a fierce kind of determinism, in which free will is entirely absent. According to this view, deliberation and action are pointless because the future will be the same no matter what we do: "Life and Death, existence and nonexistence, success and failure, poverty and wealth, virtue and vice, good and evil, hunger and thirst, warmth and cold, all revolve upon the changing wheel of destiny," wrote the Taoist Chuang-tzu.

Accepting the idea of a preordained fate—a teleological goal for each of us—is foreign to many contemporary Westerners, and yet the very act of contemplating the idea of a personal destiny brings up many interesting questions. How does destiny provoke us? Are we "called" into it by the "spirit of fate," God, or the universe? Are sudden changes—even very painful ones—meant to wake us up to our authentic destiny? Throughout history, many people thought so and, like the Greeks and their *daimon*, described a force that extends an invitation to each human being to realize his or her purpose in life by staying close to one's unique path. The Neoplatonists named this force the *ochema*, the Romans labeled it *genius*, the Egyptians called it *ka*. The Christians have *guardian angels* and Muslims have the *jinn*. Keats simply and poetically dubs it the "call of the heart." In Hindu and Buddhist traditions our true purpose or destiny is an individual expression of the life force itself, and one that can only be denied with great peril and enormous karmic indebtedness. We are awakened to our destiny and purpose by whispers and intuitions, often by shadowy hints, and sometimes by sudden changes in our life or fortune, which are almost always painful, given how most of us resist change of any kind. W. H. Auden framed this ethereal question very nicely when he wrote, "The so-called traumatic experience is not an accident, but the opportunity for which the child has been patiently waiting—had it not occurred, it would have found another, equally trivial—in order to find a necessity and direction for its existence, in order that its life may become a serious matter."

In spite of all these multicultural musings on the nature of destiny and luck, there are those who believe we completely create our own destiny through the choices we make and the paths we follow in life. In spite of the power of their mythological and religious teachings, many early Western philosophers—particularly the Sophists, Socrates, Plato, and Aristotle—argued that man could not be entirely bound by the inevitable, inescapable vagaries of the gods. Surely, not everything in life was controlled by the Fates or destiny. To these thinkers, ethics and morality were impossible concepts without this notion of choice. It was simply not realistic to believe that man did not have some effect on his destiny, they said.

Since the time of the early Greek philosophers, the nature of free will and that of luck and destiny have been pondered by theologians, scholars, and brilliant thinkers such as Bacon, Descartes, Voltaire, Rousseau, Kant, Schopenhauer, Mill, and James, among others. Another early Greek philosopher, Heraclitus, must not have liked the mythology of the Fates any more than the rest of them, because he wrote, "A man's character is his fate." Shakespeare pursued this idea further in *Julius Caesar*, when he said, "Men at some time are masters of their fates: The fault, dear Brutus, is not in our stars, but in ourselves." In the late eighteenth century, the German poet Novalis argued this same point, that we control our fate by the choices we make, and simply said, "Character is destiny."

I see these two extreme points of view—first, our fate is entirely determined by forces outside our control or, second, we determine everything about our destiny—as forming a continuum of beliefs. Somewhere in the middle of the continuum, between these two extremes, lies the concept of predeterminism—a particularly Christian term that implies that the eternal destiny of a person is set in stone by God's unchangeable decision. However, this doctrine usually insists that only our final destiny (death) is predetermined and that throughout life our actions remain free, an idea that resonates with the Eastern notion that we do, in fact, create our own karma.

As in most things in life, I tend to find a "middle way" when approaching this question. It seems to me that both of these extreme views fail to take into account the idea that the truth about fate, luck, and free will embraces a both/and, as opposed to an either/or, reality. I believe that every human being has both a destiny and a free will. Yesterday's actions set in motion the conditions that we live in today. At the same time, many events of our life seem independent of any choices that we make. If we are constantly late for work, we create a situation in which we're very likely to be reprimanded or fired. In this way, our actions are setting a course for our destiny. On the other hand, we have no immediate power over whether the executives of our company will decide to merge with a large multinational corporation that will move their operation, and our job, to Mexico. We have no control over the fact that we might be born with a genetic predisposition toward heart disease—a destiny seemingly loaded onto a snippet of DNA. But we have free will as to whether we'll engage in poor health habits, such as smoking, eating a high fat diet, and refusing to exercise, that have been shown to contribute to heart problems.

I see the two powers of destiny and free will as partners in a subtle dance in which our choices create our destiny and our fate gives us opportunity for new choices. Maybe the true measure of our lives will be found in just how gracefully we glide between the two, aware of their delicate interweaving and the power of each. Our true challenge is found in learning to better understand this subtle, though complex, dance. If we can see how these forces influence us, we may be able to live more consciously, make wise choices about when to act, learn how to wait for the right action to arise, and know when to accept our fate with grace and courage. To return to the sailboat metaphor—it's important to know when to row like hell and when to flow, when we are wise enough to let the winds and tides carry us in the directions they naturally go. Some days flowing is what is called for. To do otherwise is to exhaust ourselves in a useless task as we try to defy their power. But it's just as important to know when we should row, when we have the power to determine our own course and we are well advised to take it. A great deal of suffering emerges from making the wrong choice between rowing and flowing or, more commonly, from ignoring the fact that we do have a choice.

I rather like the idea that we create (or at the very least co-create with some higher power) our own destiny, at least at an unconscious level. This idea is one that has been endorsed by thinkers in both Eastern and Western traditions. In the third century, the great neo-Platonic philosopher Plotinus explained that our soul selects everything about our life before we were born. We choose our body, our parents, our situation, and every circumstance along the path of our life that is necessary for the full realization of our destiny. According to Plotinus, the reason that we don't understand the importance of every experience, especially those we would label as "bad luck," is simply because we have forgotten that we have chosen it.

Jungian analyst James Hillman recounts an ancient Jewish legend that speaks similarly to how we have forgotten the soul's prenatal choices about the events we will encounter in life. The story says that the truth is pressed right into your upper lip. That little indentation below your nose is all that's left to remind you of your preexistent soul-life. That's why, it is said, when we conjure up a lost thought or an insight, our finger naturally moves to that significant dent. This is, according to this tale, where the angel pressed its forefinger to seal your lips.[1]

This way of thinking, while rich in its metaphysical implications, can bring us to a New Age slippery slope in that it assumes that people create ALL of their own fate, all of their own suffering. Every illness, every tragedy that befalls a human being can be seen as yet another "soul-lesson" designed to provide insight and growth. Perhaps this is true, as Plotinus might argue, at the ultimate cosmic level, but the belief that we control every aspect of our destiny can be a dangerous one. This view creates a false sense of power and security and can cause us to feel guilt when things don't go exactly as we expect that they should. This view may also reduce our expression of compassion for ourselves and others who are going through hard times, leading to statements like one I actually overheard: "I know he has cancer, but what a great opportunity to learn his cosmic lessons." Is this not another form of determinism, an extreme view that suggests that everything that happens to us is predetermined—whether by us or by God—and that we are powerless to change anything?

Locus of Control

Lacking the poetic language of ancient cultures, contemporary psychologists refer to the perception of one's command over our present and future as one's "locus of control." With a highly developed "internal locus of control," we believe that we can control everything that happens to us. We proclaim, "I am the master of my fate, I am the captain of my soul." On the other hand, to have a strong "external locus of control" is to accept that our choices have very little influence over the events of our life; we feel like a pawn on the chessboard of the Fates or a leaf in the whirlwind of destiny. From this point of view, everything that happens to us is beyond our control. We create additional pain and suffering when we adamantly insist on sticking to our habitual way of looking at life; either we control everything, or we control nothing. I find that both extreme endpoints on the locus of control continuum are dysfunctional and inadequate to meeting the challenges that life presents to us. Many of us remain stuck in conditioned responses, insisting that the beliefs and behaviors that we've used to resolve problems in the past are the only ways to solve the ones we face today regardless of the realities that confront us. As I said, I like the middle way. I believe we can be *both* directors of our fate and subject to forces beyond our control. In fact, to accept that we do not have any control over the events of our lives is to be extremely depressed, while to believe that we have total and complete dominion over everything is certainly narcissistic, if not downright psychotic. Jawaharlal Nehru uses a familiar and accurate metaphor to describe the relationship between free will and destiny, when to row and when to flow. He said, "When the cards are dealt and you pick up your hand, that is determinism; there's nothing you can do except to play it out for whatever it may be worth. And the way you play your hand is free will." It seems to me that to be flexible—capable of both rowing or flowing as the circumstances demand—and wise in determining the right course of action (or nonaction) is a remarkable tool for living consciously.

Fully exploiting the relative powers of choice and destiny requires that we "hold the tension of the opposites," as Jung pointed out. In this dialectical process, we consciously hold both (rather than either/or) as being true and in the psychological resolution of this conflict, we allow for the emergence of an unforeseeable "third" reconciling truth to emerge. In Jungian (and Hegelian) terms, we start with a thesis such as "I have control over everything in my life" and counterbalance it with its antithesis, "I have control over nothing in my life." This confrontation of opposites generates both tension and energy. If we can only have the courage to wait for the outcome, this energy gives rise to this new "third thing," which is the truth that can be seen in this statement: "I have control over some things and no control over others." From the standpoint of consciousness, we have now reached a psychological "middle ground." Jung's analytical psychology is in clear agreement with the Eastern idea of "nonjudgment": withholding value-laden interpretations and waiting, as the *Tao te Ching* suggests, for our "mud to settle," knowing the Right Action (Jung called it the "transcendent function") will reveal itself it time. Our job is to remain conscious and open to its instruction.

Through our visitations to the Underworld, thanks to the blessings of bad luck, we begin to understand who we are and the path that our life is taking. We can more fully appreciate the nature of our human reality and discover a deep, compassionate heart along the way. It is through bad luck and suffering, the downturns that our destiny forces upon us, that we can fully value our good luck. And it is through this contact with deep truth that we discover who we are and what matters to us. Jungian analyst James Hollis points out that "most of life is a flight from the anxiety of being radically present to ourselves and naked before the universe."[2] Without the spirals created by good and bad luck we would live what Jung called "the provisional life," which he described as a life devoid of meaning, purpose, or joy. We would simply go from one event to another without the benefit of consciousness, awareness, or being fully present to ourselves and each other.

Rowing AND Flowing

When my mother was first diagnosed with leukemia, she and our family chose to fight this battle with every tool we could find. We had a very strong "internal locus of control." We were going to be warriors and determine her destiny. We made certain that the very best doctors treated her. We scrutinized their credentials and asked friends who had survived cancer for their opinion about their skills and reputations. We read medical textbooks and the latest research in academic journals so that we better understood the treatment options available to her. We even identified some clinical trials that were evaluating new forms of chemotherapy for her disease, and she participated in them. Although she had always followed a good and proper diet, my mother tried a variety of nutritional approaches that had been demonstrated to be helpful in fighting cancer. I could go on and on listing the things we did, but the point is that my mom and the rest of us made an immediate gut-level decision that we were going to row. We'd use whatever power we had to beat the cancer and restore her to health.

If I had to make the decision over again, I'd opt to do exactly what we did. From the very beginning, we knew that my mother's prognosis was poor. She had a particularly deadly form of leukemia and one that medical science knows relatively little about. I think we all knew that, regardless of the outcome, we couldn't live with ourselves if we didn't do everything possible to change what appeared to be my mom's fate.

In spite of everything we did, my mother continued to get sicker. About three months before she died, it became clear that—barring a miracle—she would not live much longer. Our worst fears were confirmed not only by her weakening physical condition (she could no longer go up or down the stairs and was exhausted by walking the few steps from the couch to the bathroom) but also by the irrefutable blood work charts that impersonally announced the advance of the cancer. Her red blood cells and platelets were going down quickly. Immature and deformed white cells were pouring out of her bone marrow by the millions. We helplessly watched those blood test numbers mount up the way an underdog football team stares at the scoreboard and realizes the game is over. There is a point of no return when time has run out. We had lost.

I remember the moment when I knew that we could no longer row against this terrible disease. My mom knew it, too. I think that we both understood this completely the day she talked to me about the music she wanted to be played at her funeral. In that instant, I knew that we had reached the place where we had to flow. We had to let go of our need to stand bravely in the face of her destiny and surrender to those forces that were so much stronger than we were. Reluctantly, we did. I think it was the right thing to do, though I'm sure some people might not agree. Some people say fight until the bitter end. But I would argue that we would have lost something precious—some extraordinary moments of grace—in the process had we taken that position.

There is something numinous, awe inspiring, in the moment when we fully accept our suffering, give ourselves over to some higher power, and become open and vulnerable to "what is." There is enormous power in being able to say—as Mary did to the angel Gabriel when her fate was revealed to her—"Let it be." Whether we think of the transcendent as God or the laws of nature, we are released from the anguish of the fight and the need to control the future. On this afternoon with my mother, I knew that we were now being held in someone else's hands. Surrender is at the heart of every spiritual initiation rite, and it was through this letting go that we discovered a transcendent perspective in which our pain became THE pain. We were bursting with spirit and an awareness of how my mother's life and our lives were part of a far bigger picture. During this time I kept the following haiku by Issa in my wallet to remind me of this when I was scared or in the throes of a grief so deep it had no bottom:

How lovely!
Through the torn paper screen,
The Milky Way

By accepting her fate, my mother was able to openly grieve and speak about her fears, her anger, and her love. In the last few weeks of her life she said things to each of us that might not have seemed important if she hadn't accepted that she was dying. But they were important. We had some of the most intimate and powerful moments of our lives together during those last days and weeks. We were tasting life in a new way, living—as May Sarton has written—"deep and hard." We lived as if every moment mattered and we had all the time in the world. I remembered something that the thirteenth-century Sufi poet Rumi had said about the incredible power and freedom that comes with living fully in the present. "Stay here," he said, "quivering in this moment like a drop of mercury." And so we did. We cried and laughed and loved each other as if those were the only things we ever had to do. And perhaps they were. I was continually awed by the depth of our relationship, the strength of my family, and my mother's honesty and grit as she moved gracefully, fearlessly, through the rest of her life.

I've always liked the Serenity Prayer precisely because it so eloquently describes the complex question of when to act and when to accept life on its own terms. It was written by Protestant theologian Reinhold Niebuhr in the early part of the twentieth century. He first uttered these simple words in a small church in New Hampshire, and today they are recited daily by people all over the world. His prayer begins, "God grant me the Serenity to accept the things I cannot change; Courage to change the things I can; and Wisdom to know the difference."

My greatest hope is that the pain in my life will propel me toward a destiny that holds serenity, courage, and wisdom. More than anything, I want to be worthy of my suffering.

A Path with Heart

Everybody suffers. But it is through the agony of pain and how we choose to respond to its challenge that we realize meaning in our life.

Discovering how to mine this gold from lead should be our ultimate goal. The "good luck" and "bad luck" events of our lives guide us toward our destiny like highway markers on the road home. Following this one true path reveals our most authentic Self, and promises both psychological health and spiritual enlightenment. So there are always blessings, though sometimes not in plain sight, even in the difficult parts of the cycles that we live through. We have only to awaken to them—choose to go through them consciously and do our best to be wise in deciding when we must row or flow.

Knowing when to muster all our resources to change our situation and when to surrender to our fate is not always easy. There are no hard-and-fast rules about rowing and flowing, about when to struggle to create our own destiny and when to stand naked before the gods. Our impulses as to whether we habitually fight against or accept our suffering are heavily influenced by culture, family, and our beliefs about the world and ourselves. Look honestly at your attitudes about life. Do you adhere to a "when the going gets tough, the tough get going" philosophy? Or are you more inclined to believe that you don't control most of the things that happen—or will happen—in your life? A flexible, conscious attitude is one that can take *either* path based on the reality of the challenges we face. The more we reflect on our life, asking hard questions about ourselves and our responses to our suffering, the more we fan the flames of awareness. Awakening to universal truths about the nature of reality forms the bedrock of living a conscious life.

I think the most important thing we can do in our lives is to be awake, to live fully and passionately through *every* experience, to be equally and completely present during the bright moments of felt grace as well as the chaos of fear and sorrow. By making a commitment to living a conscious life, we can always be grateful for the preciousness that *is* our life even in the worst of times or when confronted by a mystery that we will never fully understand. In spite of suffering that I've experienced, I am still awed by the miracle that is my life and the potential and promise it holds in spite of limitations and pain that come my way. I'm grateful. I've come to believe, as fourteenth-century Christian mystic Meister Eckhart did, that "if the only prayer you say in your whole life is 'thank you,' that would be enough."

Spiritual and wisdom traditions throughout time have clearly mapped the terrain we must travel in order to make our lives meaningful and bring love, compassion, and courage to each moment. They also instruct us in how to grow through suffering. In my studies, I've found that while each tradition is flavored with images, beliefs, and unique cultural ideas, they all say the same things about suffering and the importance of compassion and meaning in life. Many paths, same truths. And, though we might not always be aware of it, a great deal of this wisdom is already well known to us. These truths can sometimes be found in our thoughts, our rational mind, but more often we discover them in the deepest recesses of our instincts and intuitions—in our hearts. By listening closely to these inner urgings, we develop a sureness of heart, a trust in the wisdom of our own inner Self, and can face our lives directly, accepting our suffering and limitations as well as our joys and possibilities. This is the warrior's path, the one that Yaqui sorcerer Don Juan in his teachings to anthropologist Carlos Castañeda called "the path with heart." "Look at every path closely and deliberately," he said. "Then ask yourself and yourself alone one question . . . Does this path have a heart? If it does, the path is good. If it doesn't, it is of no use."[3]

In the next section, I offer some practical ideas and actions that I've learned from studying the words of wise men and women and talking with people who seem to have a knack for self-growth even through unbelievable pain. A great many of the things I now know have come from fumbling, and, finally, learning through dark times in my own life. There are no rules that apply uniformly to everyone. My thoughts are offered as gentle suggestions to spark your own curiosity and imagination. Each of us must evolve our own philosophies about life. Trust your heart. Rely on your own creativity, your inner guidance, and you will discover the answers that work for you, as you resolve to seize every bit of meaning and growth from your own suffering and as you strive to stay on the path with heart.

PART TWO

A Dozen Strategies for Growing Through the Pain

Introduction

God does not want us to be burdened
because of sorrows and tempests that happen
in our lives, because it has always
been so before miracles happen.

—Julian of Norwich, fourteenth-century mystic

    Human beings naturally want to be happy, find meaning in life, and avoid suffering. That is as it should be, and just because we've made a decision to grow through difficult, painful times does not mean that we now should invite suffering into our lives. Who would want to do that? What we must carry with us is the awareness that a great deal of suffering cannot be avoided. We must face that we age, die, and lose people we love as we travel along our path. As we get older, we'll each watch our bodies age, children will leave home, pets will pass away, and opportunities for career advancement will dwindle. These are the inescapable losses, the wrenching realities of living as a human being. We can't avoid these painful experiences, and to feel grief and sorrow when we're in the midst of them is not only understandable; it's also psychologically and spiritually healthy.

However, while a great deal of suffering is unavoidable, a lot of it we bring on ourselves unnecessarily. When I think about the needless suffering that I've experienced in my life, I realize that it always stems from my faulty reasoning or phony philosophies regarding the nature of reality. I know I'm not alone in this, for I've seen my mistakes mirrored in my clients and my friends. But, this is the kind of suffering we can bypass if we are aware of the thoughts we have that invite it. Here are the eight beliefs/actions that can add to our pain if we let them:

1. **Resistance to Change**. This is the "suffering of change." When under its spell, we grasp at illusions and do not accept the transient nature of our being. We fail to relinquish our attachments to all impermanent things (which, of course, is everything).

2. **Expectation That Life Is Always Fair**. Again, this is a failure to understand the true nature of reality. Life is *not* always fair, and we set ourselves up for a big fall if we insist that it is.

3. **The Illusion of Egoism**. The ego would like us to believe that we are separate from all other beings. This erroneous belief adds to our sense of isolation and alienation from the great cosmic dance. It also feeds the idea that somehow we do (or should) suffer any more or less than anyone else.

4. **Failure to Take Responsibility for Our Responses**. We forget that although we cannot control all the events of our lives, we have full dominion over how we will respond to life's challenges.

5. **Ruminative Suffering**. We define ourselves by our pain. We set a tape playing about how we are suffering and never turn it off. Our whole self-identity becomes wrapped up in our suffering. In popular parlance, this is the "pity party."

6. **Failure of Compassion**. We cannot feel the pain that others experience. With this inability, we add to feelings of isolation and loneliness and stymie our expression of love and tenderness for others and ourselves, as well.

7. **Unconscious Approach to Life Prevails**. Asleep to our own potential and that of all life, we carry around such a poor self-image and, often, self-hatred that we refuse to allow ourselves to be happy. In this frame of mind we don't believe that we have the right to happiness or freedom from pain and we continue to feel we're unworthy of love, respect, and concern from others.

8. **Self-Sabotage**. We make choices and behave in ways that will inevitably and unequivocally lead to suffering. We may or may not be aware of the outcomes we are setting up for ourselves.

A lot of people hold on to one or more of the above beliefs and suffer greatly as a result. That's the bad news. The good news is that we can change these viewpoints anytime we wish. We can begin to look at the world and ourselves differently. A new outlook isn't born over-night, but we can work at it and often can see results as soon as we do. We can become warriors, courageous in the face of the suffering we cannot prevent and wise in avoiding the pain that we can. I'm certain that there are thousands of ways to reduce unnecessary suffering and grow from the kind that cannot be avoided. By thinking clearly about your own behavior and beliefs, you will, no doubt, come up with some approaches that work to ease your own pain. As you do so you may want to consider the following strategies that I've discovered as I've talked with people who I think have become better, not bitter, through their suffering. Not surprisingly, these are consistent with what spiritual traditions, philosophers, and wise indigenous people have always taught about how best to live as a human being.

You'll notice that at the end of each section I've included some very practical suggestions for putting these strategies into action. You'll be amazed at how small, simple changes can dramatically alter your life. I hope that the ideas I've put forth can start you on your way and grease the wheels of your own creativity as you develop your own plan for reducing suffering in your life and growing through that which you must endure. Insight, understanding, and knowledge are necessary and important first steps in making changes in our lives, but they're not enough. Determine not to be just a wiser, though still suffering, person. We live best when we take responsibility for the directions our life will take and, to do that, we have to manifest our wisdom in day-to-day activities and behaviors. Not to act on our discoveries is akin to being at a magnificent banquet but never eating a bite. We'll still be hungry. An ancient Hindu text, the *Bhagavad-Gita*, written sometime between the fifth and second centuries B.C.E., advises us to "perform all necessary acts, for action is better than inaction; none can live by sitting still and doing nought." And in the words of a Russian proverb that teaches the same thing: "Pray to God, but row for the shore."

Strategies

1. DISCOVER A LARGER PERSPECTIVE

Four years ago, I hung a remarkable NASA photograph in my office. It's a picture of the Eagle Nebula taken by the Hubble Space Telescope. It shows eerie pillars of warming interstellar hydrogen gas and dust that serve as an incubator for infant star systems—some bigger than our own solar system—against a background of boundless indigo space. The setting for this shot is a "nearby" star-forming region that lies in the direction of the constellation Serpens. These columns in the photo resemble thunderheads, clouds that form in our sky as a powerful summer storm builds. Those in the Eagle Nebula are quite a bit larger. They tower more than six trillion miles high. It's a breathtakingly beautiful image, of what astronomers call a "star nursery." This photograph is so awesome that it sets my mind to almost unimaginable wanderings, but what's even more amazing to me than the size of this phenomenon is the fact that the Eagle Nebula is more than four hundred million times farther from Earth than our sun. While that might be "just around the corner" in astronomical terms, it means the events shown in my picture occurred more than 42 trillion miles from the earth. It took the ultraviolet light blasting from those baby stars racing at 186,000 miles per second seven thousand light-years to reach the camera lens of the Hubble and be snapped in this cosmic Kodak Moment in April 1995.[1]

When these stars were being born, it was 5000 B.C.E. on Earth. This is a mind-blowing thought to me. My recent photograph depicts events that were happening in space at the same time that human beings on Earth were living in the evolutionary period known as the Neolithic Revolution. We, as a species, had recently ceased our hunter-gatherer ways and were learning to live in communities and get the hang of agriculture. We still could not write or read. We had just discovered that we could trade with people who had things we wanted in exchange for those we didn't. However, those objects of exchange must have been small and easily portable because we wouldn't invent the wheel for another fifteen hundred years. It would take thousands more years before we built the Great Pyramid at Giza (2700 B.C.E.) or set the massive blocks of Stonehenge into place on the fertile fields of Salisbury in Britain (between 3000 and 1000 B.C.E.). (Dorothy reminds me, though, that by the time these baby stars were birthed, dogs had been human companions for more than five thousand years—domesticated dogs date back prior to 10,000 B.C.E.).

When I look at my photograph, I can't help but wonder if, at this moment, those stars are still there. Are they blazing away in the galaxy, perhaps with planets whirling around in orbit just as our Earth dances elliptically around our star, the sun? Did they explode in a roaring supernova? Or did they cave in on themselves, perhaps becoming "wormholes" that tunnel to unknown universes? Our descendants, seven thousand years in the future, are the only ones who will be able actually to see what is happening in the Eagle Nebula in this precise moment of time in *our* night sky.

If looking at that NASA photo doesn't fill me with awe, wonder, and humility, I don't know what could. The thoughts and emotions that this transpersonal point of view arouses in me are mystical, sacred, spiritual, and entirely intuitive. They come from my heart, not my head. In Eastern philosophies, such experiences are called *satori* or *samadhi*. Psychologist Abraham Maslow calls this way of looking at things the "farther reaches of human nature." But regardless of the words we use to try to express this truly indescribable and numinous feeling, there is a powerful transformation of consciousness that accompanies this perspective. Seeing myself as part of this unfathomable cosmic order casts my problems—indeed, my whole life—into an extraordinary relationship with the universe. Whatever created this grandeur created me, is the thought I am left with after pondering the Eagle Nebula. As I look up at the stars at night, I can't help but believe that I am both unique in all the world and a grain of sand on the beach. My life will be singularly my own, and yet I will face challenges that are common to all living beings. Just as there is light, there will be shadow. We're all gifted with the blessing that is life, and we'll all endure pain as we live it. When I see my existence in this universal context, I feel deeply connected to everyone and everything. Without any perception of distance between us, I am naturally aroused to compassion and connection. In this state of mind, I understand intimately what twelfth-century mystic Hildegard of Bingen meant when she said, "Every creature is a glimmering, glistening mirror of Divinity."

If we pause to look at the world around us, we will see that there is a bigger picture beyond our existence. Even if we live to be one hundred and twenty, our lives are a mere blip on the radar screen of the universe. Here now, and then gone, in an instant of cosmic or geologic time. It's clear that we have been invited—at least in our present form—for only a relatively short visit. It doesn't make sense to me that the power that formed this vast universe would waste the time or energy creating human beings for just a brief and, so often, painful ride that is meaningless. I believe that something within me, call it soul, spirit, or consciousness, must have some larger purpose. It is within this immense mystery—created by the hand of God (described by whatever name you believe in) or by forces so awesome in their power that they defy our imagination—that we live our mortal human lives struggling for meaning and purpose while suffering through its pain. Albert Einstein pointed out that making the best of our lives in this mystery is "our sacred human responsibility."

When we take our suffering out of our own dark isolation and see it in this larger context of life and stars and awesome powers, something important happens. We recognize the truth about our relationship to all of life. We are no longer alone. Our life is part of some larger plan, though we may not always understand it. An ancient Ojibway saying captures this feeling for me: "Sometimes I go about pitying myself, and all the time I am being carried on great winds across the sky." However, remembering that we do have a purpose, that we're here for some reason, may be particularly difficult during painful times. But when I find myself feeling alone on a bad day, I look up at the sky and remember that the stars are present at midday just as they are in the blackest night—they're just harder to see.

Carl Jung believed that there is only one decisive question that human beings need ask, and that is, Am I related to something infinite or not? "That is," he wrote, "the telling question of life. Only if we know that the thing that truly matters is the infinite can we avoid fixing our attention upon futilities and upon all kinds of goals, which are not of real importance. . . . In the final analysis, we count for something only because of the essential we embody, and if we do not embody that, life is wasted."[2]

Growing through suffering requires this shift of perspective from an outlook in which a person feels alone—picked on by the universe—to one in which experiences, even difficult ones, are related to something infinite. When you're suffering, think about all the other beings who have gone through similar experiences or far worse ones. I'm not advising you to ignore your pain or tell yourself that you cannot grieve or feel bad because other people may have had it harder. Just try to see your pain in the context of the big picture. Open your heart, mind, and spirit to this larger, transcendent perspective of your place in this great chain of being. With such an outlook consciousness blooms and, suddenly, we see things that we were ignorant of just a moment earlier. A single transpersonal experience can change your life forever.

Taking a larger perspective helps us put our suffering in a new context. But this perspective is not always starry and ethereal, racing out toward the edge of the cosmos. This transformed perspective can also be very down-to-earth and may come from looking at the specific events of our lives within the framework of our whole life. We can see from other times in our lives that we may be suffering now, but it will not last forever; hope will surface, and better times will come again. Like the figure on the Wheel of Fortune, we all exist in spiraling cycles of blessings and pain. Sometimes we need to step back from our current pain to see that this is true.

We need patience to appreciate our suffering in a larger context. Although patience has always been espoused as an indicator of high character (Saint Augustine pointed out that patience is nothing less than the companion of wisdom), most of us are not very good at it in our rapidly paced modern world. We often get stressed and impatient when things don't happen immediately. We want our expectations and needs met now. "Charge it!" we say as we purchase fabulous shoes on a credit card, even when we're strapped with bills and have a closetful of similar fabulous pairs. Immediate gratification is our credo in Western society. Some of us even find ourselves tightening up and yelling "Come on!" when traffic moves slowly or a Web site takes more than *ten seconds* to load, as if our demands alone were sufficient to move four lanes of traffic or digital data across cyberspace. With these expectations about the pace of life and how long we think we're supposed to delay getting the things we want, It's no wonder most of us have trouble waiting for our mud to settle or for the right action to arise following a moment of suffering.

Viktor Frankl once used a metaphor to describe the patience we must have in understanding our larger purpose and finding meaning in suffering and in our life itself. He asks us to think about a movie that consists of thousands of individual frames. Each picture makes sense and has some meaning of its own, but the whole film cannot possibly be understood until the final sequence is shown. Life is like that. We need patience. We can't understand all of life's meaning until we reach its end and sometimes not even then. Often we must simply live with the mystery. But in an attempt to grasp as much wisdom as we can about our lives, Frankl asks us to consider that our life's final meaning depends in large measure on how we've chosen to live it. He wrote, "And doesn't this final meaning, too, depend on whether or not the potential meaning of each single situation has been actualized to the best of the respective individual's knowledge and belief."[3]

Living up to our potential—living life fully and becoming worthy of our suffering—demands patience and a larger, longer view. This is part of the path with heart. You may have already started down this road, but if you haven't, here are some ideas that might help.

Some Practical Suggestions

1. Consider exploring specific religious or spiritual traditions by regularly attending a church, synagogue, mosque, ashram, or wherever people gather to ask the big questions about life. If you are not already committed to a particular approach, test the waters of different faiths by checking into short retreats that focus on discovering meaning in life. Look to your own tradition first and if the fit is good with your philosophies and beliefs about life and the Divine, get involved. If the tradition you've selected (or the one you've been raised with) is no longer right for you, investigate others. Connecting with kindred spirits, becoming part of a searching community, and deepening faith are important parts of a path with heart for many people. If you can't find a group that is right for you, then forge your own, unique spiritual path.

Pray and meditate. Simply make a point to reflect on your life every day and especially when you are suffering. But don't just talk about doing these things; *do something*, be active. Explore illumination and spiritual truths with a passion. Go forward, as Hindu sage Sri Ramakrishna said, "Like a man whose hair is on fire seeks a pond."

2. Read. Read the wisdom of your own spiritual tradition with hunger and passion. Learn about traditions other than the one you adhere to. It's remarkable to see how every faith and wisdom tradition teaches the same basic truths while maintaining its own unique character, liturgy, and form. Read history and mythology to learn how others have suffered and what they've learned through it. If you don't know where to start, read anything by Joseph Campbell. Read *Man's Search for Meaning*, by Viktor Frankl. Read *Anne Frank: The Diary of a Young Girl*. They are my favorites. Read the works of the great philosophers. Read about ancient civilizations, nature, or quantum mechanics. Read anything you can get your hands on that excites you and offers guidance about the larger nature of reality.

3. Take classes in philosophy, metaphysics, or other scholarly disciplines where people gather to study and discuss ideas about the "bigger picture" and the meaning of life. Investigate offerings of local universities or community colleges in your area.

4. Investigate your family genealogy. Understanding your own family history can put your life in a new context. All your forbearers have lived and suffered. Many have died. Ask those living to share their memories of life and of other family members. What can you learn from their lives?

5. Look to nature. It's hard not to appreciate the big picture when you're standing at the edge of the ocean watching the waves crash against the shore or looking at a horizon filled with magnificent mountains. Stare up at the night sky from a place where city lights don't obscure the radiance of the stars. Buy a telescope or join a local astronomy club to get a closer look. Take a walk in the woods and be aware of all the sights, sounds, and smells you experience. Or if you have access to a park, yard, or garden, look closely at the intricate design of petals and leaves or the number of living creatures in just a small handful of soil. Sit quietly in places and take in their majesty. What do you come away with after a bit of reflection?

6. Buy a small notebook or journal in which to write or sketch some of your thoughts and reflections. List other ideas that come to your mind about ways to put into practice some of the points you're reading about and the ideas you've come up with.

2. TURN TOWARD COMPASSION
AND HELP OTHERS

After Dan Maslowski was captured by the Viet Cong and held as a POW, he was interrogated, put in isolation for three days, and ruthlessly beaten. He was told he would be killed if he didn't reveal what he knew. His captors asked him about military plans, numbers of troops, where they were camped, and where they were headed. They demanded to know what his mission was. "I told them I was basically a stinking pilot. I'm a taxi driver—it's an expensive taxi but a taxi nonetheless. I was only delivering supplies from one place to another. I wasn't in the intelligence loop for big plans," he said. He knew that there was nothing else he could divulge because he didn't know the information that they desperately wanted. Then they asked him: "How many other men were aboard your aircraft?" This was a different kind of question. He knew the answer to that one.

"That hit a chord," he told me. "I said to myself, they obviously haven't captured all of us." While he was in isolation—terrified that his life would be snuffed out with a single pull of a trigger maybe after digging his own grave in the muddy ground of Cambodia—he made a decision that he would *not* answer that question regardless of the consequences. "I knew that I wouldn't give them that information no matter how much they beat me, even if they threatened to kill me. I knew that if they had only found a few bodies—maybe none—they'd know more were still alive and continue to hunt down the others. I thought about one of those five other guys getting caught, maybe killed, just because I'm a little scared and tell the bad guys what I know. I knew I couldn't live with that. My life is important to me, but why is it any more important than his life is to him?" Dan never answered that question about who was with him in the helicopter when it went down.

Dan's heroism is a striking example of a person acting selflessly for the greater good. He cared about another's life even when he was suffering terribly and his own life hung in the balance. A deeply felt concern for others, the ability to imagine ourselves in their place without distance or pity, and to act on these feelings as Dan did is true compassion.

In spite of their many differences, all religions and spiritual traditions place great emphasis on the importance of compassion. In every tradition, we're taught the "Golden Rule" of treating others as we would like to be treated ourselves. We are told to, quite simply, love one another. Jesus was clear in his teachings: "Do unto others as you would have them do unto you." Buddha says, "Consider others as yourself." All but one of the one hundred fourteen verses of the Koran begin with the same phrase: "Allah is merciful and compassionate." This holy text teaches that no one can be a true Muslim "unless he desires for his brother that which he desires for himself." Jewish, Hindu, Confucian, and Taoist teachings mirror this same loving ideal, as do the cosmologies of Native American and other indigenous peoples and the ethical works of Greek philosophers. The expression of compassion is a universal central feature in living a meaningful, connected, and spiritual life.

Seeing the suffering of others puts our own trials in a new perspective. If we keep our eyes, ears, and hearts open, we cannot help but be moved by the suffering around us. Suffering is everywhere, from the war-ravaged mountains of Kosovo to the devastation in Taipei, Taiwan, after the 1999 earthquake jolted buildings off their foundations, leaving more than two thousand people dead and hundreds more missing amid the debris that was their city. In our own hometowns, children battle cancer, neighbors grieve the deaths of loved ones, and people sit alone, sometimes die alone—isolated from community, with no relationships to salve the sting of their own inevitable suffering. Our own suffering, and the realization that we are not alone in it, breaks our hearts open so that we can fully receive the truth that we all experience pain and loss. Most often, it is our wounded, softened heart that invites this power of compassion into the clear light of awareness.

While writing this book, my home of southeastern Virginia was visited by two major hurricanes in less than a month's time. First, Hurricane Dennis gave us a major soaking, raising water levels of rivers and turning the ground into sloppy mud that could barely support the root systems of trees that were being pounded by accompanying eighty-mile-an-hour winds. Then just two weeks later, Hurricane Floyd dumped twenty inches of water on us in less than twenty-four hours—that's more rain than usually falls in this region in six months' time. The water table was so high that the ground simply could not hold another drop. Trees fell, gutters and streets flooded, swollen rivers crested fifteen feet above normal, and the wind howled. The wind and rain tore up the small trees and the wooden fence in our backyard and left them scattered down the block.

The downpour of Floyd came upon us suddenly. We had no time to prepare. I still feel lucky that I made it home at all. When the storm struck, I was at a meeting about three miles away from my house. I drove through torrential rain and streets filled with four feet of water to reach the relative safety of home. The trip took almost two hours. Nancy and I were both lucky. Our telephone and electric power were out for days, and my biggest worry was how I would finish this book by deadline given my dependence upon my computer. My problems were only minor inconveniences.

More than forty people drowned during that storm. Throughout southeastern Virginia and northeastern North Carolina, thousands of others barely escaped by boat from raging torrents that swept away their houses, farms, crops, and livelihood. In Tarboro, North Carolina, a john boat searching for stranded people capsized in the rushing water—six more lives lost. Before the storm, the little town of Franklin, just south of where I live, had 181 small businesses. The day Hurricane Floyd hit, every single one was under at least six feet of water. More than a million cows, hogs, and chickens were drowned and farmers' incomes with them. Diesel and gas storage tanks, ripped from their moorings, split open and spilled thousands of gallons of petroleum products into wild streams, creating rainbow-colored slicks of pollution and danger. Caskets and burial vaults, unearthed from the muddy ground, floated to the surface and whirled through churning brown water like macabre fishing bobbers. The little town of Princeville, North Carolina—a historic African-American community—was demolished, its rich history and tradition wiped from the map in less than a day.

However, in spite of their great losses, neighbors helped neighbors. Our television and newspaper were filled with altruistic images long after the wind and rain had subsided. Time and again people who had lost almost everything shared the little bit of food or clothing that they still had with those who had less. Individuals and groups throughout the area raised money, donated blood, and assembled massive quantities of blankets, food, and household supplies for the tens of thousands of people forced out of their homes and into shelters around the area. In Tarboro, Carol Clayton McClancy hung a Christmas decoration—a white dove—in a window of her damaged home as a symbol of enduring hope. "This is all going to pass," she told a reporter for the *Virginian-Pilot*. In spite of the near-devastation of her house, Carol took in a stray cat, a stray dog, and two homeless people. Her son brought more than one hundred gallons of fresh water from Raleigh that she shared with her neighbors. "I feel like the ark," she said. "Everybody can come here. We need to celebrate life."[4] Why is it so often in the midst of great suffering—like that which Dan Maslowski or the people whose own lives were devastated by this storm endured—that we most easily turn toward compassion for others?

In my book *Ordinary Grace* I set out to examine the roots of compassion through real-life stories of ordinary people who have helped others in extraordinary ways. As I explored this subject, I compiled incontrovertible verification that empathy is a natural element of human nature. Evidence from research conducted with indigenous people, newborn babies, and even animal studies with primates, our closest nonhuman relatives, confirms this fact. Neurological research has even identified the part of the brain—the amygdala—that appears to regulate the biology of empathy. From every direction, the evidence mounts: we're prewired to care about each other.

We're born with the innate ability to share others' suffering. Day-old human infants respond to the sound of another baby crying by bursting into tears themselves. We have a natural bent toward equanimity. But it is when we consciously, willingly, open our hearts to another's pain—not from pity or sentimentality, but with a deep desire for connection and relationship—that we achieve true compassion. This compassionate state of mind means that we go beyond the desire ever to harm another. We expand our hearts with the wish for others to be free of their suffering with the same vigor as we wish ourselves to be free of our own. We hold others with the kind of selfless love that a mother feels for her only child. In such moments, we are filled with such love that we take on the pain of another and offer whatever resources we have to reduce her or his pain. When we act with compassion, we assume responsibility, respect, and commitment to those suffering. This feeling is best expressed in the actions we take in response to another's pain or loss. Compassion, it seems, should be understood as a verb, not a noun.

Some of those seen as the most sacred in many of the world's religions bear a title that acknowledges great compassion, and there are terms and tales that point to its import as well. In Buddhism this ideal of compassion is a *bodhisattva*, one whose essence is perfected wisdom and compassion. This is a person who, on the brink of entering Nirvana, relinquishes this prize in order to help his fellow man toward salvation and freedom from pain. The *bodhisattva* lives for the benefit of others. Christianity speaks of the "Christ-within" as the epitome of deeply compassionate living. Jesus said, "This is my commandment, that you love one another as I have loved you" (John, 15:12). Here are simple and clear directions to the compassionate heart. Judaism offers powerful tales about compassion in the many stories about the *lamed-vav*. The *lamed-vav* are thirty-six just men whose caring and heartbreak for the suffering of others are so profound that even God cannot comfort them. The thirty-six are secret saints who pass as ordinary mortals, and, in fact, some are not even aware of their station. It is said that when one dies, another arises in his place. The deep love and concern these three dozen individuals carry for others is what allows the world to continue to exist at all. For if even one were lacking, the sufferings of mankind would be so great that the souls of newborns would be poisoned and all of humanity would suffocate with a single cry.

To feel great compassion for others does not mean that we should deny such tender feelings to ourselves. Very often I see good-hearted people who do not let themselves grieve and have no compassion for their own pain because "other people have it worse than I do." Self-regard and love toward ourselves is not self-pity.

When it is best expressed, compassion flows out in all directions—toward others and toward our own wounded hearts. Care for others but also be gentle with yourself.

Some Practical Suggestions

1. Look at the things you say to yourself when you are suffering. Think about both extremes of self-acknowledgement: "No one could ever feel this pain that I'm feeling" versus "I shouldn't complain. Others have it much worse than I do." Each of these viewpoints lacks compassion. In the first case, the lack of compassion is toward others and shows a failure to "suffer with." This is the plaintive wailing that resonates with a false sense of separation from others and the truths about the universality of suffering. It is a refusal to acknowledge our deepest spiritual connections. In the second case, there is lack of compassion for oneself. Find the middle way. Know that your suffering *does* matter and can lead to great lessons if you face it with an open spirit. You're allowed to feel pain and grief for yourself. It is healthy and good when the events of our lives break our hearts open to life. At the same time, acknowledging that others are suffering, too, connects us to one another as nothing else can.

2. Fuel your compassion with action. Volunteer. Help others. My research for *Ordinary Grace* demonstrated that people who actively help others are happier than those who don't. Read stories to kids in a pediatric oncology ward. Cook in a soup kitchen for the homeless. Visit isolated older people at a local nursing home. Volunteer for the Special Olympics. Read your local paper and find ways you can help in your own community. Find your own passionate way to help relieve the suffering of others. Spend a lot of time or just a little reaching out. Do what you can. The world needs your compassion. You can help ease others' suffering and change your perspective on your own suffering with the same action.

3. Most of us could use some more compassion toward ourselves. Here's one way to help yourself release those feelings more easily: Find a picture of yourself as a child. Look at it often and use it as a reminder to treat yourself with tenderness and concern especially when you are in the midst of painful times.

3. RECOGNIZE AND STOP
SELF-IMPOSED SUFFERING

When you think about illness, aging, death, the loss of loved ones, and natural disasters, it becomes very clear that a great deal of suffering is simply unavoidable. Although this is true, there are two areas of our lives that often create great pain and that each of us has the full, individual power to change. The first is what I call "preventable suffering," and the second is our self-image.

Under the heading of preventable suffering are all those terrible outcomes that result from our decisions (or lack of decisions), choices, and behaviors that we can see will lead to very predictable pain. Think about how adultery creates crisis in a marriage, how addictive behaviors result in serious health problems, illegal activities land us in jail, and how unwise, unsafe risk-taking can cause injury or even death. A significant number of events that we prefer to label as "accidents" or "fate" do not really just happen out of the blue. Enormous suffering and even many injuries and fatalities occur in predictable patterns, and many are quite preventable. For example, recently, one of my friends called me late at night and in tears. He told me that his wife had left him when she discovered that he had been having an affair for more than a year with a co-worker. My heart broke for all of them. But two months earlier, when my friend first told me about his situation, I asked him what he expected to happen if he continued to cheat on his wife. He said he knew his wife suspected that he was seeing someone else and that he was sad, depressed, and guilty about how his behavior was hurting her. But he just couldn't make a decision or stop seeing this other woman. He took no actions to solve his problem. I urged him to explore what he wanted in his life, even see a therapist to help him sort out his feelings, and then make conscious, responsible, and respectful choices about his needs and those of the women his behavior was affecting. He is not a womanizer nor is he usually cavalier about his moral responsibilities. His affair was causing him guilt and pain, but he truly felt torn between his love for his co-worker and that for his wife. His inner conflict in no way justified his dishonesty with his spouse, but his suffering was authentic and deep. I told him that it saddened me to know what he was doing. Looking at his life seemed like watching two trains speeding down the same track toward each other. In this situation, a train wreck is inevitable. After all, what else can happen? I think my friend knew that he was headed for a catastrophe, but still he made no intentional decisions about what direction he wanted his life to take. Instead he just kept going forward as if he were impervious to the realities and predictable outcome of his situation. Now his suffering has increased with his failure to make wise and conscious choices.

Everyday decisions in large and small matters set us in the direction toward good outcomes or disaster. When I was a teenager, a neighbor was killed when a ladder collapsed and he plunged to the ground and broke his neck. He knew before he put his foot on the first rung that the ladder was dangerous and unstable. In fact, he mentioned to one of his friends that same morning that he needed to buy a new ladder because the one he had was an "accident waiting to happen." His prophetic words came true. He made a bad decision but, still, this is huge suffering. My neighbor lost his life, and his widow and two children grieved terribly. It might be easy to say, "How could he have done that? Why was he so foolish?" To blame or criticize him for his poor choice to climb that ladder is not kind or productive. He and his family deserve our compassion, as does anyone who suffers. But when we think about this tragic loss, we can't escape the idea that had he only been more careful and fixed the ladder first or bought a new one, all this pain could have been avoided.

We might like to distance ourselves from this man's poor decision to rely on a faulty ladder. "I would never do anything like that," you might think to yourself. But every single day, intelligent people suffer brutally because they make poor decisions like my neighbor, are unconscious about preventable dangers, or put off doing things that they should. For example, have you ever postponed getting your brakes fixed because you haven't had time to get around to it, even when you know that they're not working properly? Have you checked your smoke alarms lately (or ever) to make sure the batteries are fresh and that they still work? Have you ever ignored a physical symptom that might be potentially serious because you're afraid to know more about it or just haven't gotten around to checking it out with your doctor? Have you ever skied down an expert slope or tried any other activity that you really didn't have the training or skill to attempt? "Just this once I'm going to try it," you might say. "I'll be really careful." Did you build your new house on a floodplain or on the edge of an eroding beach? Do you ever leave your pets or children in your hot car because you're just quickly dropping something off at a friend's house? Have you ever driven with your children while they're unrestrained by car seats or seat belts because you're "just going around the block to the convenience store?" If you have, you may want to know that injuries are the number-one killer of children in the United States. In fact, more kids die from injuries than from all childhood diseases combined. Each year ten thousand young people between birth and fourteen years of age are killed and more than fifty thousand are seriously hurt in a variety of ordinary but dangerous situations, many of which could have been prevented. Thousands of children are poisoned because their parents fail to lock up cleaning supplies and hazardous chemicals. Every day, fourteen American children under the age of twenty are killed or wounded by guns that were not locked safely out of the reach of their little hands. These injuries and deaths create enormous suffering for families who must now also bear the guilt and self-blame for not having done anything to prevent these tragedies.

The list of possible ways we can avert at least some of our future suffering is endless, but to be conscious and alert to those opportunities doesn't have to turn us into frightened people locked behind closed doors in order to avoid the potential dangers in life. We can live large and still avoid unnecessary suffering. I've discovered that a lot of pain and catastrophe can be prevented by small decisions and changes, taking personal responsibility for our lives and safety, and being alert to the wake-up calls that are given to raise our consciousness and motivate our actions. Sometimes life gives us irrefutable warnings about the importance of overcoming the denial or laziness that keeps us from doing very simple things to prevent future suffering. I like to think of myself as a reasonably intelligent and cautious person about personal safety, but I had put off fixing a broken window lock in my kitchen for almost six months because I just didn't seem to have the time to fit it into my schedule. I kept telling myself, I'd do it over the next weekend and, of course, those weekends filled up with other more important or fun things to do. Soon I forgot about it all together. Then one morning I came downstairs to see this window wide open and the wind whipping through the kitchen blowing napkins and dish towels across the room. During the night, while I was home and asleep in my bed, someone had broken in and stolen some money and a portable tape player. My two sweet dogs, Portia and Clancy, were old and almost deaf at the time. Both slept through the whole break-in snuggled up on the floor in the next room. Immediately, I knew that I had been incredibly lucky. I could have been raped, seriously hurt, or even killed if the intruder had done anything other than steal and get out quickly. The police came to investigate and dusted for prints, but no arrest was ever made. But I had that window lock fixed ten minutes after they left. Then I went around my house and scrutinized every other window and door. I changed my plans for the morning and repaired and bolstered everything that was not secure. These safety measures took me less than two hours and cost no more than twenty-five dollars in hardware and locks. Then I said, "Clancy and Portia need a playmate, and I want a dog who can hear." That's when we brought Dorothy into our family, knowing that in addition to her fine company and sweet friendship, her acute hearing and relentless barking when something seems amiss to her offered an additional measure of protection against intruders. Imagine. I could have done all these things a year ago. "Forewarned is forearmed," the old expression says, and there is wisdom in those words. Heed the wake-up calls that life gives you. Paying attention to the details of our lives and acting to remove potential sources of suffering pay off in the end.

The second source of preventable suffering requires reflecting on our self-image. How we think about ourselves and the philosophies and worldviews we believe in hold very powerful emotional, cognitive, and evaluative components. Our self-image is all encompassing and affects every aspect of our life, including our abilities to meet the challenges of life's dark times.

Look at your own self-image. Does it contribute to your suffering in life? To assess that, let's look at a few questions. Do you feel unworthy of good things? Listen carefully to your inner voice. Do you hear excessive negative self-talk? Do you put your negative self-image into action by consciously or unconsciously confirming your unhealthy, unloving views of yourself? Simply, do you love yourself enough?

A sign that you do love yourself enough is a healthy self-image that engenders a personality that is confident but not overbearing. It is an ability to act with courage without bravado and practice self-reliance without isolation. There is great humility in true self-love and it's expressed in deliberate movement toward life, toward consciousness, and away from fear and judgment. To love oneself is not selfish, egotistical, grandiose, or conceited. Instead it is the full awareness of our fundamental lovability, our authentic identity as Self rather than as mere ego. It's an acceptance and awareness of our place in the universe, and of our truest nature, which is that of a "divine spark." It is the simple understanding that, as the mystic Julian of Norwich said in the fifteenth century, "We have been loved since before the beginning." Bishop John Lancaster Spalding put it into these words at the start of the twentieth century when he wrote, "Self-love, in the true sense, is the love of one's real good—of truth, of virtue, of beauty, of God. It is the strongest in those who are most alive in their higher nature. It is the opposite of selfish love."[5]

A self-loving internal image is reflected in the belief that one deserves to be happy, and it is the foundation for meeting the challenges of life with grace, courage, and confidence. It's the bedrock of the ability to feel love and compassion for others. For if we don't know how to love ourselves, how can we expect to practice it with others?

The importance of a healthy self-image, self-esteem, and self-confidence cannot be overstated. Just think of a day when you have been "down on yourself." Is there any feeling that's worse than that self-generated, self-contained, self-loathing, or hypercritical self-judgment? The lack of such self-love has been shown to create enormous amounts of suffering, especially if it is a long-standing state of mind. Research has demonstrated very clearly that the lack of self-esteem contributes to increased delinquency and crime, teenage pregnancies, drug and alcohol abuse, depression, suicide, and a host of other psychological problems such as panic disorder, free-floating anxiety, anorexia, and bulimia.

Even without spawning outwardly negative behavior, a negative self-image is a potent source of suffering in and of itself. Feeling unworthy of life's blessings is a pain-filled state from moment to moment. What's more, espousing this view contributes to additional suffering because we have fewer psychological resources—less confidence and less strength to deal with the other challenges and losses that will no doubt confront us during our lifetime.

Here's a metaphor that explains this latter point: Think about yourself as a drinking glass. Imagine that each challenge in life comes in the form of liquid being poured into that glass. When the glass is full, it spills over. It's no longer able to contain what it needs to. In human terms, this is a psychological crisis. How long will it take the glass to spill over? Well, it depends on two things: how much is poured into it from life and how much is already there that we have brought along in ourselves. A poor self-image immediately fills the glass almost to the top. It's not hard to imagine that when even a small amount of additional liquid (stress, challenges, losses, pure suffering) is poured in, the glass will overflow. A glass that is almost empty can be filled with a great deal more of life's obstacles before it spills over. Because challenging and difficult times in life will be poured into our glass, we owe it to ourselves to get rid of what we add with a negative self-image. We can take full control of how we view and treat ourselves. If we work to create a positive, loving approach to our human condition, we will find so many more resources at our disposal when we need them.

In chapter 3 ("Brick Houses and Straw Houses"), I brought up the example of Anna, who had a series of disastrous marriages to abusive, alcoholic men. In her present marriage, to an alcoholic, she suffers greatly; her glass is spilling over with stress and pain. Her husband is unreliable and verbally abusive, and has alienated her from her friends and family. Like all who suffer, Anna deserves our compassion and concern, even when we can see that a great deal of her pain has been self-created by her own poor choices, which were based heavily on her negative self-image. Anna didn't believe she deserved to have a better life than the one she had. Even in this very difficult circumstance, Anna has choices.

She can continue to suffer as she has or she can take action to reduce her suffering. Think about what we might do if we were in Anna's place. We could join an Al-Anon group and find comfort and support in the company of others who are experiencing similar problems. We could work with a psychotherapist (something Anna, thankfully, has done) who could help us discover options and support our positive, life-affirming decisions. We could gain insight into why we've made some of the choices that we have, not with self-blame but with self-understanding and with the goal of avoiding similar self-defeating choices in the future. We could express "tough love" and tell our husband that he must get help and overcome this addiction—we'll help him. But we will not stand by and allow our life to be destroyed by his addiction. Just as we might, Anna can make many choices that have the power to reduce her suffering and change her life. But she can't or won't do any of those things until she first accepts that she is deserving of a happy life.

Regardless of where the blemishes in our self-images began, each one of us has the power to move in the direction of greater self-love. In order to change our self-image, we must first honestly look at the way we feel about ourselves. We must understand that we did nothing to deserve poor treatment or trauma as a child, if that was our experience. Our parents or other family members were simply not up to the task. Perhaps, they themselves were treated badly and never learned how to express love or protect their child. Perhaps, we've been carrying around hurt and anger all our life. We must let go of old, inaccurate ideas and go about the business of reimagining ourselves. This can take the form of a meditation. Simply sit quietly and create a new image of yourself. Imagine the details of how your life will be without the anchor of these negative feelings. Use all your senses to create a new image of who you are and who you can be. In the process of moving forward, you will encounter all kinds of emotions. Let yourself feel grief and anger but continue to imagine yourself in positive ways. Continue to move forward in this imagery in spite of the ache of long-ago hurts. This is the path that leads to forgiveness and self-healing.

Grief and anger are natural feelings when we've been badly hurt. Even if our wounds are deep, we can learn to forgive and in forgiving let go of a past that continues to cause suffering in our lives. "My grandfather always hit my father when he was angry. That's why my father hit us kids." "My mother really wanted to be an actress. No wonder she was so critical of her children. She really didn't want to be there." "My mother had to work at two jobs to support us. Now I understand why she could never come to my baseball games." To be able to make these statements, and ones like them, though filled with childhood anguish and disappointment, is evidence of a highly evolved, conscious personality. This is a personality that can understand and—though not forget—can forgive. Note that forgiveness doesn't just come because we want it to or because to pardon those who have hurt us is the right "spiritual" thing to do. Forgiving is not easy when you've been hurt badly. As author C. S. Lewis pointed out, "Everyone says that forgiveness is a lovely idea, until they have something to forgive."

Authentic forgiveness is the reward for having acknowledged and accepted our righteous anger, moved beyond it, and felt compassion even for those who have hurt us deeply. Buddhists refer to the practice of *tonglen*, which in Tibetan means "giving and receiving." *Tonglen* is an opening of the heart, an acute awareness of the suffering of another—even when that person has been cruel to you. To come to this level of awareness, one must have walked through the pain and suffering of life, grieved for disappointments, and only then emerged into the bright light of true forgiveness for our less-than-perfect parents and experiences.

As a psychotherapist, I've seen many people who cannot seem to leave their past behind. In fact, their whole self-definition seems to rely on past abuse and pain. At the other extreme are people who refuse to revisit the trauma of their past in spite of the fact that it continues to exert its very painful influence in the present. "There's nothing I can do about what happened to me. So why even talk about it?" they say. Once again, I think the best approach to healing the wounds from the past and reducing their correspondent suffering in the present lies in taking the middle way.

The example I often use with my clients is that childhood trauma is like having fallen off your bike when you were younger. Imagine that you crashed onto a gravelly roadway and hurt your knee badly. You've healed—sort of. But, even after many years, there are still pieces of that gravel in your knee. You can get around—you can function. You might be one of the "walking wounded." Still, you can walk. But what you cannot do is dance. And there is pain. Sometimes when the weather is damp (things you can't control) or you move in a certain way (unconscious things you do that aggravate the pain), an intense and blazing pain runs up your leg. You're knocked down. You're suffering even now from something that happened a long time ago. It seems to me that the only way to heal this injury is to cut open that scar and remove the stones that are still in there. This is a terribly difficult task—the wound is ugly, and has been festering, under the surface, for years and years. And so, you must carefully, painstakingly, pick out the gravel, wash it clean, and remove all the obstacles to healing. Having done that, you stitch it up. And then? And then, you leave it alone. It will never heal if you continue to pick at it. Let it heal. But this time around, let it heal cleanly. If the wound is particularly serious, it's wise to get some professional help with it. In order to heal cleanly, it is sometimes necessary to revisit our painful past and then consciously get beyond it, let it go, and move courageously into our future.

No matter how painful your past has been, you can change yourself now. It will not be easy and it will take time. But you can begin today, right now if you choose to. As in any journey, the first step is usually the hardest; but once you take it, you can begin the ascent out of the ashes of pain and negative self-images and into the clear light of self-love.

Some Practical Suggestions

1. Listen to your wake-up calls about the things you can do in your life to avoid suffering in the future. Get out of your denial or laziness and fix things *before* they create problems. First, look at your personal safety in your behaviors and your surroundings. Literally do a room check of your house to make certain that doors and windows are secure and that children and pets, if you have them, are protected from things that could hurt them. Make a list of things that need to be repaired and then fix them now. Be honest with yourself about ways you put your life (or others) in potential danger and change those habits. Be honest about your own abilities and, if you choose to try daring things in your life, be willing to train and condition yourself so you have the knowledge, skills, and experience to undertake those risks. Taking personal responsibility for our lives and having a cautious attitude doesn't mean we can't take any risks, or that we must worry all the time. I believe in living passionately, and we are freer to do just that when we've taken care of the things that could cause us pain. We can't blame fate when we break our ankle on that broken back step that's been there for a

year. An old Arabic saying speaks to our personal responsibility to take care of ourselves: "Trust Allah, but tie your camel."

2. Honestly look at your feelings about yourself. If your self-image, your self-esteem, is not what it could be, then actively change it. Begin with reimagining yourself. Practice *visualizing* this reinvention of yourself every day. Sit quietly and close your eyes. Breathe smoothly and evenly. Then bring to mind the vision of yourself as you would like to be. Focus on creating the details. What is the expression on your face? Are you sitting, walking, dancing? How do you feel in this picture (happy, confident, optimistic)? Where are you—in your favorite armchair, on the beach, or walking into the entrance door of a great new job? Who surrounds you, or are you alone? To bring a reality into being, first you have to know what you are driving at. Revisit this picture of your ideal self regularly and embellish it with new details each time. We get good at what we practice.

3. Surround yourself with good company. Look at the places and people in your life who reinforce your negative feelings about yourself. Create loving ways to avoid them. Instead find people who will celebrate you and your life. Think of who would be supportive and see you as the person you just visualized. Those are the kind of people you want to gather close. Writer Natalie Goldberg once said, "When you walk in the mist you get wet." Being around negative, demeaning people makes us sick—psychologically and spiritually.

4. Forgive yourself for your mistakes. Make a conscious effort to learn from them and then let them go. Remind yourself that humans make mistakes and you are human. Mistakes are a normal part of life and will always be.

5. Change the way you talk to yourself. Listen carefully to your inner dialogue, identify negative self-talk, and change it to reflect the ways you would speak to someone you love.

6. Be wary of setting unreasonable, perfectionistic goals for yourself. You can set your standards high so they are a challenge, but beware of irrational goals. They ensure that you will fail. Play with your expectations of yourself and find the level at which they are high enough but not out of reach. Make a note of your attainable goals and post them in a prominent place—like on the refrigerator, on the wall by

your bed, above your desk, or on the bathroom mirror. Seeing them will help you remember to focus on them and celebrate them when you've achieved them.

7. Celebrate your strengths and achievements. Have a celebratory meal or throw a party for yourself when you finish a class or a project, or achieve an important personal goal. Share your excitement and your accomplishments with the world. Let your gifts and spirit shine, casting a wide glow of light around you.

8. Avoid comparing your life to others'. We all travel our own paths and have different lessons to learn along the way. Looking at others often leads to the "tyranny of the shoulds," as in: "I should be this." "I should have that." Look inside to find out what you truly need. What makes you happy? These are clues for your way.

9. Believe that you can change. William James wrote, "The greatest revolution of our generation is the discovery that human beings, by changing the inner attitudes of their minds, can change the outer aspects of their lives." He's right. You might want to remind yourself of the power you have over your life by hanging this great quote (or another that resonates with you) someplace where you will see it every day.

4. PRACTICE MINDFULNESS

There is a story that is often told about the Buddha. It's said that after his enlightenment, he was walking down the road and passed by a man who was struck—almost overcome—by his extraordinary radiance and peaceful presence. The man stopped Buddha and asked, "My friend, what are you? Are you a god or celestial being?"

"No," said Buddha.

"Are you a magician or a wizard?" Again Buddha said, "No."

"Are you a man?"

"No."

"Are you an angel, then?"

"No."

"Well, then, my friend, what are you?"

The Buddha replied, "I am awake."[6]

With these simple words, "I am awake," Buddha describes the power of truly living, of being fully alive in every moment and appreciating each one for exactly what it is. Whether the moment be one of absolute bliss or great pain makes no difference. Buddhists refer to this practice of being focused, centered, and attentive to *this* moment as "mindfulness." This concentration on "what is" and the appreciation of the reality of any given moment are important practices in Buddhism. Learning to be in each moment without judging, reflecting, thinking about the future, or being attached to outcomes is a way to enlightenment and an important element of the *Eightfold Noble Path*. Zen masters refer to life when it is lived fully and completely, always in the moment and with nothing held back, as the "supreme meal." We can benefit greatly if we espouse a similar approach to life. Others have.

An awareness of the importance of the present moment, while richly described in Eastern traditions, is neither exclusively Eastern nor particularly mystical. In just one instance, Native American traditions look to the immediacy of nature as instruction in living in the present. Lakota shaman Black Elk speaks beautifully about "coming to our senses," in *Black Elk Speaks*. He describes the moment of oneness when we are wide open to our immediate reality hearing, smelling, tasting, seeing, and feeling all that fills each moment. At these times, he explains that we are connected to the heart, our concentration moves from head to heart.

Twentieth-century humanistic psychologists also speak of the importance of living in the "here and now" as a measure of good mental health and transpersonal enlightenment. Psychologist and author Jon Kabat-Zinn reminds us that the present moment is all we ever really have by simply reminding us that "wherever you go, there you are."[7] Thoreau, Emerson, and other naturalists and philosophers have written masterpieces about the clarity open to those who are truly present and aware in the present moment. "In eternity, there is indeed something true and sublime. But all these times and places and occasions are now and here. God himself culminates in the present moment, and will never be more divine in the lapse of all the ages," Thoreau wrote in *Walden*. Many contemporary writers such as Annie Dillard, Diane Ackerman, and Terry Tempest Williams, speak eloquently to the crystal-clear simplicity of the present moment. But a short poem by William Carlos Williams captures for me the essence of the present and is a wonderful example of his admonition to "write about things that are close to the nose." His poem is called "Thursday."

> *I have had my dream—like others—*
> *And it has come to nothing, so that*
> *I remain now carelessly*
> *With feet planted on the ground*
> *And look up at the sky—*
> *Feeling my clothes about me,*
> *The weight of my body in my shoes,*
> *The rim of my hat, air passing in and out*
> *At my nose—and decide to dream no more.*[8]

When we enter deeply into each moment as it occurs, we more clearly see the true nature of reality, and it is this insight that liberates us from suffering and pain.

So many of us so often forgo the present moment for memories of the past or expectations of the future. I have some good friends who love to eat gourmet meals. Their knowledge of food is astounding. They're well traveled and have sampled cuisine from around the globe. I love them dearly and enjoy their company, but at every meal I've ever shared with them, they talk mostly about other dishes they've had in the past or ones they're going to have in the future. In spite of their love of good food, I have to wonder if they've ever actually enjoyed one of the meals while they were eating it. After all, we'd had meals in lovely restaurants with gorgeous views and delicious food they seemed oblivious to. I wondered, as they talked about other meals, did they notice the way the color of the water outside the window just then changed as the sun went down and cast its pinkish glow over the glassy surface of the bay? Did they savor the tang in that horseradish-dill sauce on the salmon? Did they notice the woody, understated bouquet of the merlot? Did they actually taste anything at all?

Being present-centered, in the here and now, or mindful can be a very difficult task for those of us raised with the frenetic, future-oriented pace of modern life in Western societies. Trust me, I know! I struggle to stay mindful, present in this moment just as everyone else does. More times than I'd like to admit, my friends have jerked me out of some distant musings with an "Earth to Kathy" comment because I've been so thoroughly "not-there" that I've missed something interesting or important in the present moment. Remember the thoughts that were going through my head after my father and Deanne's accident? I was walking with Dorothy in their backyard. If I had been focusing my attention and concentrating on the moment, I would have been in better touch with the smell of the grass and the way the moonlight gleamed on the water of a small pond behind their house. My feelings would have been clearer to me. Instead my thoughts were stumbling around Greek myths, conversations I'd had with my clients years earlier, and what was going to happen in the future. Judging from many of my own experiences and listening to others describe their days, it seems as if we're always having something akin to "out of body" experiences in which our thoughts are projected very far from where we are, looking more clearly into "might be" or "what was" instead of "what is." In an effort to prepare for the onslaught of future events, information, and expectations others have of us, we plan for the future, look toward tomorrow, and in the process miss the vitality and aliveness of today. However, our preoccupation with trying to control the future is a great source of suffering. It is often such a futile gesture because we can guess at but never really know the future. Our life doesn't exist there; it is here, now, and unfolding from moment to moment. And this moment—this one right now—is the only one that we can truly know. This does not mean we shouldn't plan for the future. That's fine. But we can diminish a lot of our anxiety and unnecessary pain if we avoid spending time trying to wrangle all the "what ifs" up and ready ourselves to face each one. To do that, we have to loosen our hold on the fear of the unknown. Perhaps we may also have to let go of the fear of directly and completely experiencing all our feelings because they will flood us when we focus on right now. If we lived fully in this present moment, we would have to experience the full measure of our pain as well as our pleasure. This can be challenging; however, unless we do so, we may pass through our lives without ever experiencing them.

Animals and children have a great deal to teach adult human beings about the importance of the present. In fact, I often refer to Dorothy as my "four-legged Zen master." Not only does she teach me about the importance of unconditional love and nonjudgment, but her mere presence informs me about just how alive each present moment can be. She is not concerned with what happened last week or what will happen later today; at every moment she is fully entranced by what is. If she's lying in a spot of sun on the living room floor, she is there, embraced by its warmth. If she's walking down the beach, I am certain that she feels each salty breeze just as it happens and is alert to the changing shadows on the sand that let her know there's a bird to chase. Her eyes, her whole face, and how her body moves speak to Dorothy's keen appreciation of each moment.

Children at play are great teachers for learning to stay in the moment. When kids are fully engaged, you can see it in their expressions, their eyes, and their movements. Their attention to what they are doing evinces that, to them, the only thing that matters is the very moment at hand. When I was in elementary school at Holy Trinity, our teacher would call the class roll every morning. With more than sixty fourth-graders, this roll call took some time, but it was our ritual that started every school day. The teacher would call each one of us by name, making a careful checkmark next to each entry in her hardbound notebook. We knew exactly how we were expected to respond. "Kathleen Brehony?" Sister Eileen Cordis would call out. "Present, Sister," I would respond. Present. I'm here. I am. You don't need to look around for me, Sister. I'm really here sitting behind Mary Alice Riley and in front of James Joseph O'Connor. At that moment, we were expected to be fully present to our teacher. There was to be no fidgeting, no talking, no passing notes back and forth, and no slinging spit wads at each other. And for the most part, we sat at rapt attention, listening and making this simple response to the sound of our name. A small matter, this calling of the roll, but our responses said something important about where we were. We were here. Right now. Present.

If you want to learn more about mindfulness, watch children at play when they are passionately involved in what they're doing. When my niece, Katelyn, was four or five years old, she revealed an early interest in visual arts. Today, at seventeen, she wants to make her career in directing films, so I guess it's true what they say about children revealing their deepest passions early in life. She would sit for hours working on what she called her "projects," usually a drawing with crayons and colored chalk. As I watched her, I realized that her whole being, her entire attention, was wrapped up in the drawing of a particular line or filling in an open space with a color that she would select with great care. Similarly, when my nephew, Matthew, took up the guitar in his midteens, he would become so immersed in the struggle to learn a new chord, so focused on the frets and the placement of his fingers, that his attention was concentrated on just that one thing no matter what else was going on around him. In the midst of the noisy conversation and laughter that characterize my family gatherings, Matt would sit at the edge of the group and by the calm and focused expression on his face and the way his tongue protruded just slightly through his teeth, I could see that his whole reality was wrapped up in this one blissful moment of discovering the intricacies of an E-flat diminished ninth or some other complex chord. Matt is now twenty-three and a professional musician. Still, when I watch him play, I see that same focused and harmonious facial expression, his eyes closed, his hands gliding fluidly down the neck of the guitar, and his body swaying to the beat. This is pure harmony; he is fully in this moment. He is fully in this music.

Mindfulness doesn't require any special setting or circumstance. Instead it's a decision and a dedication to experience the reality of whatever you are doing in the present moment, the "precious present." You can experience mindfulness while you're driving, eating, making love, walking, or working in the garden. It's just a matter of letting your consciousness be exactly where you are whether you are snapping beans or picking tomatoes. In *Refuge*, writer Terry Tempest Williams describes her immersion in the present moment with these words: "This afternoon, I have found quiet hours alone picking tomatoes," she writes. "As my fingers find ripe tomatoes, red and firm, through the labyrinth of leaves, I am absorbed into the present. My garden asks nothing more of me than I am able to give. I pull tomatoes, gently placing them in the copper colander. Pulling tomatoes, pulling tomatoes. Some come easily."[9]

I have found that mindfulness can be more easily tapped during experiences that require my full attention and total concentration. Like my nephew, Matthew, when I'm learning a new song on the guitar or keyboard, every fiber of my being is engrossed in grasping a particular chord or sequence of notes. When I'm writing and into the flow of it, my entire consciousness is directed at the words that appear on my computer screen. Sometimes it even feels that the words come through me rather than from me. There is nothing else at those moments. Time takes on a different feel; it's suspended, and hours can pass without notice. I'm called to dinner and realize I never stopped for lunch. I don't quite know what happens to my sense of time in those instances, I only know that I've been absorbed, concentrated right here, right now. I'm certain that I'm not alone in this experience. My artist friends describe with enthusiasm this same phenomenon that takes place when they are working on a painting. They say they become totally absorbed in each moment as colors take shape, blending and merging into a form that they had only vaguely imagined.

I've noticed how quickly worries and cares evaporate from my consciousness when I'm skiing downhill. I'm not a great skier, so every bit of my attention is focused on getting down the hill alive and with the least amount of social embarrassment I can muster! Many sports are excellent teachers of mindfulness, even the ones that don't sometimes include tumbling through the snow head over heels. In a way, mindfulness is to life what keeping one's eye on the ball is to tennis. In *The Inner Game of Tennis*, author Timothy Gallwey wrote, "When a tennis player is 'on his game,' he's not thinking about how, when or even where to hit the ball. He's not *trying* to hit the ball, and after the shot he doesn't think about how badly or how well he made contact. The ball seems to get hit through an automatic process that doesn't require thought."[10]

To practice mindfulness and live in the moment reduces negative and chaotic thinking. Psychologist Mihalyi Csikszentmihalyi (he must need a great deal of attention and mindfulness just to spell his name correctly!) calls the experience of mindfulness "flow" and defines it as the psychology of optimal experience in which an individual is calm, enjoying him or herself, and focused all at once. During "flow" we become tantalized and seduced by the process of our concentration itself, and goals or outcomes melt away. At these moments we feel strong, alert, unselfconscious, and in effortless control. We experience high levels of joy and creativity. An exhilarating sense of transcendence replaces pain and emotional problems. During those rich moments, no matter what else is happening in life, we are one with the moment. Suffering stands aside. Time disappears.[11]

There are many paths that lead to mindfulness, to flow. The first step is understanding the importance of this state of mind in improving the quality of our lives by reducing the pain of suffering, diminishing stress, and offering an entryway into transcendent experience where the full spectrum of our consciousness resides. When we are mindful, we are, as the Buddha was, awake. This most desirable state of mind is, perhaps, most easily attained through the focused attention of meditation. And one does not have to retreat to an ashram or remove oneself from daily life in order to enjoy the riches of meditation and mindfulness. It's a simple activity that can be practiced almost anywhere, though it does not always come easily.

For more than ten years, Jon Kabat-Zinn has taught mindfulness practices to all kinds of people and found amazing results in enhancing the quality of life and reducing stress and pain through very uncomplicated techniques. He suggests that we can begin a practice of mindfulness by simply stopping, sitting quietly (being rather than doing) for a few minutes, and following our breath. Try this for a moment. Just let all your attention focus on your breath. Observe its temperature and sound. That's all. In and out. In and out. Feel your breath as you inhale and then exhale. Notice it. There is nothing else at this moment but this breath. After you do this for a few moments, take a mental scan of your body and your thoughts. Do you feel more relaxed and, perhaps, sense a slowing of your thoughts? These are the sensations meditation can bring. They are the foundation for a life built in the moment.

Kabat-Zinn calls mindfulness the "art of conscious living." He explains that in practice, there is nothing magical nor mysterious about it. It is just being alive to and in the moment. "It is simply a practical way to be more in touch with the fullness of your being through a systematic process of self-observation, self-inquiry, and mindful action," he says. "There is nothing cold, analytical, or unfeeling about it. The overall tenor of mindfulness practice is gentle, appreciative, and nurturing. Another way to think of it would be 'heartfulness.'"[12]

Many paths lead to mindfulness: meditation, sports, art, picking tomatoes, being in nature, watching children at play, or observing the behavior of animals. Even tangerine Life Savers can point the way as they did for one client I came to know. I met John when I was conducting group therapy at the psychiatric hospital where he had been admitted for severe depression. I liked him immediately. In group therapy, John talked about his current situation. I could see that he was a good man, but he was suffering. He was going through a painful divorce, the loss of his business, and financial devastation all at once. He was terribly depressed and had no hope for the future he told us as we sat in a circle. In fact, all of his thinking was focused on the future and how bleak and terrible it was going to be. John had lost his way.

After one group meeting, John and I struck up a conversation in the hallway. I asked him what he had liked to do before his world came heaving in around him. At once, a gleam came into his eye. I could tell that although he couldn't imagine a happy future, John could remember happiness in the past. He told me about his love of fishing and his great passion for the Outer Banks of North Carolina. It was easy for me to smile back and share his enthusiasm because it is one of the places I love most in the world. Then his expression changed, and he fell back into the pain of hopelessness and despair.

We sat down in the day room, and I handed him a tangerine Life Saver and said, "For just this one moment, I don't want you to think about anything except the taste of this candy. It's sweet and it's sharp all at once. You'll like it." John looked at me a bit like I was nutty, but agreed. While he was eating it, a tear rolled down his face. His shoulders relaxed and he sighed. If I had him hooked up to measuring instruments, I'm certain his heart rate, respiration rate, and blood pressure would have gone down. But even without this empirical information, you know, you can just tell when people are in pain and when they're not. It shows in everything from their facial expressions to the way they hold their hands. It was obvious to me that for the first time in months, John was not worrying about the future or ruminating about the past. He was immersed in the moment. He could feel what was. For the first time in months, he was fully in the present.

John was released from the hospital after a week or so and I didn't see him again. I didn't expect to. Then one day, years later during a fishing tournament on the Outer Banks, I literally ran into John again. Even though it had been a long time since we'd seen each other, we recognized each other immediately. We hugged. John introduced me to the smiling woman he was with who was going to become his wife. His work life was great, he said. As it turned out, the loss of his old business had been something of a blessing in disguise for John. Now he was back on his feet financially, had a new job, looked forward to going to work more than ever, and loved what he was doing. He looked strong and healthy. His face was open and bright. He was happy again and said he was glad about that. But he told me he had learned something very important during his suffering that had changed the way he lived his life now. He said that he had learned to love the moments on the beach when his fishing line was whirring with the sound of a big bluefish on the line. John now noticed what the air smelled like and how he could sense a shift in the wind just by a slight movement on the water. He said he had learned to appreciate moments that were here now and would never come again. Then he reached into his shirt pocket and offered me a tangerine Life Saver. We laughed. Tangerine Life Savers, I thought. I guess it's true that enlightenment doesn't care how you get there.

Some Practical Suggestions

1. Practice a daily meditation, even if it is only for five minutes. Observe your own breath. In and out. Feel the warmth or coolness of where you are. Hear the wind as it races into your own body. Give life to yourself through your observed breath. The great Indian poet Kabir tells of the importance of breath to the transcendent: "God is the breath inside the breath," he says. That is a good line to remember when you are doubting whether you can spare that five minutes a day. The key word here is *practice*. As in anything else in life, the more you focus on your breath and body here and now, the better you get at it.

2. Read books and access information about mindfulness and meditation. Jon Kabat-Zinn's book, *Wherever You Go There You Are*, is a great one to start with. Read almost anything by Thich Nhat Hanh, *A Path with Heart* by Jack Kornfield, and *Breath Sweeps Mind: A First Guide to Meditation Practice*, edited by Jean Smith, which contains short excerpts about meditation by many different writers. It's a good introduction to the many styles and techniques of meditation. In addition to books, there is a plethora of videotapes, audiotapes, and computer

programs that give detailed instructions for starting a meditation practice. You can identify those that most resonate with you and follow up by learning more about them.

3. Tap into community support. Yoga in its various forms is also an excellent path to mindfulness and the consciousness it bestows with its emphasis on breathing, meditation, and body awareness. In fact, the word *yoga* in Sanskrit means "union with the Self" or "Self-realization." Both meditation and yoga classes are widely available in most cities and towns. Search through the Yellow Pages or look up these terms on any search engine on the Internet. You'll find many resources that can direct you to classes and practice groups. Check into them.

4. Find your own path to mindfulness. Discover ways and places in which you are in the great flow of life itself. Do you feel awake and alive in the garden, by the sea, hiking in the hills, sewing, strumming, singing, or dancing? Do you feel it in the kitchen when you are preparing a special meal or when you are walking your dog? Ask yourself: Do I engage in some activity during which time floats away and I lose myself? If the answer is yes, can you continue them or incorporate them more often into your life? If not, explore a variety of actions and options until you find those places and activities that help bring you into this calm state of mindfulness. Make a commitment in your own heart and mind to be present in each and every moment of your life.

5. Learn to relish and appreciate each and every moment. It's the only one you can be absolutely certain you will ever have.

6. Be where you are as often as possible. Don't think about how you will be mindful later, on the golf course or working in your garden. Focus on being present while you're making widgets at the factory. Be mindful of each widget. Those moments are as precious and full as any others. Remember full mindfulness, being purely in the present, is as close as your next breath. Do it now.

7. Let yourself feel everything. Try to be aware of when you are avoiding confrontation, pain, or loss. To enhance your awareness of avoidance, try to think of a pleasurable activity and scan your body for how you feel in anticipation of that. Then think about an unpleasant activity and note how you feel when facing that. This latter group of sensations most likely accompanies your avoidance reactions. Then, do

your best to embrace those feelings fully. Life is lived in moments of darkness as well as light.

8. Buy some tangerine Life Savers (or your favorite flavor) and sit quietly somewhere while you open the package and pop one in your mouth. Do nothing but savor that piece of candy until the last solid fragment melts on your tongue. No biting it, either.

5. GRIEVE

By November 1997 it was obvious that my beloved Aunt Teresa was going to die. Like my own mother, just five years earlier, my aunt had fought courageously against cancer. Teresa's battle had taken a torturous path. Remarkable responses to chemotherapy that seemed to put her non-Hodgkin's lymphoma into remission were followed, sometimes less than a week later, by the devastating news that the cancer was once again metastasizing into her healthy cells. Aunt Teresa's illness was a wild, twisting journey of celebration and despondency as our spirits soared and were then suddenly yanked back into sorrow by a prognosis that seemed to change from minute to minute. I went to visit Teresa in New Jersey as much as I could, and we spoke often by phone. Without fail, we talked every Friday morning from nine o'clock to ten. This hour was sacrosanct—written in my appointment book in pen and the best part of my weekly schedule. I'd make a cup of tea before dialing her number and sink into the warmth of our relationship and our riveting honesty with each other. I loved Teresa. She was the good friend you can call at three o'clock in the morning. She was my second mother. We always had great conversations, and sometimes we'd still be on the phone long after the clock struck ten. We'd talk about the cancer and Teresa's optimism about beating it. Sometimes, she'd talk about her fears. Her biggest worry centered on how her husband George and her kids, Patty, Mike, and Mary Ann, would be able to cope with her death. She'd update me on the latest news from her doctors, but mostly we'd talk about our family, catching up on happenings and gossip. We often talked about God and her philosophies of life. We talked about writing a book together. She wanted to write about the deep connections that all people have, about how we all have more in common than our differences pretend. She hadn't written a word of it yet, but she did have a title. She called it "One Size Fits All." In spite of nausea from chemotherapy, the loss of her hair, the constant blood transfusions and unending stream of visits to doctors, Teresa kept her great sense of humor, and even in our great sorrows we always laughed together.

However, while many of our conversations still carried a lot of humor, as Teresa got sicker, my heart became heavier and heavier with the sorrow of letting her go. The reality of losing her seemed more inevitable as each day passed during that cold fall season. I continued to work and live my life, but my sadness was obvious to me and palpable to my friends and family. I was preoccupied, easily moved to tears, and my usually ever-present sense of humor went flat. I looked tired and wanted more time alone than is usual for me. One good friend, who loves me dearly and meant only to help, called me and during this time kindly suggested that I shouldn't feel so sad because, after all, Teresa's soul was going to a better place: one where she wouldn't feel any pain. She went on to say that, someday, we'd be together again. My friend followed that up with "I know you have very strong spiritual beliefs. You know that death isn't the end of things. It's just like Teresa is going to California."

"What?!" I yelled into the phone. "What do you mean to not feel so sad?! California?!" I can't remember exactly what I said next but it was a crushing rebuttal, filled with several words that are not printable here. None of what I said was particularly kind. After I calmed down, I called my friend back and apologized for my explosion but not for my feelings. Of course, I knew my friend meant to help me and was certainly right about my strong spiritual beliefs. I have faith and I believe unequivocally that the soul, or Self, or some form of consciousness does not die with our mortal body. I have a sense that our physical form is merely a short-term vehicle that manifests and gives form to the life force. But do you know what? I didn't care about all that at that moment. I *wanted* my sadness. I needed to feel the pain of letting Teresa go. I had to grieve for the Friday-morning phone calls that would be gone forever and the end of our beautiful relationship as I had known it for almost fifty years. Teresa wasn't going to California. If she were, I wouldn't feel this utter sadness. I could call her there or catch a plane for the coast. If she were there,

I could still look forward to seeing her face, touching her hand, and hearing her voice and her laughter. But I would not have the luxury of these pleasures any longer. Teresa wasn't moving to California. I looked ahead and saw a future in which all our moments of closeness and contact would be gone. Knowing that Teresa's energy, her soul, was infinite gave me some comfort, to be sure, but not nearly enough to quench the ravaged and vulnerable feeling I had when I thought of life without her. I do not believe that to accept suffering as a part of life means that we should go through terrible losses with cold detachment or callous resignation. The great French writer Marcel Proust once wrote, "We are healed from suffering only by experiencing it to the full." I believe him.

There's a danger with faith and metaphysical leanings that refuse to acknowledge the deep suffering that loss creates. Many of us tend to turn away from the dark side—the shadow that is cast from the bright light of life. We are afraid of darkness, and ancient ideas of life and death as being two sides of the same coin seem to have vanished from our modern sensibilities. We've lost sight of our suffering that courses in the form of melancholy and sadness, as being "touched by Saturn," a belief of our ancestors that colors our pain with mythic and cosmic significance. In earlier times, the Roman god Saturn, and the planet of the same name, were thought to rule over memories, yearning for days gone by, and the sense that time passes too quickly. Saturn is the reaper, the patron of endings, and the god of the harvest. The festival honoring Saturn, the Saturnalia, is the winter solstice in mid-December. This is a time when the earth seems to die, the weather becomes chilly, the nights grow longer, and cold winds loom on the horizon. It is the ending of the yearly cycle, the gray and reflective time that must come before the verdant illumination of spring. These are the earthy seasons that our ancestors paid heed to. But today, we don't talk about these cycles or Saturn's influence; instead, we believe that suffering is to be avoided, and Prozac is the prescription that's immediately written for the person experiencing even normal grief. Many of us hide our sadness, sometimes even from ourselves, as if somehow our sorrow and tears are signs that we have failed spiritually. And yet, the loss of people we love *is* the "pain so utter" Emily Dickinson wrote of and is worthy of grief. Grief is, as Victor Hugo called it, "a divine and terrible radiance." We are human. We need to mourn when we've lost a precious part of our lives, be that in the form of a family member, friend, pet, job, marriage, health, or youth.

Grief is the natural and normal human response to significant loss. The words we use to describe this experience fully express the pain of the passage. "Grief" comes from the Latin *gravis* meaning "heavy" or "burdened." "Bereavement" from *reave* means to be "dispossessed or robbed." In our grief we often feel as if we've been robbed. When a gaping hole exists where a loved one used to, we feel loneliness and sometimes isolation. When we are suffering such a loss, the world seems to be going about its business as usual, but we don't feel our part in it is the same because our hearts are broken. As we grieve, it's not uncommon to be anxious, extremely sad, and sometimes angry—which can lead to sleepless nights or ones filled with nightmares. We often cannot eat and have a hard time concentrating on any task at hand. Grief expresses itself in every aspect of our being. We feel it emotionally, mentally, spiritually, and physically. There's even research showing that the tears that spring from our eyes in sadness are chemically different from those caused by slicing onions or a brisk wind blowing in our faces. It's as if our loss is being felt by every cell in our body.

Well-intentioned friends may try to help you through your grief by rushing you along, suggesting that it's time to get back into the swing of things. "You should be over this by now," many will tell you at different points along the way. Because our pain is great and we want it to end, we tend to believe them. "Time will heal all wounds," I've heard. "Keep busy. Don't think about it," is offered as good advice. But grief knows its own rhythm; its pace can only be honored and endured, not accelerated. Grieving a significant loss is best measured in months, often years, rather than days and weeks. Often just when you think you're better, perhaps when the sharp sting of loss has given way to a chronic ache, an anniversary, a birthday, a song on the radio, or the first Christmas without her appears and it's as if you haven't healed at all. It takes a long time to recover from terrible losses, but time alone is not enough to heal the wounds created by life's suffering. It is our full experience of grief itself that heals as we go, day by day, through our life. If we are alive through every moment, accepting our pain, we can find joy amid the sorrow, and comfort for our tears.

Sometimes, in the midst of grieving, we go numb. When I was talking with Beth Nielsen Chapman about grief, she offered some wise words about this aspect of mourning. "Grief has its own agenda," she told me. "It's just being open to staying open to it when it knocks on your door. You can't make it happen any faster. A lot of people I talk with who've lost someone don't feel anything. I spoke to this woman and she said, 'I feel like a monster. I don't feel happy or sad. I don't feel anything. I feel dead.' I said, 'You'll get around to it. You just have to honor where you are at the time.'" There is not a prescribed way to feel or a time line to follow when we cope with significant losses. We are individuals and have to chart our own course. Kahlil Gibran, in *The Prophet*, places grief in its rightful perspective as an integral part of life—sometimes waxing, sometimes waning—when he says: "And you would accept the seasons of your heart, Even as you have always accepted the seasons that pass over your fields. And you would watch with serenity through the winters of your grief."[13] When the dark and cold of grief comes it helps to remember that spring lies ahead.

As we live through the winters of our grief, we can find solace in the companionship of good friends and family. Sometimes we are wise to seek a therapist or a support group of kindred spirits. Look for small ways to introduce moments of comfort or joy into your dark or low days. Be awake as you move through this time and know that you can draw as much knowledge about your soul and this world from the mourning as you do when rejoicing.

Ritual can be a tremendous help in times of loss. Joseph Campbell suggests that ritual is so important because it is the enactment of myth that holds the rich meaning of all man's experience in it. By participating in ritual, we share in the dimension of myth that brings our troubles and our suffering into wider context and helps us to keep sight of the larger perspective. Ritual serves to bring our own pain into the realm of *all* pain. Through ritual we can often ease the sense of isolation and loneliness loss brings our way. We are connected with all mankind as we throw the first handful of dirt on the coffin, or spread the ashes on sacred ground, or as we light a candle.

People throughout history have evolved rituals to help them deal with the profound suffering that surrounds the death of a loved one. Born from man's search for meaning and healing, rituals represent a way of participating in the events that have jolted our sense of control over our lives. Understanding, as T. S. Eliot did, that "the end is where we start from," every culture has created unique ceremonies and rites to bestow meaning on the particular suffering from the loss of a loved one. Jews sit *shiva* for a week, the Irish keen and hold wakes for days, Mexicans celebrate both death and life in a yearly festival called *Los Días de los Muertos*—Days of the Dead. And in an act of elegant simplicity, the Balinese carry the ashes of a loved one in a coconut shell to the sea, where they are ceremonially released to the great waters. Participation in our culture's process of mourning can help heal the pain of grief. But, if you find that your family or societal customs don't work for you, then create your own.

Although I have found great comfort in the religious services and family customs that honor my Aunt Teresa, my mother, and other loved ones who have died, I've discovered my own rituals that bring their spirits close to me and help me heal my pain. Every year on the anniversaries of the deaths of my mother and Teresa, I plan to spend about an hour alone on the beach. My mother died in early November and Teresa on New Year's Eve day and so, at these times of year, the beach is deserted. The air is usually quite chilly, and the ocean is rough and windblown. On that quiet beach, I think about them, listen to music that was special to them or is to me, meditate, and, one by one, toss a bouquet of their favorite flowers into the ocean. I feel my own pain washing away as I watch the ocean take the yellow tulips for Teresa or the yellow roses for my mother. To me, these are powerful moments of connection and remembrance. I cherish them as they arrive each year. Allow yourself the freedom to explore your own self-expression of the pain you have inside. Develop your own ceremonies and moments of meaning and reflection. Honoring and acknowledging your feelings of pain, loss, and mourning will help keep dark and light balanced in your inner landscape. You may find that these moments you used to dread become welcome opportunities for remembering a loved one as you make a special time and activity for her or him in your life.

Grief can be activated by events that occur suddenly—an accident, an act of violence, the sudden death of a friend—or by ones that have been anticipated for a long time, like a lingering illness or the loss of a job at a company that has been in financial crisis for a long time.

Many people immediately, and wrongly, assume that grief is a response only to the death of someone we love. In fact, grief is engendered by losses of all kinds: the end of a marriage, financial security, a job, our health, or a dream. Recently one of my clients spoke about her feelings after her husband of thirty years left her for a much younger woman. "I almost wish he had died," she said. "It might have been easier, because I just don't know what to do with the incredible anger that I'm feeling." Over many months my client cried and raged in my office. She gave voice to her anger at her estranged husband. She even wrote him a scathing letter, which she chose not to mail. She said that there was something in the process of writing and getting those feelings off her chest that was healing to her. Beneath all her anger was a deep grief for the loss of her dreams and expectations. Slowly, by honestly reflecting on her feelings and talking them out, she began to move past her suffering and see that life still held many blessings and opportunities for her. When you are suffering, the most important first step toward healing is to accept that significant losses of all kinds create normal grief.

In the midst of grief, it's important to remember that you will heal. A day will come when you will be free of the unbearable pain. Time is part of the process of healing, but there are things that you can do that will help you grow through your grief and heal cleanly. It's important to remember that even in the darkness of the deepest grief, you will once again find hope, once again be happy. You will find a new "normal," you will make the choice to become bitter or better through your experience, but you will never be the same again.

It's been more than six years since my mother's death and, still, I walk into a department store and smell Estee Lauder perfume and think about her, missing her presence in my life. This was my mother's favorite fragrance, a spicy aroma that will always remind me of her. Because I think of my mother at these times is not to say that I go into a deep depression and am unable to function for the rest of the day. No. This is no intrusion into my life, no tumbling from my normal day into one filled with heartache. Instead it's a sweet passing, a longing, a brief but powerful reminiscence that keeps me in touch with my relationship with her, my love for her, and my desire to—one day—see her again. In the same way, I never want a Friday morning at nine to pass by unnoticed. On my way to work or somewhere else, I want a few moments to think about Teresa. I want to remember.

Practical Suggestions

1. When you are in the wake of a great loss, recognize and acknowledge that you are grieving. Some characteristic feelings you may experience are: shock, denial, anger, guilt, sadness, anxiety, emptiness. Allow yourself to feel these fully. Have patience with yourself as your broken heart heals.

2. Let yourself feel the pain. Give in to it. Accept that grief's emotions come in waves, in cycles. Let yourself cry. Viktor Frankl reminds us that tears are no cause for shame. ". . . For tears bore witness that a man had the greatest of courage, the courage to suffer," he wrote. Many people have told me that they were afraid to cry for fear that the tears would never stop. I can only tell you that, after more than twenty years of working with grieving people and suffering grief myself, I have never seen that happen. If the tears go unshed, however, the fear of their torment can continue until they are released.

3. Express your sorrow. Talk about your grief. Write about your feelings in a journal. Express your sadness through art of any kind. Paint, dance, sculpt, write, or sing into the world. Release the pressure of the pain and don't be ashamed to let it out.

4. Forgive yourself for all the things you think you should have done or wish you had said and didn't. Let go of your regrets. However, pay attention to what you wish you had done and let your grief about chances lost impel you to change now and in the future. Show your feelings to others you love. Let grief help you to treasure each moment you have. Let it encourage you to express your tenderness but forgive yourself for what you cannot change.

5. Take care of yourself. Maintain a balanced diet and good exercise habits. Take care of your physical body. Meditate. Grief is exhausting, and we often get distracted from our normal routines when it visits us. When you're grieving is a particularly good time to become very committed to caring for yourself.

6. Find diversions. Although it is important to sit with your grief—doing nothing but experiencing "what is"—it is also necessary to take

some breaks from it. Go out to a lighthearted movie with a friend. Be frivolous. Have fun.

7. Be aware of "anniversary reactions" and know that certain, special days are likely to be particularly tough ones for you, especially in the early stages of grief. Plan activities that commemorate your loss. It will ease your pain. Plan some different activities than the traditional ones that you shared with someone you've lost. Some feelings of loss will be triggered throughout your life by a wide array of reminders. These can be all kinds of sights, sounds, smells, and events that recall your loss. If grief is not fully worked through, if most of it lies beneath the surface in the underworld of the unconscious, these triggers can engender major psychological reactions rather than a passing feeling of loss or nostalgia. Be aware of the intensity of your responses to these memories. If you break down completely when something triggers a memory of a lost loved one, explore ways to mourn your loss more consciously.

8. Get help if you need it. Be aware that sadness can turn into depression. There are many resources that you can turn to for help: a therapist who specializes in grief, bereavement groups, or support groups for people who are going through divorce or the loss of a career.

9. Help others. Nothing puts our own grief in perspective as much as helping others who are struggling with their own sorrow. Volunteer and share with others your experiences. Listen to theirs. Find the healing that this simple transaction brings.

6. BUILD GOOD CONTAINERS

After Teresa's funeral, I stood near her grave site as my aunt's amazing and vast collection of family and dear friends mingled in small groups or walked toward their cars. An Irish bagpipe continued to play the melancholic strains of "Amazing Grace" and a brisk wind burned my face, though the day was unseasonably sunny and warm for the beginning of January. I remember clearly my feelings of deep sadness mingled with the warmth and connection I had when I saw the hundreds of people who came to mourn my aunt's passing. I knew they shared my pain. I watched my Aunt Jean and Uncle Pete and thought about the fact that they were the only ones left of the five children in their generation of the Kelly family. They had lost their brother Jim—an Army pilot—in a helicopter accident in 1964. Their sweet-hearted little brother who rescued chickens as a child just went out to work one day and never came home. Jim died at twenty-eight and left his Mary, widowed with three very young children, to raise. Mary, my mother, died five years before. Today, they were saying good-bye to Teresa. They had their arms around each other. My cousins were clustered in small groups, holding one another; some were crying. Three- and four-year-old children too young to understand the tragic reason for this family gathering ran across the broad, flat lawn of the cemetery, chasing after one another. Babies cried and were rocked by tearful mothers and fathers.

My cousin Mary Ann's little girl, nine-year-old Alex, ran over, threw her arms around me, and sobbed. Her pain was enormous. But how could it have been otherwise? Teresa was her grandmother and lived just a few houses down the street from her. Alex had seen Teresa almost every day of her young life. It was Teresa who coached her Little League team and Teresa who was always there to celebrate birthdays and put Band-Aids on scraped knees. I remembered one night, just a little over a month ago, before her health began to deteriorate rapidly, when I was moved by the close relationship between Teresa and her granddaughters. I was visiting for the weekend. Teresa was hosting an impromptu "girls night in" party. Teresa, my cousins Patty and Mary Ann, and Mary Ann's two daughters, Alex and Jackie, and I dressed down for the occasion in comfortable sweatpants and baggy flannel pajama tops. By then, Teresa had lost all her hair from the chemotherapy and wore little cotton caps that she insisted were not her idea of the latest things in fashion. But as she looked around at our casual and rumpled attire, she knew it didn't matter. This was family. Teresa, Alex, Jackie, and I made comfy beds on the floor from blankets and pillows while some opportunists immediately grabbed good spots on the long sofa. We ate popcorn and ice cream and watched videos, slumber-party style in Teresa and George's living room. By the time the *The King and I* started, everyone but me was asleep. It was our third video of the evening, after all. As the video played, I thought about the movie's ending and all the sons and daughters the king leaves behind. As the song "Shall We Dance?" came on and Anna polkaed with the King of Siam,

I thought about Alex, and her little sister Jackie, and how much they would miss Teresa when she was gone. They knew their grandmother was very sick but they were too young to fully understand that she was dying. I looked at Teresa, Alex, and Jackie curled up on the floor together, snuggled under blankets. It was that image that filled my mind now as Alex held on to me, crying so hard that her little body was shaking.

"It hurts so bad. How can I ever live without my Grammy?" she struggled to say as her sobs tangled the words in her throat. I hugged her tight. "Look around you, sweetie," I said as my own voice clutched through tears. "Our family and how much we love each other are the only things that make any of this even the least bit bearable. Without those, I wouldn't have a clue." Alex looked around and though her tears continued to run down her cheeks, she smiled up at me. "That's it," she said quietly.

Feeling that you belong to others, that you're part of a clan, a tribe, a family is not a luxury in life. Inclusion in a group is a human necessity; it is the enduring cement that holds us to one another. It's a basic need that we require only a little less than air. In his early work, psychologist Abraham Maslow described a hierarchy of human needs. He said that, after the most basic ones are met—food, shelter, and protection from wild animals and the environment—human beings must satisfy their needs for love, affiliation, acceptance, and belonging. This quest for belonging is not about "fitting in," conforming, or moving up some social ladder; instead, it is the deep, resonating sense that we are part of a group that surrounds us and holds us with love.

Feeling included, loved, accepted, and part of a community is such a powerful human need that the absence of these felt connections leaves a gaping hole in our lives. If we don't have it, we hunger for it. Many religious texts, spiritual leaders, and philosophers speak to the importance of community that we rely so strongly upon. The Bible teaches about the strength that comes from the strong bonds of relationship: "And though a man might prevail against one who is alone, two will withstand him. A threefold cord is not quickly broken" (Ecclesiastes, 4:12). Buddhist priest Thich Nhat Hanh reminds us, "We are here to awaken from the illusion of our separateness." In his excellent book, *Care of the Soul*, psychologist and writer Thomas Moore argues passionately for the deep and stirring importance connected to the experience of family. Whether our "family" members are attached to us through bloodlines or the connections of the heart makes little difference. "The soul needs a felt experience of family, whether we are children getting most of our family experience at home, or adults looking for family in the workplace or neighborhood," he writes. "In the extended sense, 'family' is no mere metaphor, but a particular way of relating that can take many different forms. It always provides a fundamental relatedness that doesn't depend upon attraction or compatibility . . . When we hope that our nation can hold together as a family, or that the family of nations can live in peace, these are not metaphors, but rather the expressions of a profound need of the soul for a special, grounded way of relating that offers deep, unconditional, and lasting security."[14]

Throughout life, but especially at times when our hearts are broken, when the emptiness of suffering and grief surround our every breath, we need the container of love and inclusion to get through it. It is when our lives are filled with pain that we can most clearly see where our lives may be lacking this fundamental belongingness. When we are suffering terribly, we might suddenly discover that we're unprotected and we have been working without the net of belonging.

The word *container* comes from the Latin *continere*, which means "to hold together" or "to enclose." While this word is often used to refer to bottles, boxes, or jars, it's rarely used to describe the surrounding environment we need to live fully as human beings. But I think *container* implies a lot about the importance of relationships in holding us together or enclosing us in a space filled with love and belonging. I think of my biological family—and my family of friends—as the container that encloses me and holds me together during hard times in my life. I have discovered through the deep sense of connection I have with my loved ones that suffering finds it's truest meaning when it's shared.

Each of us makes decisions every day about the kinds of containers we are willing to create in and around our lives. We determine how well—or not so well—we'll be in containing others we meet. I think the answer about how much we need to belong to a warm and loving group is thoroughly clear. Throughout time, poets, philosophers, and the great myths of every culture have instructed us in the importance of friendship and family, of containers that salve the wounds of suffering and bring joy to times of celebration. There are many wonderful expressions of the importance of belonging, of feeling a part of family, but my favorite is an uncomplicated one. Rumi, a thirteenth-century Sufi mystic, writes, "Friend, our closeness is this: anywhere you put your foot, feel me in the firmness under you."[15]

The only thing that matters is love. We've heard this pronouncement from every religion and wisdom tradition there is. We may speak of love in its moral and religious sense. We may accept the spiritual importance of loving one another and base our lives on this abstract moral imperative but neglect to build the real, earthy relationships in which love is best expressed. It's clear that love *is* the container in which broken hearts are rebuilt. Many have echoed this sentiment. Robert Burton, a noted writer and clergyman of the seventeenth century, wrote, "Let the burden be never so heavy, love make it light." George Eliot: "No soul is desolate so long as there is a human being for whom it can feel trust and reverence." Ralph Waldo Emerson: "The moment we exercise our affections, the earth is metamorphosed; there is no winter, and no night; all tragedies, all ennuis vanish—all furies even." And Emily Dickinson, with her typical and elegant economy: "Love can do all but raise the dead."

My life is blessed by the sure and strong containment of a biological family that loves and embraces me. I realize that not everyone is so lucky. Perhaps you come from a small family, separated by great distances. Maybe your family is not emotionally close even if they live in the same town. Regardless of your particular circumstances, your need for inclusion, for feeling loved and held by the sense of family is no less than mine. If you weren't born into these connections, then you must make them. If I didn't have a single blood relative, I realize that I would still have a family. I'm equally blessed by my friends of the heart; many are people I've known for more than twenty years. We've seen one another through good times and bad. Everyone needs this. Community is not a luxury. It's like air for us.

I reflect often upon how I've been surrounded and protected by this same wide net of people throughout my life—this firmness under me. In grief and celebration, we are always in it together. I recall sitting at my cousin Mike's wedding. At that time, my father was dying of liver failure. Everyone knew that without a transplant, he wouldn't live for many more months. I remember my sadness, as I looked at my father sitting at the head table with Teresa and George, and all my other aunts and uncles. I thought, "This could be the last time my father will join the family for a wedding or other celebration." But that was not the case. Two weeks later, my father was given the gift of life through the grace of a grieving family who offered their son's organs for transplant. In that same two-week period of time, Teresa was diagnosed with cancer. It was her last family wedding. Life is like that. It turns on a dime and when we think we know what to expect, fate steps in and tells us something different.

Another day. Another wedding. My cousin Matthew Kelly marries Tara in an elegant ceremony followed by a rousing reception. The food is outstanding, the champagne exceptional and flowing with abandon. Two new families are coming together with music and soul. My cousins are toasting the bride and groom. My brother and sister-in-law are dancing. My father and Deanne are standing, swaying to the music. Dad's still using a walker—the automobile accident was only six months ago, and his recovery will take years—but that's not going to stop him from getting out on that dance floor. I've been dancing with my cousin Paul and now my Aunt Mary and my cousin Shannon at the same time. I look around and see that everyone's dancing. Is that my brother doing the cha-cha with my cousin Patrick? I take a moment to glance at all the familiar faces, many of whom I've known since the day I was born. My Uncle Pete, the father of the groom, takes the hand of my Aunt Jeannie, his only surviving sibling, and they move to the dance floor. To the slow, sweet beat of a Frank Sinatra standard, I overhear him say to her, "It's just the two of us left now, Jeannie." Still, they dance. Just as I do, I think they feel the firmness under them.

Practical Suggestions

1. You need to belong. You need a family. If possible, shore up the connections in your family of origin by frequent contact. Tell people you love them. Email your cousins, nieces, and nephews if you have them. Stay in touch.

2. If you don't have a strong biological family, and even if you do, create a family from friends. Cultivate friendships with people you love and admire, the kind you can open your heart to even with a phone call at three o'clock in the morning.

3. Build your containers before you need them, before suffering demands that you be held in the clear, warm light of loving relationships.

4. Be a good container to the people in your life. Listen and love unconditionally.

7. COUNT YOUR BLESSINGS AND DISCOVER THE POWER OF OPTIMISM

Last year I bought a new computer. On a freezing and windy winter afternoon just after Christmas, I eagerly opened the boxes containing its various components and marveled at how much easier everything was to set up compared with the old Windows 3.0 dinosaur I had worked on for many years. Even the printer and mouse cables were color coded at each end with colors that corresponded to the ports on the back of the CPU. "This is going to be a breeze," I said as I started to hook things up. With all the hardware easily and correctly configured, I turned my computer on and opened the preinstalled Windows program. From that very moment, my good luck went south. Everything I tried to do was met with an error statement that I didn't understand. I spent hours poring through the manual, until finally I just couldn't take it anymore. I called the manufacturer's tech support number where I was treated to forty-five minutes of droning "elevator" music punctuated by an occasional robotic voice that pleasantly assured me that I was a valued customer, all technicians were tied up, and that they'd be with me soon. I was caller number eighty-four. *Argghh!* When I finally spoke with a human being, I was beyond irritated and way out of patience. This nice young guy spent over an hour on the phone with me; we tried various fixes, but to no avail. Finally, he concluded that there was nothing else he could do. He said it must be a "hardware" problem and, since it was brand-new, I should just return the computer and get another one.

I didn't want to do what he suggested. I wanted this computer working now! I had already dismantled and given away my old computer (so there was no backup). This particular, rotten computer now sitting on my desk was the very last one of that model in stock and I would have to wait weeks to get another one. Besides, Dorothy had already chewed up those Styrofoam things that hold everything in place. I swore at the computer one more time and then went downstairs to get a glass of water. I was steamed.

I turned on the tap, drew a glass of cold water, and drank it. Then something came over me. For the first time in hours, I stopped being upset and some—probably more enlightened—part of me said: "Calm down. Look at how lucky you are. You're blessed to be in a position to be able to afford a nice, new computer. By tomorrow this problem will be solved even if it means exchanging your computer. Now think about this. You can walk right downstairs and get a glass of cold, clear water that is safe to drink and will refresh you. Do you know that most of the people in the world can't walk only a few steps to find cold water? Do you know that people all over the world get terrible diseases because they don't have access to clean, safe water?" As these thoughts rumbled in my head, I watched the sleeting rain cascade against the kitchen window. The wind was howling outside, but my house was cozy. A blazing fire burned in the fireplace and I was warm and safe. Nancy was watching a movie on HBO and Dorothy and Miss Maude—my sweet and bossy old calico cat—were snoring on the carpet, in the glow of the fire. Suddenly I became very aware of just how lucky and blessed I was. At this very moment and not very far from my house, there were homeless people living outside, shivering in this storm. There were others who didn't have the money to buy food or little holiday gifts for their kids, much less a new computer. I thought about the people who were having a difficult time on this day, struggling to find shelter or something to eat. I thought about the parents sitting with their sick or dying children at the hospital, just down the street from my house. I said a little prayer for them and one of thankfulness for myself. My thinking was not a self-imposed guilt trip, but rather a change in perspective, a new context in which to see my own small problems. No wonder I had been in such a bad mood. I had taken many good things in my life for granted. I had forgotten to count my blessings.

When I went back upstairs to my office, my whole attitude had changed. I was calm and patient. I'd solve this problem or return the computer (sans Styrofoam inserts). In my new frame of mind, whatever was going to happen would be just fine. I had detached myself from the outcome. Once again, I turned the computer on. Surprisingly it worked flawlessly. There were no more unexplainable error statements, no more crashes. Later, my good friend Leslie, who is something of a computer expert compared to me with my techno-peasant abilities, told me that she thought the problem was a "corrupted file" that Windows had repaired on its own. (Windows, it seems, has a proclivity to both create and fix errors that defy reason.) I suppose that could be, but I will always believe that I fixed it. I think that my change in attitude put out a calmer, less frenzied, electromagnetic energy field that wasn't in such conflict with that of my new computer. I think my computer's turnaround matched my mood. It was case of mind over matter.

I readily admit that my stress about this computer does not constitute suffering on a grand scale. Instead, it was one of those frustrating, stress-producing incidents that take the fun out of life for the moment. I think most of us are quite familiar with this state of mind, at least from time to time. But what was most interesting to me about this incident was how quickly I was able to forget all the blessings in my life simply because I was irritated when things weren't going my way. I'm not proud of that. But I was even more amazed at just how easily I changed my experience of that moment by simply revising the way I was thinking about things. Consciously changing my mind had changed my whole mood, and my whole reality. Just consider the enormous power our mind gives us over all kinds of experiences in our life. I remember a similar and sudden change of mind at a time when I was really suffering. This was not mere frustration—like the glitchy computer—but full pain, deep and authentic sorrow.

After my mother's funeral, a large number of us went from the cemetery to my brother and sister-in-law's house. There were many people there, lots of food, and a warm fire burning. People were talking quietly in small groups. Someone had brought out an old photo album and pictures were being passed around. In spite of the loving compassion that surrounded me, I felt empty and sick, filled with grief, and missed my mother more than I had ever imagined I could. Her absence, especially here, especially now, when I was surrounded by her sisters and brother, carved a hopeless emptiness into my soul. As I sat there with my heart broken so wide open that I thought it could never come back together again, I looked around me. My cousin Mary Ann was pregnant at the time. The baby girl she was expecting was due in less than a month and was to be named Jacqueline Mary; Mary, after my mother. My niece and nephew and multitudes of my cousins' older children were playing quietly on the floor with the smaller kids. I looked at each one. Perfect children. All born healthy and thriving. What are the odds of that? I thought. With so many children in this big family, what are the odds of having every single one born without any disability, disease, or infirmity? I looked at my sweet brother, my sister-in-law—and all her family—my cousins, my father, my aunts and uncles. We, too, were healthy and had good relationships and satisfying work. We had one another for comfort and support in hard times like this. In spite of my grief, I could feel the tenderness of knowing just how much my life and all of our lives had been blessed. We had our share of anguish, especially right then, but there were many other gifts present in that room as well, blessings that couldn't be ignored in spite of the pain. In this moment, I grasped the larger picture. My mind was still, quiet, and peaceful. American poet Theodore Roethke once wrote, "In the dark time, the eye begins to see."[16] He's right. Through the darkness of my own grief, I saw clearly the cycles of life here in this house, and I was humbled by my observation. Here in my own family, some had died and some were busy being born. This change of mind—change of heart—is not denial of pain, not the time-worn notion of a "silver lining in every cloud," but a truth and a challenge. Those who take it recognize the context in which our suffering takes place and acknowledge that even in the midst of suffering we have the power to focus our mind, determine our reactions to our losses, and count our blessings.

One who seems to maintain a serene and loving outlook in the face of many challenges is the Dalai Lama. I read a remarkable interview with the him just after he won the 1989 Nobel Peace Prize. A British reporter asked him how he was able to maintain such compassion, lack of anger, and forgiveness for the Chinese in spite of the fact that their actions had forced him to live in exile from his beloved Tibetan home-land for almost forty years. Since the Chinese army invaded his country in 1959, over a million Tibetans have been killed, including many Buddhist priests and nuns. More than six thousand sacred Buddhist sites, shrines, and temples have been razed. Tibetan culture has been all but annihilated and, even today, people in Chinese-occupied Tibet are tortured and killed for their nonviolent expression of political opposition. In spite of these atrocities, the Dalai Lama is filled with peace and forgiveness. He refers to the Chinese as "my friend, the enemy" and he responded to the reporter's questions by saying, "They have taken everything from us; should I let them take my mind as well?"

The power of mind—of consciousness—is awesome. It's the only equipment we really need to grow through suffering and find happiness in life. The Dalai Lama is a living example of this truth. Through practice we can learn to tame our frenetic monkey mind, as the Zen masters call the ego, and see deeply into the true nature of things. A Buddhist text from the fifth century B.C.E. called the *Dhammapada* speaks to the importance of cultivating our mind: "It is good to tame the mind, which is difficult to hold in and flighty, rushing wherever it listeth; a tamed mind brings happiness." Refining our mental states like compassion, kindness, counting one's blessings, and seeing the larger picture quite naturally leads to a more optimistic view of life in general and our own in particular.

Optimism is not the Candide-like belief that everything always happens for the best in this, the best of all possible worlds. Nor is it the denial of problems or avoidance of our responsibility to feel deeply the wounds of our lives. It can be described in many ways. Which one speaks to you? Rather it is the state of mind we adopt no matter what our situation is. It is what we do when challenged and how we think about our experience. Optimism allows us to see the future as worthwhile and positive. With it as our guide we know that present problems will pass. It's the impulse to say "I can," not "I can't." It's the glass as half full and not half empty. And research by psychologist Martin Seligman and others has shown that an optimistic view of ourselves and the world is like a "protective armor" against depression, low self-esteem, and the pain of disappointment and loss.[17] Optimism is the opposite of pessimism, which sees the present as always difficult and the future as bleak and hopeless. Optimism is wide-open in contrast to pessimism's closed heart. Optimism is joyful searching; pessimism is a prison of fear and a clutching at illusionary safety. As Helen Keller pointed out, "No pessimist ever discovered the secrets of the stars, or sailed to an uncharted land, or opened a new heaven to the human spirit." Alexander Graham Bell succinctly commented on this dialectic between optimism and pessimism when he said, "When one door closes, another opens; but we often look so long and so regretfully upon the closed door that we do not see the one which has opened for us." Look for the open door.

Here are some thoughts and practices I have found helpful in cultivating my optimism and keeping it strong. Maybe they will be useful to you as well. Give them a try.

Practical Suggestions

1. At all times, but particularly during difficult ones, look around you at the blessings in your life. Some people find it helpful to keep a journal or small notebook where they can write these down. That's a good idea. Reflect often on your blessings and record them if you like.

2. Calm your mind through meditation, yoga, spending quiet time alone, and experiencing nature. Remember the importance of staying alive in the present moment. Even in the middle of suffering, your mind can be clear and peaceful. Focus on your blessings. Do not discount your anguish, but see your pain in the context of all you have in your life. When difficult times are upon you, try to be here and now.

3. Look at your own levels of optimism and pessimism. How do you rate yourself? Remember, earlier I wrote about optimistic attitudes as explaining events in ways that are temporary, specific, and impersonal. Pessimism is characterized by explanations that are permanent, pervasive, and personal. Listen carefully to your inner voice. What do you hear? Translate pessimistic thoughts and self-talk into optimistic ones.

4. Share the blessings that you have with others. Volunteer or just be generous with your gifts of time, care, love, and material things with your loved ones, friends, family, community, and strangers.

8. FIND COURAGEOUS ROLE MODELS
AND THE HERO WITHIN

Throughout history human beings have been spellbound by stories about heroes. From wide-eyed children sitting around an ancient campfire in a tiny Inuit village listening to a storyteller relate the tale of Raven stealing the light to contemporary kids mesmerized by the Dolby-enhanced sound effects and 70 mm, twenty-four-frames-per-second thrill of the young Anakin Skywalker taking on the bad guys in his pod racer, we are motivated and inspired by heroes. It's not just children who are enraptured by heroes and their courageous acts—we all are. It's as if the hero story is part of our very souls, nestled in the deepest, most authentic recesses of our psyche. While its production values and presentation may have changed from the oral tradition to Hollywood blockbusters over time, the story hasn't.

In spite of this story's many and variant retellings, the archetype—or primary characteristics—for the hero remains remarkably consistent across time and cultures. Mythologist Joseph Campbell called it "the one, shape-shifting yet marvelously constant story." There is no gender that defines a hero. The hero can be male or female. From a psychological perspective, the hero's journey is an apt metaphor for the emergence of consciousness through trials and tribulations. The hero starts out one way, goes through difficult times—sometimes even a symbolic or physical death—and comes home another way. According to Carl Jung, the hero can always be identified by certain specific characteristics: the experience of a divine birth, a descent into the underworld, heroic actions that must be performed, the presence of helpful companions (sometimes in animal form), and the process of defeat, death, and rebirth. Heroes always return transformed through their struggles.

Why are we so drawn to and inspired by heroic acts, by mere humans who take on superhuman attributes as they fight for justice, save the village, or slay the dragon to return home with some valuable gift for the rest of us? I think we are attracted to the myth of the hero because, like him or her, we instinctively understand that we, too, will undergo trials and tribulations in life. In hero stories we find images that reflect our own pain and our own suffering. In his PBS interview with Bill Moyers, Joseph Campbell remarked on the significance of the difficulties and tests the hero must endure. He said, "The trials are designed to see to it that the intending hero should really be a hero. Is he really a match for this task? Can he overcome the dangers? Does he have the courage, the knowledge, the capacity, to enable him to serve?"[18] When we consider our own struggles in life, aren't we really up against the same challenges as the heroes we encounter in myth, literature, and art? The question, then, becomes personal: Will *we* have the courage, the knowledge, the capacity to serve, and to use our struggles as a launching point for consciousness and growth?

We can learn so much from our heroes. Psychologist and author Carol Pearson writes, "The heroic quest is about saying yes to yourself and, in so doing, becoming more fully alive and more effective in the world. For the hero's journey is first about taking a journey to find the treasure of your true self, and then about returning home to give your gift to help transform the kingdom—and, in the process, your own life."[19] At all times in life, but especially when we're suffering, our heroes can be companions and illuminate the path as we forge ahead on our treacherous way. There are many people I admire, and I even have a few heroes, but ever since I was a very young girl, my greatest heroine and role model has been Helen Keller. You might not be surprised to know that since quotations from her life and work pepper this book—as they have the other books I've written. The way Helen Keller approached life offers many lessons about growth through suffering, extracting the gold from lead, in the hero's journey.

In Alabama in 1880, Helen Keller was born a perfectly healthy, thriving baby. But when she was nineteen months old, she caught a vicious fever that was never conclusively diagnosed but was most likely scarlet fever and almost died. She survived, but the illness deprived her of both her sight and hearing. Because the fever struck her during the early stages of speech development, the loss of her hearing made it almost impossible for her to speak as well. But in spite of her cruel sensory deprivation, Helen Keller made great efforts to experience the world and share her reactions and thoughts on it with those around her. By the time she was five years old, Helen had created more than sixty different signs that she used to communicate with her family. These signs were inventive and clever. If she wanted bread and butter, for example, she would pretend to cut a loaf of bread and butter the slices. For ice cream, she wrapped her arms around herself and shivered. But as she grew older, Helen became more and more frustrated, enraged at her difficulties in communicating more complex ideas. At this stage, it seemed that Helen's remarkable intelligence was becoming less a blessing and more a curse as she struggled to express herself.

As she found herself imprisoned in darkness, silence, and isolation, Helen became increasingly wild and frenzied. She flew into rages that became more and more violent. She would snatch food from her family's dinner plates and eat it on the run, knocking into cupboards and chairs. She'd fling fragile objects to the floor. She'd scream, then kick and bite anyone who tried to stop these outrageous tantrums. Not knowing what to do next to help their beloved but increasingly intolerable daughter, the Keller family hired a tutor just before Helen's seventh birthday. Helen's tutor, Annie Sullivan Macy, had been blind as a child and terribly unruly herself. She had been given the nickname Spitfire at the Perkins School for the Blind in Boston because of her own rudeness and bad behavior. Successful surgeries restored Annie Sullivan's sight, but her personal experiences with blindness and how she overcame her own frustration gave her an insider's view into Helen Keller's pain and suffering. She believed that Helen's rages were caused by her powerlessness to communicate and that, if she could help Helen learn to do this, the rages would abate.

Annie Sullivan was right. She taught Helen the manual alphabet, which is a sign language in which each letter is signed onto the hand of the deaf-blind person so that it can be felt. With this alphabet, Helen could spell out words and sentences. She could communicate the complex ideas that she yearned to share with others. Though at first brutally resistant, Helen soon became a remarkable pupil. Later, Helen learned to read and write in Braille and to read people's lips by holding her fingertips against them, feeling the vibration and movement of air. This latter technique, called Tadoma, is one that few people ever master. Helen even went beyond all expectations, learning to speak a little bit, which is a daunting task for someone who cannot hear.

In spite of her profound disabilities, Helen Keller graduated *cum laude* from Radcliffe College, where she studied Greek, Latin, German, French, and English. Motivated by an incredible dedication to social justice and inspired by deep religious faith, Helen set up the American Foundation for the Blind, worked tirelessly to end poverty, and became a suffragist demanding equal rights for women and a socialist committed to fair treatment and honest wages for working people. She lectured throughout the world bringing hope, courage, and inspiration to people with and without physical disabilities. She urged everyone who came to hear her speak to reach for the stars and strive for the highest levels of self-fulfillment. "I thank God for my handicaps," she said in one lecture, "for through them I have found myself, my work, and my God."

After Helen's death in 1968, Helen Keller International, an organization that combats blindness in the developing world, was established and continues her brilliant legacy of compassion and determination to decrease the world's suffering. Helen Keller's extraordinary life is an example of the hero's journey. It's a beacon to people with disabilities, in particular, because of the exceptional role model she provides for the power of determination even in the face of profound physical limitations. Helen Keller's advice about the kind of effort required to accomplish what you desire in life was simple and clear-cut. She said, "We can do anything we want to do if we stick to it long enough."

Helen Keller's life is an inspiring model of triumph over tragedy. If you are curious to learn more about her, you will find a lot of material in several different media. Many books have been written and several plays and films produced about this exceptional woman. The story of Helen Keller is beautifully told in her own words in *The Story of My Life* (1903), which she wrote when she was a twenty-three-year-old college student. The 1962 film *The Miracle Worker* accurately portrays her amazing life-story and, in particular, gives wonderful insight into the deep relationship between Helen and Annie Sullivan. Both Anne Bancroft (as Annie Sullivan) and Patty Duke (as Helen Keller) won Academy Awards for their performances. And in an interesting Hollywood moment, this film was remade in 1979 and, this time around, Patty Duke Astin plays Annie Sullivan to Melissa Gilbert's Helen Keller.

By studying and reflecting on the hero's journey of Helen Keller and others, I find that I am more able to connect with the hero within me. When my life is tough and I'm in the middle of pain and suffering, I often think about Helen Keller and the struggles she went through in her life. I even keep a few of her quotes taped up on the walls in my office at home. I think it never hurts to be reminded of another's journey and inspired by those who have demonstrated extraordinary abilities to meet the difficulties in life with courage and determination.

Like all of us, I have a part of me that is abundantly courageous and confident of my abilities to meet the challenges that my life will deliver to me. This is the hero who will leave the village, the safety of the known, to search for the Holy Grail or the magic elixir—nice metaphors for consciousness—that offer growth, life, and hope. I also have a part of me that's wimpy and scared, which I call my "whoosie" complex. That's the apathetic, cowardly villager who would rather have someone else—the real hero—bring that magic elixir home while I sit safe and secure, drinking grog at the local pub. The blessing in suffering is that it gives me no choice to be this latter character. The pain in my life tosses me out of the village pub, as unwilling as I might be to leave this safe and friendly place, and onto the path of the hero. My success along the way will be determined by the choices I make, my responses to a series of opportunities for defining moments. And I will be called upon to make *many* choices along the path of the journey. Will I choose to be compassionate and brave or avoidant and self-defeating, complaining about the rotten circumstances that life has handed me? Will I live up to my full potential or find myself—at the end of my life—never having grown, learned, or realized the truths about myself? Do *I* have the courage, the knowledge, the capacity for the hero's journey?

Each of us has a hero living inside us. Suffering in life helps us to discover the enormous power of that archetypal force that has been freely given us as part of our human birthright. The stories of our personal heroes can point us in the right direction in our search for our own inner hero. Even those heroes with swashbuckling external adventures give us lots of instruction for our own inward-looking hero's quest, the soul's journey that requires only metaphorically that we leave our house or village. In Helen Keller's view, the choice to fulfill the hero's call is the path well worth taking. "Avoiding danger is no safer in the long run than outright exposure," she said. "Life is either a daring adventure or it is nothing." Which do you choose?

Practical Suggestions

1. Sit quietly and reflect on your heroes. Who are they? Have they changed over time? Who were your heroes as a child? Who are they now? Why? Make a list of your heroes.

2. Learn more about your heroes. Read books and watch movies that explore their life and journey. Study the great myths from all cultures. Some of our best heroes are fictional characters (books and films that inspire and instruct don't always have to be based on the lives of real people). I've found a great deal of motivation for striving and having the courage to overcome difficult times or great odds from films like *Star Wars*, the Indiana Jones movies, *Life Is Beautiful*, and *The African Queen*, as well as those about real people like *The Miracle Worker, Braveheart* (Scotland's William Wallace), and *My Left Foot* (about disabled artist Christie Brown). Many films made for children quite explicitly lay out the terrain of the hero's journey. Adults can learn something, as well, from *Mulan, The Lion King, Fly Away Home*, and even *The Bad News Bears.* Books like Paule Marshall's *Praisesong for the Widow, Bastard Out of Carolina* by Dorothy Allison, and *Beloved* by Toni Morrison give us enduring and enlightening characters who overcome great pain and loss and emerge transformed. There are hundreds of thousands of wonderful role models for overcoming hardships and growing through suffering. Take a cruise through your local library, bookstore, video rental store, or neighborhood movie theater to find them and bring them to life in your heart and mind.

3. When you are going through a difficult time, write a story about the circumstances you're in and how your hero might deal with the same crisis or problem. Don't worry about your grammar, punctuation, or typing. Just relax, breathe easily—follow your breath for a moment or two—then let the story write itself. Put it down for a day or two, then read it again. Ask yourself how you might apply your hero's choices and decisions in the story to the real situation in your own life.

9. KEEP A SENSE OF HUMOR

On a cold January Super Bowl Sunday in 1981, my good friend Kathryn, a television news photographer at the time, was returning to Roanoke, Virginia, after covering a story at Smith Mountain Lake for WDBJ-7, the ABC affiliate in the area. Kathryn was driving, accompanied by news reporter Kelly, when the road took a sharp twist, the wheels spun on gravel, and the car lurched out of control. They clipped a mailbox and smashed head-on into the only tree within sight. Both women were rushed to the emergency room at Community Hospital and into surgery. Kelly had broken her femur and received multiple cuts to the arm that she had used to brace herself against the shattering windshield. Kathryn suffered massive internal bleeding, and surgeons removed her damaged spleen before they could even begin to deal with her broken hip. Later Kathryn was wheeled back into a post-op recovery room with Kelly. As Kathryn was waking up from the anesthesia, her doctor began explaining what they had done and why. "We had to remove your spleen. It was a life-threatening intra-abdominal injury," he said. "The good news is that you can live a healthy life without a spleen. The bad news is that now you'll always be more susceptible to infections and your immune system will always be a bit more compromised than if you had a spleen." Kelly overheard the doctor talking about surgery, Kathryn's spleen, and her immune system. She looked over at Kathryn. "Where . . . where is your spleen, anyway?" she asked anxiously. Kathryn motioned across the room to a large plastic wastebasket. Without missing a beat, Kathryn said with her typical dry humor, "I believe mine's in that garbage can over there." There was silence for a second, then the three of them burst out laughing.

Humor and laughter are powerful strategies for making the best out of the worst situations. At that moment in the emergency room, I have no doubt that Kathryn's wit was as potent a medicine as anything the doctor could dish out. Laughter broke the tension, reduced stress, and brought both the doctor and his patients into a heartfelt connection, creating a memorable shared and positive experience. For a moment, Kathryn and Kelly's physical pain and fear were suspended by laughter.

Modern science has revealed the healing power of laughter and humor, demonstrating their power to reduce stress, boost the immune system, and ease suffering. A lot has been written about the mind-body interconnection, but the word *interconnection* is not strong enough to describe the exquisite dance among our physical, cognitive, emotional, and spiritual selves. It is becoming clear that our bodies and minds are two parts of one whole. Research into the nature of neurotransmitters, peptide molecules such as interleukins, interferon, and endorphins, and receptor sites has revealed that every cell in the body is capable of responding to chemical messages, which were thought to exist only in the brain. Professor of Physiology and Biophysics at Georgetown University Medical Center Candace Pert is a leading figure in the emerging field of psychoneuroimmunology (PNI), an interdisciplinary specialty that involves the study of the relationship between mental (psychological) functions and the immune system via traditional neuronal connections. The research findings that have emerged are so compelling that Pert finds it almost impossible to think in traditional terms of a mind and a body. She says that she has come to see the human being instead as a single, integrated entity, a "bodymind."[20]

Studies have corroborated what those of us who like to laugh a lot have always known intuitively: laughter brings about a wide variety of benefits. A good laugh triggers many positive psychological effects and physiological changes. Through the "reverse exhalation" capacity of the lungs, the physical contractions of laughter cause extra oxygen to enter the body, moving stagnant air and increasing our body's blood oxygen levels. In other words, laughter is aerobic. I like to think of it as "inner jogging." The muscle movement of laughter increases peripheral circulation, which is associated with the innervation of the parasympathetic nervous system and the "relaxation response" of the body. In some ways, the breathing patterns created by laughter are similar to those that naturally occur during meditation. So, laughter sends calm and soothing messages to all our cells. Other studies have shown that laughter lowers serum cholesterol, reduces stress-related hormones, and increases virus killer cells, B cells, and activated T lymphocytes, all of which improve immune system functioning and offset the immunosuppressive effects of stress and suffering. There is even some growing evidence that a good, healthy laugh releases endorphins, the body's own natural opiates, which diminish both physical and emotional pain.

Editor and writer Norman Cousins was one of the first to call public attention to the power of humor and laughter in his best-selling book, *Anatomy of an Illness*, in 1979.[21] This book recounts his extraordinary battle for his health fifteen years earlier. In 1964, Cousins was the well-known and highly respected editor of the *Saturday Review* when he was stricken with ankylosing spondylitis (AS), a serious connective tissue disease that is painful, progressive, incurable, and can often be severely disabling. Cousins became immediately aware that his regimen of boring—perhaps toxic—hospital food and routines coupled with powerful anti-inflammatory drugs would not be enough to heal him and, in fact, might even make him sicker. After only a few days he wrote, "I had a fast-growing conviction that a hospital is no place for a person who is seriously ill." With his open-minded physician, Dr. William Hitzig, as a partner in his plan, Cousins checked out of the hospital and into a nearby hotel where he could determine his own diet and not be awakened at all hours of the day and night for blood tests, medication, and other procedures. In addition to these obvious benefits, Cousins was delighted to point out that the hotel cost only about one-third as much as the hospital did. He stopped taking all pain-killing and anti-inflammatory drugs, slept whenever he felt like it, and consumed mega-doses of vitamin C (which American chemist Linus Pauling, a two-time Nobel Prize winner, had emphasized as a way of enhancing immune system functioning). He also gave himself a steady diet of laughter by watching *Candid Camera* reruns, old Marx Brothers movies, and reading humorous books. After several weeks, Cousins felt an improvement and his doctors corroborated those results with their tests. His plan seemed to be working. Cousins wrote, "Ten minutes of genuine belly laughter had an anesthetic effect and would give me two hours of pain-free sleep." Luckily, his physician understood the importance of what Cousins was doing to mobilize the natural resources of his body and mind to combat disease. When Dr. Hitzig checked Cousins's sedimentation rate, a measurement of the degree of inflammation, immediately after a laughing spell, it had significantly decreased. This was an empirical, objective measure of improvement and one that validated Cousins's belief that laughter is, indeed, some of the best medicine there is.

Norman Cousins's excellent book was a wake-up call to all of us about the power of laughter, humor, and positive thinking when it comes to reducing pain, illness, and suffering. But his insight was not a new one. Plato, Aristotle, Kant, and Hume had all addressed this subject. At the turn of the century, psychologist and philosopher William James wrote, "We don't laugh because we're happy; we're happy because we laugh." In fact, knowledge about the specific medical benefits and healing properties of laughter dates back to the 1300s. During the Middle Ages, Henri de Mondeville, a noted professor of surgery, wrote the following advice to his students: "Let the surgeon take care to regulate the whole regimen of the patient's life for joy and happiness, allowing his relatives and special friends to cheer him, and by having someone tell him jokes."

The *Journal of Holistic Nursing* recently published the results of a study of the effects of humor in which some patients were told one-liners after surgery and before painful medication was about to be administered. The patients who heard the jokes reported experiencing significantly less pain than those who didn't. In 1986, Duke University Hospital and the University of North Carolina at Chapel Hill Hospital teamed up to create the Duke Humor Project in which volunteers distribute funny books, tapes, games, and videos to patients in their care. A roving cart—called the Laugh Mobile—is equipped with yo-yos, water guns, crazy glasses, and rubber chickens and makes the rounds so children and adult cancer patients have a variety of funny stuff to play with and laugh at. The positive responses in both physical healing and patient outlook and mood were so remarkable that additional "humor intervention" programs have been instituted in medical centers in Phoenix, San Diego, Philadelphia, Dallas, and Brooklyn. In addition, more than a dozen professional groups have sprung up to study and implement humor in medical settings, foremost among them the American Association of Therapeutic Humor. Many of us have become familiar with the integration of humor into medicine through the movie *Patch Adams*, in which Robin Williams portrayed a real-life Virginia doctor who treated his patients while wearing a red rubber clown nose. So powerful is the effect of humor and laughter on healing that Dr. Lee Berk, of Loma Linda University in California, one of the major researchers in the field, said, "If you took what we now know about the capability of laughter to manipulate the immune system, and bottled it, it would need FDA approval."

In addition to many profound effects on the immune system and overall health, laughter and humor give us a sense of empowerment over the suffering we encounter in life. They help us to see new perspectives and feel some mastery over our circumstances even when the events of our lives seem to be spinning painfully and wildly out of control. One study presented in 1990 in England at the Eighth International Conference on Humor—an interdisciplinary and scholarly organization dedicated to the advancement of humor research—showed that participation in a "humor training course" in which subjects laughed and joked increased internal locus of control as measured by a valid and reliable questionnaire. Nursing researcher Patty Wooten and her colleagues, the authors of the study, concluded that humor allows people to understand that although they may not control all the things that happen to them, they do have control over how they view these events and how they choose to react to them. They summarize these findings by citing comedian Bill Cosby: "If you can laugh at it, you can survive it."[22]

In looking at the characteristics of people who grow through suffering, who become better not bitter through its savage teachings, it's hard to miss the sense of humor that each one of them brings to his or her life. In Jeff Beaton's office, I'm talking to a man who hasn't moved a muscle below his neck for thirty years, and yet we spent a good deal of our time together laughing about growing up in the seventies and how we both have earnest conversations with our pet dogs. Beth Nielsen Chapman spoke openly about "coming from her joy" in everything that she does. Her humor is evident in the quick wit that comes through in her conversations and lyrics. In my research for *Ordinary Grace*, I spoke with many people who were bringing extraordinary goodness into the world, many of whom were surrounded by the suffering of orphaned children, homeless people, and crippling diseases, and yet, there was humor, laughter, and joy radiating from each of them. The people I interviewed seemed to have an endless capacity for seeing the world's problems honestly while never taking themselves too seriously. They seemed to experience genuine joy and pleasure at the opportunities and challenges before them, and I noticed that they laughed often and had a good time. Their sense of humor was creative, spontaneous, philosophical, and even slightly self-deprecating, but never hostile or condescending toward others. Instead, it expressed itself in an easy-going attitude that seemed naturally to embrace the humorous edge of things. In talking about "self-actualized" people, Abraham Maslow described exactly what I had seen. He wrote, "Psychologically healthy people are more able to enjoy, to love, to laugh, to have fun, to be humorous, to be silly, to be whimsical and fantastic, to be pleasantly 'crazy.'"[23]

In my own life I have seen that even in the midst of terrible loss and pain, humor and laughter have their own healing place. The day after my mother's death, my brother, J. P., went to pick out the cemetery plot in which my mother would be buried. He was grieving terribly—both of us were extremely close to our mother. In spite of his own deep loss, J. P. wanted to spare my father the difficult task of picking out the coffin and grave site. But the humor he sees in life and had made me laugh with since we were kids came out to help him through even in those days just after Mom died. At the cemetery, J. P. was in this little office with a rather officious woman—dare I call her a sales representative?—who was showing him the various sites available and telling him the costs for each one. We all had discussed it and thought that my mother would like to be buried in the section near the cemetery's large and beautiful statue of the Blessed Mother. As it turned out, there were several available plots in this area. "This one is about eight-thousand dollars more than the other," the woman said to J. P. as she pointed to the site plan with perfectly manicured, bright red nails. "Really? Why?" he asked. She cleared her throat and said, a bit pompously, "Why, it has a better view, of course." J. P. stood there for a minute. He thought about what she had just told him, smiled, and said, "Oh, of course. I understand that. I'm a builder and land developer. Just like you, I charge higher prices for lots with better views." The woman smiled at him. "But there is one big difference in our markets," he said. "My customers are alive!"

When J. P. replayed this scene and those lines for my dad, Nancy, and me, we cracked up and fell all over one another laughing. Here we were in the middle of the biggest loss, the most painful experience of our lives, and we were laughing like crazy. That's how laughter can be, though. It's not that we have to grieve *or* laugh. We can grieve *and* laugh. Both give clear evidence that we are alive and feeling everything in each moment. By the way, we picked the site nearest to the statue of the Blessed Mother. We didn't care about the view.

Humor is like a magnet. It has the power to pull us together just as grief does. Laughter is like the songs of birds, acoustic, natural, immediately understood by others of our species. You might be interested to know that the human laughter "call" is emitted as a series of short vowel-like syllables—"ha-ha-ha," "hee-hee-hee"—each about one-sixteenth of a second long and a quarter of a second apart. Regardless of our own unique versions of laughter, it always follows the measurements and vowel patterns described above, increases with volume over time, and doesn't interrupt the structure of a sentence. I love this research that has examined hundreds of thousands of, in the words of researchers, "laughter events." Though its expression can be altered by culture and attenuated with age, children laugh from two hundred to four hundred times a day; adults average only twenty times a day. Laughter is not learned; it's innate. It's observed in infants and even in children who are congenitally deaf and blind and have never seen or heard anyone laugh. It's ubiquitous in every species of primate and, get this, even rats have been known to laugh when they're tickled.[24] Like tears, laughter cuts across every cultural and language barrier that threatens to separate us from one another. Humor and laughter have the power to bring people together in good times and in bad. This is an important thing to remember when life's challenges leave you feeling lonely.

The day after my father's liver transplant at the University of Virginia Medical Center in 1995, Nancy, J. P., Deborah, and I took a short break from the hospital to get some lunch and walk around outside for a while. Though he was asleep, we had seen my dad and talked to his doctors. Everything looked good so far, and his prognosis was excellent. Deanne, Shelley, and Dick, were with my dad while he slept off the effects of fourteen hours of anesthesia. He was going to be moved from ICU into a regular medical-surgical unit bed later that afternoon and so this was a good time for us to get some fresh air for an hour or so, then return and give the others a chance to do the same. The four of us had lunch, browsed around Charlottesville, and then walked into a little store that sold Virginia products: T-shirts, mugs, key rings, souvenirs of all kinds. The travel slogan for our state is "Virginia Is for Lovers." I've never quite understood exactly what we are trying to say with that slogan. Often I've wondered what it does to entice visitors to our fair state.

As we're meandering around this little boutique, happy to be away from the hospital sounds and smells, Deborah lights up as she does when she gets a real good idea. "Virginia is for lovers?" she said. "That's right," we agreed. How could we deny it? After all, we were surrounded by coffee mugs and teddy bears and dolls wearing little shirts that proclaimed this to be true. "With all the organ transplants they're doing here, don't you think what they really mean to say is that 'Virginia is for LIVERS!,'" she said. With the suddenness of big cats charging after a herd of tired wildebeests, we started snatching up T-shirts and bears, bumper stickers and coasters, balloons and bookmarks. We also bought Magic Markers and tape, and soon every item carried *our* new state slogan—"Virginia Is for Livers."

When my dad was wheeled out of ICU and into his hospital room on a gurney—still groggy from pain medication—he was greeted by an entire nursing staff wearing their new T-shirts and a large banner draped across the door to his room, all proudly proclaiming: "Virginia Is for Livers." He looked around. His first response to his newfound chance at life curled at the edges of his lips. His eyes sparkled. And he laughed.

Practical Suggestions

1. Even in the worst of times, humor and laughter heal and help. Don't ever be afraid that because you're suffering you cannot step back from the moment of heartbreak and laugh anyway. Remember that laughter and grief are two sides of the same whole; both are alive and rich with the possibility of meaning. Make it a point to keep humor in your life by hanging out with positive, happy people. My friend Margaret is so naturally funny and makes me laugh so hard that no matter what is going on in my life, she always cheers me up with her irreverent and witty view of things. Find your Margarets. Different people have widely varying senses of humor, but discover what makes *you* laugh and then seek out those people, movies, books, and other activities and fill your life with them.

2. The only thing we have to give one another in this lifetime is our true and authentic Self. Share your laughter with others. Let yourself relax and find the humor that surrounds you even during tough times.

God must want us to laugh and view the world with humor. If not, why have we all been blessed with this natural gift? Laughter is a blessing. Use it. Reinhold Niebuhr once said, "Humor is a prelude to faith and laughter is the beginning of prayer." Give yourself permission to laugh even when you're suffering.

10. EXPRESS YOUR FEELINGS

Suffering relentlessly insists on expression. The pain of suffering, if left unexpressed, incubates, over years, decades, even lifetimes, and festers into a growing inner wound that will not heal. American poet Henry Wadsworth Longfellow once wrote that "there is no grief like the grief which does not speak." Longfellow was right, and we now know empirically that it is critically important for us to express our feelings about our pain always and particularly if our loss has been sudden or traumatic. Nightmares, anxiety, depression, dissociation, flashbacks, alcohol or drug abuse to anesthetize the soul—the anguishing symptoms of post-traumatic stress disorder (PTSD)—are all too common in people who have witnessed or directly experienced threats to their own or others' lives and felt the fear, horror, or helplessness of those moments. Suffering that is not taken in or processed and expressed is suffering heaped upon suffering. There is first the initial horrendous event and then years, sometimes a lifetime's worth, of more pain and anguish from reliving its memory.

During the first two world wars, the symptoms of PTSD were often lightly dismissed and referred to as "shell shock." It was not until after the Vietnam War that we began to understand the profound long-term effects of suffering initiated in dangerous and terrifying circumstances. Today, we know that these serious symptoms are created by many kinds of trauma in addition to the horrific experience of war. Serious accidents, suicides, sudden deaths of loved ones, natural disasters, family violence, rape, violent crimes—in fact, the abrupt loss of anything that one holds near and dear—can later lead to serious psychological symptoms. In 1998, more than forty thousand people in the United States were killed in traffic accidents, leaving behind thousands of grieving families and friends. In 1996, more than seventeen million people survived seventy-five major disasters and eight national emergencies in the United States, including floods, earthquakes, tornadoes, and wildfires. Police officers, fire fighters, EMTs, disaster relief volunteers, and all those who work in emergency rooms experience a dark and terrifying side of life on a daily basis. All those people could face the effects of PTSD. Many universities, communities, and the U.S. government have conducted studies about how professionals can work with the survivors of trauma and help them avoid suffering from its long-term effects. The conclusions are abundantly clear. An immediate priority in the wake of disaster and trauma is to offer survivors support by listening to their stories and allowing them to express their feelings, cry, and get their pain, and often anger, out.

If this opportunity to immediately face the feelings they have in the wake of trauma is not available, many survivors will try to turn away from the anguish or rage they feel. Such attempts to deny or circumvent the full awareness of suffering simply cover up pain momentarily. But these feelings don't go away just because we're uncomfortable with them. They simmer in the underworld of the unconscious and seep out when we least expect them to. We have two choices about expressing our pain: Do it now, cleanly and consciously, or do it here and there in unconscious bits of anguish throughout a lifetime. The longer we deny our feelings, the more power they take on until, finally, they explode out of the shadows and into our lives. Repressed emotions like these need only a spark to detonate.

Images, sights, sounds, tastes, smells, and symbols that are associated with the initial cause of our suffering *generalize* to other situations that have some association or share common elements with the initial traumatic or painful event. Here's an example. Your father has died and his final days were spent in a large city hospital. You were with him at the end of his life, and it was a tragic and painful experience for you. At this hospital, you were surrounded by many different stimuli, some of which you were aware of and some not. In the months and years after your father's death, you begin to heal from your loss, and one day you visit a friend who has just had a baby in another hospital. This is a happy day. You pick up some flowers, a nice card, and you go off to visit your friend. As you're waiting for the elevator to take you to the maternity floor, you feel melancholy wash over you. You also start feeling some tension or anxiety. Why do I feel this way? you ask yourself. Your day is going fine. You're delighted to visit your friend and her healthy new baby. Where are these feelings of sadness and stress coming from?

Difficult, painful times in our life brand our memory forever and record our history in our very soul. While you are standing and waiting for the elevator to visit your friend, your senses and your unconscious mind are taking in lots of information that you aren't thinking about and may not even be aware of. The smells of the hospital, the gleaming, clean floors, and the nurses' uniforms are all stimuli that are reminiscent of the loss of your father years earlier. Our bodies and souls respond to these cues, these sparks, these "triggers," whether we're conscious of them or not, for memory can be stubborn and ruthless and we never forget the moments of deep pain. As Pearl S. Buck once observed, "It is indeed exasperating to have a memory that begins too young and continues too long. I know, because this is my memory. It goes back too far, it holds everything too fast, it does not forget anything—a relentless, merciless, disobedient memory, for there are some things I would like to forget but I never forget."[25]

Talk about your feelings, make them conscious, haul them into the arena of your awareness. All living creatures have an innate need to express feelings vocally—to bring deep, inner experience into the outer world. Instinctively, spontaneously, and even in our ancestors' preverbal cultures, we yell out in pain, scream when terrified, "*ahhh*" with delight when something pleases us or feels good, and "*mmm*" when something tastes great. We don't have to learn these self-expressions— they're natural gifts of our human nature. Suffering, especially, demands its expression. Throughout the world, cries of anguish, dirges, lament-filled chants, and wail-like sounds, the keening of grieving women, fill the air and resonate in the outer world with our inner sorrows.

The first evidence of our life force is the breath made audible—the sound of an infant's first cry. Almost immediately, babies spontaneously call out both their pain and pleasure, and at about three months of age—when they figure out that these marvelous sounds are coming from them—they begin to babble musically and squeal with pleasure, delighted by the sound of their own voices. Vocal expression is so critical to the human species that our physiological design locates this important ability in the same pathway as the one we use to breathe and to eat. Giving voice to our inner states is an ancient and vital human need. As language developed, we became even better equipped to describe complex feelings and states of mind, though sometimes this gift of language can be a mixed blessing. On the one hand, it gives us a wider range for expressing the nuances and depths of our emotion. On the other hand, language can also be used to keep us from communicating the real truth of our experience by rationalizing and minimizing our pain rather than expressing it as utterly as a scream or moan might.

When you're in pain, experiencing the full heartbreaking depths of those feelings and honestly expressing them to a trusted friend, support group, or therapist can be the important first step in healing "clean" from your wounds. Some people are naturally better at this than others. Many of us, though, have been raised with stoic demands that prevent us from fully and honestly talking about how we feel or showing our pain and grief to others. "Don't let anyone see you cry" is uttered like a mantra by lots of people who believe that there must be something noble in suffering in silence. Many people, men in particular, have been raised with the myth that they shouldn't cry, ask for help, or ever need somebody to talk to. This is an unfortunate and dangerous belief. It keeps all our feelings locked into the underworld of the unconscious and, just when we think we have healed from a deep hurt, some innocuous event will consciously or unconsciously remind us of our pain and hurl us back into the suffering that we thought was over. Memory can be a cruel master when it comes to pain in our lives.

Suffering in all its forms demands self-expression. One need not undergo a traumatic and violent experience to benefit from the power of giving voice to an inner anguish. Using words to talk about feelings is a good way for lots of people to express what they're feeling, but it's not the only way. In fact, words may not even be enough. Tennyson wrote:

> I sometimes hold it half a sin
> To put in words the grief I feel;
> For words, like Nature, half reveal
> And half conceal the Soul within.[26]

Suffering demands our imagination and creativity, as we struggle to express our own unique story through any and all means possible. Art in all its forms has great power and passion for healing—it validates our human experience, transmits universal truths, and reminds us of what we already unconsciously know. Creating it is a way of going deep—under the surface of what we think we know about ourselves. It is in those depths where we often find our most fundamental truths. Allow yourself to plunge deeply into your pain, reaching for everything that will help you bring it to the surface of your consciousness.

To express yourself and your pain symbolically doesn't require an MFA in creative writing or a degree in sculpting. It doesn't matter whether you are skilled or unskilled in technique because it's the process of self-discovery, of connecting with your feelings and giving form to them that is the important aspect of this exercise. Acts of creation and imagination keep us centered in the moment, where we can meet and directly experience our authentic feelings in all their passion and pain. There is an old story of a Chinese potter that speaks wonderfully to this point that the process is more important than the outcome and that what we learn about ourselves is the real treasure. The story begins as a nobleman is riding through a small town. There, he sees the most elegant, graceful pots being made by an old man. "How were you able to make these pots that possess such outstanding beauty?" he asks. "Oh," says the potter, "you are merely looking at the outward shape. What I am forming is within. I am only interested in what remains after the pot has been broken."

You can begin the process of giving form to your suffering in a spiral notebook by writing poems or a daily journal that you may choose never to show anyone. You can express your pain in the disharmonic chords you've discovered on your keyboard or with the black-and-gray doodles you make in a sketch pad you purchased at the drugstore. You do not have to be a talented painter, musician, writer, poet, actor, sculptor, or dancer to use these tools to get at your own, deep inner truth. You don't have to sell your wares, play your tunes, or strut your stuff before anyone else. You just have to look deeply into your experience and express your feelings the best you can. In the thirteenth century, mystic Meister Eckhart reminded us, "The outward work will never be puny if the inward work is great." It is enough that you have discovered and given shape to the deep, wordless source of your pain. Art is not an intellectual affair, devoid of spirit. As poet and artist Alain Arias-Misson has written, art is rather "life, intensified, brilliant life."

Practical Suggestions

1. Give voice to your suffering by talking with a friend or therapist. Investigate support groups where you will meet and communicate with people who are having similar painful experiences.

2. Find symbolic ways to express your suffering through art or ritual. Make a private, personal altar that speaks of your grief and memories. If you're having trouble getting started, seek out art or music therapy programs in your area.

3. Listen to others when they need an ear. Let yourself feel their story—unique and universal all at once.

11. SILENCE, PRAYER, AND MEDITATION

I'm walking Dorothy outside my cousin's house in upstate New York. It's the evening before Thanksgiving and the weather is cool, almost bracing when a breeze blows. The pungent scent of newly cut grass and burning wood drifts through the crisp air. The bright red and orange leaves of less than a month ago have fallen to the ground, and the Adirondack Mountains loom brown and gray in the waning light. A huge yellow moon hangs in the sky. It seems so close, and it appears to brush the tops of the trees on a nearby peak and illuminates the entire landscape. Dorothy and I sit quietly and listen. There is barely a sound. If I close my eyes and focus, I can hear only the rustle of the languid branches of the weeping willow tree next to me. Occasionally, I can make out the sounds of crickets or frogs, but even the birds have turned in for the night and there isn't a man-made noise in this soundscape. If I turn my attention inward, I hear only silence. It is here, in this moment of quietude, that I can listen with my inner ear, turn off the chattering, monkey-mind of my ego, and hear the voice of my true Self. Silence. Pure Beingness. The quiet wisdom of my heart is within reach here. *Peaceful* and *wonder* are the closest words to describe this sense of inner peace, bliss, that I feel at this moment.

The Thanksgiving holiday is only hours away. It seems appropriate that I say a prayer of thanks. After all, I certainly meditate and pray intensely when I'm suffering. It's easy to take our many blessings for granted. In *The Prophet*, Gibran wrote, "You pray in your distress and your need; would that you might pray also in the fullness of your joy and in your days of abundance." And so, I pray in silence, giving thanks. Nancy and I have driven eleven hours to get here. Through fog, rain, and unfamiliar roads we're safely "home." Tonight we'll take great pleasure in the company of Karen and Steve, and their children, Brittany, eleven, and Matt, nine. We'll play games together, and the kids have enthusiastically prepared a concert for our enjoyment—Britt on flute and Matt on his recorder. It's going to be an eclectic program of Christmas tunes, scales, and themes from major nursery rhymes. They've made paper tickets and marked our reserved seats on the couches in the living room. I give thanks for this night, this visit with people dear to my heart. I offer up a grateful prayer for the good food we'll be sharing together tomorrow afternoon—the turkey and cran-berries and Karen's famous sweet potato soufflé. For the warm house we'll be sleeping in tonight. For my family and friends living through-out the world. For Nancy. For my good health and that of the people I love. For Steven Cook—the young man who died and whose liver when transplanted into my father gave him a second chance at life—and his compassionate family. For the remarkable healing of my father and Deanne after their accident. For Dorothy and the loveable and ornery Miss Maude who's old and will leave me soon I know but at the moment she is here. For all the good and wonderful things in my life. For having had my mother and my Aunt Teresa and my nana and for still feeling their presence in my life here on a dark night in the moun-tains. What a feeling this is: a powerful inward connection, during which I feel abundantly alive and filled with joy. In the eighteenth cen-tury, Saint Alphonsus likened these quiet, meditative moments to a "needle after which comes a thread of gold, composed of affections, prayers, and resolutions." He's right, but what a challenge it is to find those precious times amid the rush and noise of our everyday lives.

Silence and solitude are compelling instruments of transformation granting us moments of perfect opportunity to look deeply inside. When we're suffering, silence offers a cool oasis from the burning pain of the moment and imparts the opportunity for a full experience of our deepest feelings as our inner wisdom points the way to healing. Yet, many people are afraid of silence and scared to be alone. Many of us are not accustomed to experiencing the depth of feelings that emerge in solitary, silent, meditative moments. Still others of us have never cultivated ways or places or times to look inside in moments of silent solitude, even though they're always as close as our next breath. That's very unfortunate. Throughout time, silence has always been known to be golden; a direct pathway to God and the bigger picture.

Meister Eckhart understood the importance of solitude and quiet as being essential to knowing the Self and experiencing authentic spirituality. "There is nothing in all creation so like God as stillness," he wrote. Psalm 46:11 advises, "Be still, and know that I am God." Native American philosophies tell us, "Listen or thy tongue will keep you deaf." Poet Rainer Maria Rilke writes, "Our task is to listen to the news that is always arriving out of silence." Christian mystic Saint Teresa of Avila gently reminds us that the world of Spirit is ever-present, and that no long-distance travels are necessary to feel the immediacy of our divine connection: "We need no wings to go in search of Him, but have only to find a place where we can be alone—and look upon Him present within us."

Silence and the attention to inner, not outer, space allows us to create a psychological and spiritual environment in which prayer and meditation naturally arise. These bring mindfulness, concentration, Self-reflection, and a deeply felt connection to God and the universe. It is here, in the moments when we are most completely *within* that we discover our strongest times with that which appears to be *without*, beyond our rational comprehension. In silent contemplation we encounter the mystery, the nature of being, and the paradox of life itself. This focused introspection and reflection trains the mind to become tranquil and pure. It puts our suffering and pain in new perspective and we become stronger for it. Practices of meditation and prayer change our ways of seeing things and, in spite of the darkness that surrounds us while we suffer, they guide us to a brilliant, inner light.

Consciously, willfully engaging in inner contemplation is the core of all meditative practices. When those practices express devotion and communion with God, we may rightly call these reflections and invocations prayer. The need for prayer and meditation is universal and, as always, every human culture, religion, and spiritual tradition has advanced its own unique forms. Prayer and meditation are expressed through a wonderful variety of liturgies, rituals, and practices. Whether we are chanting a devotional Hindu prayer or a Jewish Psalm, sitting in pure silence in a Quaker meeting, whirling around a blazing fire in a Native American dance ceremony to the pounding rhythm of drums, saying a Catholic rosary, spinning a Tibetan prayer wheel, sitting on a Muslim prayer rug or in the Buddhist posture of *zazen* with silent awareness to each in-breath and out-breath, the goal for each is the same. All forms of prayer and meditation strive for a perfect state of physical and mental calmness, the seeking of Self-perfection, or an act of communion with God or some higher power.

States of relaxation, increased awareness, mental clarity, and peace-fulness are created when we turn our normal state of chaotic conscious-ness in the direction of God or the Self. In fact, empirical studies have shown the profound and beneficial effects of even short diversions from our normally overactive, monkey-minds. Prayer and meditation offer substantial physical and psychological payoffs. They can lower blood pressure and heart rate, reduce pain and stress, slow our meta-bolic rate, and have positive impacts on healing illnesses of all kinds, including cancer and heart disease.

Most of us are content to accept the power of prayer and meditation on faith alone. Recent surveys reported in popular magazines like *Time* and *Newsweek* suggest that more than three-quarters of all Americans pray at least once a week. Even among the 13 percent of people who label themselves as agnostics or atheists, one in five admits that she or he prays daily. Nine out of ten Americans are unequivocal in stating that God has answered at least some of their prayers. Physician and writer Larry Dossey, the former co-chair of the Panel on Mind/Body Interventions at the National Institutes of Health, has been at the fore-front of the research about the spiritual aspects of healing. In his book *Prayer Is Good Medicine*, Dr. Dossey reports that more than a third of the medical schools in the United States have developed courses in alternative/complementary medicine which emphasize spiritual issues in health, including prayer.[27] Even the most rationally minded among us—those who believe that classical physics holds *all* the keys to unlocking the secrets of the universe and insist upon the I'm-from-Missouri philosophy, "show me"—are becoming convinced of the power of prayer and meditation. A wide range of studies using the controlled and experimental methods of science to investigate these beliefs of the heart are producing compelling results. One classic study in the field, conducted by cardiologist Randy Byrd at San Francisco General Hospital in 1984, investigated the effects of prayer on the health and healing of cardiac patients in a coronary intensive care unit. A computer randomly assigned 192 patients to an experimental group and 201 patients to a control group. Both groups were matched for age and severity of their cardiac condition. The experiment was designed as a double-blind study in that none of the patients, nurses, or doctors were aware of which group a particular patient was in. Thus any difference in the results of the study could not be attributed to the expectations of the patients (e.g., a placebo effect), the subtle (and sometimes not so subtle) influences of the experimenters, or the beliefs of the attending team. This same classic experimental design for many empirical research studies has often been used for evaluating the effectiveness of a certain kind of medication or other clinical treatment. In this study, the intervention being studied was prayer.

The experimenters recruited clergymen and -women of a variety of different religions and faiths throughout the United States. All the clergy were given the first names and the diagnoses of specific patients and asked to pray each day for their "beneficial healing and quick recovery," but they were not given instructions about how to pray. Every patient in the experimental group, none of whom was aware he or she was being prayed for, was placed on the prayer list of five to seven people. The results of this study were presented at the 1985 meeting of the American Heart Association, and the findings were stunning. On measures including the number of antibiotics prescribed to control infection, the presence or absence of pulmonary edema, and whether or not a respirator (to help with breathing) was necessary, the experimental patient group who were prayed for fared consistently and statistically significantly better than the un-prayed-for control group. In addition, although the result was not statistically significant, fewer patients in the prayed-for group died compared with the control group.[28]

Modern-day metaphysical theories derived from quantum mechanics, the observation that matter and energy are indistinguishable in the subatomic realm, *psi* experiences like telepathy, precognition, and ESP, revolutionary notions about the space-time continuum, and the idea that consciousness exists and travels in "morphogenic" fields are cracking open our limited views about the nature of reality and the universe. These new findings suggest that thoughts and prayers themselves are a form of energy that is as real as electromagnetism or gravity and just as capable of an impact on matter despite the fact that the extent of their power is just beyond the reach of our measuring devices as yet. Startling incidences of prayer-based spontaneous healing confound rational thinking, and yet more than four decades of laboratory experiments very clearly demonstrate that mind can have significant power over matter. But these views about the intimate relationship between consciousness and the material world are not the handmaidens of modern physics and a new scientific revolution. They've been articulated in and believed by every civilization since the dawn of time. Ancient metaphysical traditions taught that thoughts are energy and that our mind radiates out into the world in real physical space. Sacred texts speak of the power of mind to move matter and levitate one's body in highly practiced yoga masters. Buddhism teaches that all the energy of life extends from mental forces called *Sankhara*. In the sixteenth century, the alchemist Paracelsus wrote, "The vital force is not enclosed in man but radiates around him like a luminous sphere, and it may be made to act at a distance. In these semimaterial rays the imagination of a man may produce healthy or morbid effects."

The healing powers of silence, meditation, and prayer are available to every one of us. Especially when we are suffering, these quiet channels to the Self and to God ease our pain and give us comfort. They grant us immediate access to the true nature of being and an experience of our life and reality that is larger, more mysterious, and numinous than we ever think possible when we are immersed in the trials of life. Perhaps, especially when we are suffering, we should meditate and pray. At such times, the pathway to the divine and the divine within ourselves are most clearly present. In the eighteenth century, Rabbi Israel ben Eliezer, now known to us as the Baal Shem Tov, described the power of suffering to bring us into the light. "Each prayer has its own meaning, and it is therefore the specific key to a door in the Divine Palace," he wrote. "But a broken heart is an axe that opens all the gates."

Practical Suggestions

1. Set aside time each day to meditate or pray. If it's possible, set aside a specific place where you can comfortably sit, stand, or kneel. Turn off your telephone, turn on your answering machine, and ask your family to give you this time without interruption. Decorate your prayer space as you would decorate your soul. Use fresh flowers and quiet music. Set up a small altar that contains objects and symbols that are close to your heart. Try to spend at least thirty minutes a day in this quiet space or walk silently in places that are alive with the beauty of nature. Either one will allow you to be quiet and open yourself to your own soul and its mysteries. Buddha wrote, "If you wish to know the Divine, feel the wind on your face and the warm sun on your hand."

2. There are many types of meditation and prayer. Read, practice, and learn more about them. Many communities offer courses in meditation, yoga, chanting, or other forms of Self-reflection and worship. Check them out.

3. Discover the joys of prayer and meditation with others through participation in a church, temple, synagogue, mosque, ashram, or other place where people gather to pray and worship.

4. Learn to love silence. Find places and times when you can be truly alone with your own thoughts. Many people find these moments in the quietness of nature. In fact, the Celts referred to certain locations as "thin places," where the divide between the human world and that of the Divine, between past, present, and future becomes very narrow, sheer. These are sacred, magical places. Find your own "thin places." Nature is a good place to start.

5. Ask your friends and family to keep you in their prayers and hearts when you are suffering and need support and love.

12. COME TO YOUR LIFE LIKE A WARRIOR

Concealed in a remote valley between towering peaks of the majestic Himalayas in the far northern reaches of Tibet lies the hidden kingdom of Shambhala. Each of the eight regions of this mystical kingdom is surrounded by a ring of icy mountains. When viewed from above, Shambhala is said to resemble an eight-petaled lotus blossom illuminated by crystalline light. At the center of the innermost ring lies the capital city of Kalapa and the king's palace, which is composed of gold, diamonds, and precious gems. This kingdom is said to be inhabited by enlightened warriors who are both gentle and fearless. They've been described as perfect and semiperfect beings, immortal, living in complete harmony, and guiding the evolution of mankind with wisdom.

Throughout this awakened, utopian society, the full dignity of the human experience is expressed in the balancing of many pairs of opposites: spiritual vision tempered with practicality, discipline with spontaneity, decisiveness with open-mindedness, action with contemplation, fearlessness with gentleness, and compassion with courage. Here, in Shambhala, each individual life manifests its own unique expression of the life force within a flourishing culture.

Directions to this magical place are so vague that only those already initiated into the teachings of the *Kalacakra*, the highest and most esoteric branch of Tibetan mysticism, are able to understand them. But even if an explorer should stumble upon it, the borders of this land are said to be guarded by beings with superhuman powers. Those who have searched for this hidden country never return, because they have either found it and stayed or been destroyed in the attempt to locate it.

Does Shambhala really exist, or is it merely an interesting story enriched by centuries of legend and myth? Ancient Tibetan texts contain long lists of the names and dates of its kings, each ruling one-hundred-year terms, which correspond to known events in the outside world. To thousands of adepts, Shambhala is no myth but a real and tangible place, where human beings live as warriors in the most enlightened ways, though modern research expeditions and technology have failed to reveal its location. In the West, we are most familiar with the mystical story of Shambhala through the novel *Lost Horizon* written by

James Hilton in 1933 and, later, through the film of the same name directed by Frank Capra in 1937. Hilton called this paradisiacal kingdom, Shangri-la, and the name itself has become a metaphor for a perfect society, in which inhabitants exist in harmony with one another and all of nature, enjoy spiritual transformation, and all reap a long and meaningful life. Franklin D. Roosevelt liked the concept and image of Shangri-la so much that he named the presidential getaway in Maryland after this lofty ideal, though now we know it as Camp David.

Throughout time, all cultures have sought the utopia of an enlightened society in which everyone lives up to his or her fullest potential and, in so doing, achieves the pinnacle of the human experience itself. Whether we call this idealistic metaphor Shambhala, Shangri-la, El Dorado, Atlantis or refer to it by names that have emerged from Africa, Native American traditions, or the Japanese samurai, each is informed by the same powerful psychological archetype of transformation and spiritual enlightenment. It is the way of the warrior. But make no mistake, warriors, in this sense of the word, are not war makers but peace lovers who live mindfully and with a genuineness and courage that are deeply rooted in the heart.

Whether Shambhala or any of the other utopian societies ever existed in reality is of less importance than the lessons they teach us now and always. For the kingdom of Shambhala exists in our hearts. Its lessons about the way of the warrior lead us to discover the truest path to face the challenges of difficult, painful times and emerge through them better rather than bitter, more enlightened and compassionate, and increasingly confident of our abilities to grow through all the struggles of our life. Though the training for a warrior lasts a lifetime, initiation into a warrior's life can be instantaneous and can involve simply changing your point of view. Believing that we can be brave in the face of danger and strong in the midst of profound suffering changes everything. Do you remember how Yacqui shaman-warrior Don Juan described the difference between a warrior and an ordinary person? "The difference is that a warrior takes everything as a challenge while an ordinary man takes everything as either a blessing or a curse," he said.

The warrior path is well laid out, fully known, and beckons to each of us. In fact, the warrior already exists within us all as a natural, archetypal element in the human psyche. Without warrior instincts, our species would never have survived as it has, and so we share these characteristics as part of our human heritage even though we may not always be in touch with them. Psychologist William James wrote, "Ancestral evolution has made us all warriors." Chögyam Trungpa Rinpoche, the late Tibetan meditation master who introduced Shambhala warrior philosophies to the West in the mid-1970s, emphasizes in his teachings that our warrior nature always takes the form of genuineness, power, dignity, and wakefulness, is inborn in every human being, and is always accessible no matter how difficult our lives might be. He wrote, "As human beings, we have a working basis within ourselves that allows us to uplift our state of existence and cheer up fully. That working basis is always available to us."[29]

Different cultures describe warriors and their training in their own unique ways, but all hold the same characteristics in common. Although there are many adjectives to describe our warrior nature, I believe that there are four that are critically important during difficult times in life. You might want to think of these as the "ABCs" of living as a warrior: Awareness, Bravery, Compassion, and Discipline.

Awareness The warrior understands that every experience—regardless of how wonderful or painful it might be—offers an opportunity to become more vital, awake, and alive. For example, Shambhala warrior training is based on the concept of "basic goodness." This term does not compare "goodness" to "badness" but refers to something even more fundamental than that. Basic goodness is the capacity to experience the world with absolute attention and awareness throughout each moment. Taoists teach a similar idea and emphasize that the warrior nature essence lies in the principle of immediate responses to ever-present change. Warriors take in everything directly and authentically, without hiding anything from themselves or others. They are open to knowing and understanding all there is to know about themselves—the good, the bad, and the ugly. Everything is real. To a warrior, the world and oneself are apprehended directly in each and every moment. The beauty of pain mingles with the beauty of pleasure in a ceaseless flow of consciousness and ever-present, mindful experience. Basic goodness is best understood as a primordial energy, just below the surface of awareness, that is open to beingness itself. We can best describe it by looking inside ourselves and discovering what is most basic, most intrinsic to our very nature no matter what is happening in our lives. In other words, we are pushing past the ego and searching here for the Self. Whether we are rich or poor, happy or sad, in good health or ailing, basic goodness is the capacity to incorporate every moment of experience just as it is, without bias or judgment. That is the way of the warrior.

Bravery Living as a warrior requires a brave, unconquerable spirit, perseverance, and courage in facing both life and death, good times and bad. Warriors are men and women of relentless action who choose to act on instead of reacting to the events of their lives. A true warrior avoids nothing, no matter how painful it might be. In fact, in the Shambhala tradition, the word *warrior*, itself, comes from the Tibetan word *pawo*, which simply means "one who is brave."

Bravery shines like a beacon through all life-forms. Courage is there in the savage protection a mother bear shows when her cubs are threatened. It is there as a herd of zebras stomp and kick a predator in order to rescue a baby or an injured member of their group. These actions are innate, instinctive, aimed at survival alone. Nature gives us many teachers about how to be brave. Most Native American traditions associate the way of the warrior's courage with the direction north. This is the home of Father Sky and the many winged creatures. They say that during difficult times in life, we should model ourselves on the dignity, power, and grace of our winged brothers and sisters, embracing our challenges with our full-bodied presence rather than running away from them in fear and trembling. Facing our fears, our anguished feelings, and moving forward in spite of them is the first, and most important, step in seeing our suffering as a challenge rather than defining each event as a blessing or a curse. It is the first step in acting as a warrior.

Many people mistakenly believe that courage is the absence of fear when, in fact, it means moving through our fears and other painful feelings. To a warrior, fear can be useful in making conscious decisions; it is just another tool to help understand the true nature of the situation. But fear does not constrict the warrior or distract her from bravely doing what must be done. Courage is the determination to keep walking when the path is plagued with danger or our hearts are broken wide open. It's the realization that something else is more important than our own fear or suffering. The importance of courage to living an enlightened, meaningful life and enduring suffering cannot be overestimated. The Bible teaches, "If you faint in the day of adversity, your strength is small" (Proverbs 24:10). Winston Churchill once remarked, "Courage is rightly esteemed the first of human qualities . . . it is the quality that guarantees all others."

Compassion The warrior's regard for others and desire to alleviate their pain is paramount. Warriors make every decision based on what is to the benefit of others, what works best for the greater good. Warriors are dedicated to the sacredness that is life and avoid aggression whenever possible. They never use their powers to hurt others. Even when strength or force must be employed, it is always a last resort and utilized to protect the weak and innocent or maintain the righteous beliefs of all such as justice and freedom. Warriors don't cause others to suffer. Given that so much human suffering is created by what we, as human beings, impose on others, can you imagine what our world could be like if we all behaved like warriors?

The warrior is a genuine hero who seeks to shield the vulnerable and care for those who need help. In Eastern traditions, the way of the warrior is indistinguishable from the path of the *bodhisattva*, a way of selfless action in which a practitioner relinquishes his place in *nirvana* and commits himself to helping others obtain enlightenment and liberate themselves from the cycle of suffering. It is in this depth of compassion, this awakened soft-heartedness, that warriors have the power to shape the destiny of the world. "When you awaken your heart, you find to your surprise that your heart is empty," wrote Chögyam Trungpa. "If you search for the awakened heart, if you put your hand through your rib cage and feel for it, there is nothing there but tenderness. You feel sore and soft, and if you open your eyes to the rest of the world, you feel tremendous sadness . . . It occurs because your heart is completely open, exposed. It is the pure raw heart . . . It is this tender heart of a warrior that has the power to heal the world."[30]

The warrior is humble, kind, respectful, and protective always. In a beautiful phrase of utter simplicity, Native American traditions simply observe that warriors are always the "first to help and the last to eat."

Discipline In our society in which so many things are easily granted, discipline has gotten a bad reputation. There's a tendency to think of this quality as puritanical, harsh, unenlightened, and strict, like the stereotypical rigid piano master who smacks our hands with a ruler when we miss a note or attempt to go off on a spontaneous riff of our own. The word *discipline* comes from the same root word as *disciple*, and it simply means "to teach." With this connotation, discipline means mastery over our own body, mind, and the resources at our command to solve problems and meet the challenges in our lives. It means taking the responsibility for keeping ourselves healthy, vital, and strong. It means practicing self-control and being ready for anything. Through personal discipline we set the stage for realizing our full potential. It's no surprise that the training hall for modern-day warriors studying the rigorous discipline of the martial arts for self-defense and spiritual growth—like aikido and Shaolin kung fu—is called a *dojo*, a Japanese word that literally means "a place to practice the way of enlightenment."

With the strength of self-discipline come many advantages in withstanding physical and psychological pain. At times when we are suffering, in particular, it helps greatly to maintain good habits, disciplined practices of self-care.

A good friend called me one day in the midst of great pain. Her five-year relationship had just ended and she was feeling great despair, sorrow, and hopelessness. "Can you focus on just this one moment?" I asked her. "Don't worry about what will happen next or how you will feel tomorrow. What is going on right now?" There was silence for a moment and then she said, "I'm cold and my stomach hurts." Her pain at the loss of an important relationship was so profound that she hadn't eaten in days and was sitting in her cold living room crying. She lives in a little cabin that's heated by a wood stove, and this conversation was taking place in the middle of January. Of course it was cold in her house. "Do two things and then call me back and I'll talk with you as long as you want," I said. She agreed. I asked her to put some wood in the stove to warm up the room and then make a bowl of soup and eat it even if she wasn't hungry. She did both those things and then called me again. The soup and the heat didn't stop her heartache or bring her partner back to her, but they did give her strength. She was better able to handle her pain after she took care of herself in those small ways. When we're suffering, it's easy to forget to do the very things that keep us physically and psychologically strong. Warriors get into good habits of self-care and self-discipline, so that when an inevitable challenge arises in their lives they can rely on these practices to sustain them, help them think clearly, grit their teeth, and do what they must to move through the crisis.

When we're suffering, it's easy to forget that each of us has a warrior inside who is up to the task that confronts us. By looking inside courageously we will find that we have strength and resources that we never imagined. Each one of us can be a warrior, if we only step back from the distracting, chattering mind of the ego and into our natural state of steadfast wakefulness. It is in this quiet place where we will find the warrior's confidence. Chögyam Trungpa Rinpoche emphasizes the deep inner resources that we can apply to overcoming any challenge when he says, "If we feel we are without resources, if we feel incompetent or as if we are running out of ideas, it is said that we are being attacked by the enemy of our warriorship: our own cowardice. The idea of warriorship is that our human potential allows us to go beyond that, step over the enemy of cowardly mind and discover further banks of resources and inspiration within ourselves."[31]

Practical Suggestions

1. Gently but honestly look at yourself and your life in relation to the four warrior characteristics: Awareness, Bravery, Compassion, and Discipline. Where are you strong? What areas need development and work? Begin now to build up those areas that need strengthening by setting up a personal plan. Write it down. Start by making a separate page for each of the four warrior characteristics. Draw a line down the middle of each page and label the left side "Got 'em" and on the right side, "Need 'em." Then take a few breaths, relax, think clearly, and write down the ways in which you are already living as a warrior with regard to that characteristic. When you're finished, go back and read the corresponding section on that warrior characteristic and think

broadly about how those attitudes and skills can apply to your life. Then go back to your paper and write down suggestions to yourself about how you can best develop those areas in which you are weak. For example, if you discover that you are deficient in the area of bravery, think about your fears and set up a hierarchy of least- to most-fear-provoking situations. Begin to actively seek out opportunities to test yourself in those frightening circumstances. Start small; you don't want to set yourself up to fail. You want to succeed. Reinforce yourself for each positive step. Share your accomplishments with a few trusted friends or family members who support your efforts toward self-growth. Each week take one more step on your hierarchy until the thing you were afraid of no longer stops you.

2. Work out a specific plan to keep yourself physically, psychologically, and spiritually strong. Dorothy and I walk a mile and a half every day unless there's ice on the road or a hurricane blowing. This simple practice doesn't stop suffering in our lives, but it does provide an exercise that keeps us both physically, psychologically, and spiritually strong. Even in the midst of downturns or grief, our regular habit gives us balance, reduces stress, eases pain, and helps us recover from whatever disappointments we encounter. Make a list of regular habits that will keep you strong and bad habits you need to lose. Write down a stepwise plan to accomplish your goals. Please don't write that you're going to run a marathon if you haven't exercised in twenty years. Instead, start with achievable goals that you can accomplish. If you are really out of shape, it is advisable to consult with your doctor or health care provider before beginning a new exercise or nutritional program. Use good common sense about how quickly you can progress. It's wonderful to want to run a marathon, and—if that is what you want to do—by all means list it as a future goal. But begin by walking around your block first and then two blocks and then a half mile and then two miles, and so on. Again, reinforce yourself for your accomplishments. Behavioral psychologists maintain that if you can keep at a new behavior for just thirty days of regular practice, it can become a habit. Mark Twain offered good advice on making progress with new practices: "The secret of getting ahead is getting started," he wrote. "The secret of getting started is breaking your complex, overwhelming tasks into small manageable tasks, and then starting on the first one."

3. Every morning upon arising ask yourself this one question: "What do I need to do today to take greater responsibility for my life and live with the passionate vitality of a warrior?" Then do it.

It may seem a daunting task to make big changes in your life. But remember that we're here to grow, to become everything that is within us. You already have what you need. Sometimes it's just a matter of believing that you can have the life you want and that you can live courageously and compassionately in spite of what happens in your life and the struggles you must endure. Making changes begins by starting out boldly and blazing new trails. With regard to implementing the suggestions I've made and ones you've come up with on your own, I'm reminded of some good advice. The early-nineteenth-century German poet Goethe wrote words that have always inspired me to start out on paths that might seem difficult or frightening. Perhaps his words will help you, too, as you create the life you want, reduce your suffering, and grow through that which you cannot change. Goethe wrote, "Whatever you can do or dream, you can begin it. Boldness has genius, power, and magic in it. Begin it now." Begin it now.

Conclusion
"Living in the Guest House"

*It is by going down into the abyss
that we recover the treasures of life.*

—Joseph Campbell

🖋 The metaphors about growing through suffering are so commanding that it can be easy to distance our real pain from them. The story of Job, the hero's journey, the birth of the Self, the alchemical transformation of lead into gold can feel like bigger, more important, stories than our own little lives. Sure, we might think, those are powerful images, but what do they *really* have to do with me as I shiver with nausea from chemotherapy, feel the jagged emptiness after a loved one has died or left me, or struggle to recapture some sense of self-worth and pay the bills after the loss of a job or financial security? Any one of a thousand scenarios can threaten to crush our spirit, blind our senses, and bring suffering into our lives like an uninvited guest. But the truth is that each of our lives *is* a powerful story about life itself, suffering, and the potential for enlightenment and wisdom that can emerge in the light of such brutal teachers. It is precisely when we can see our lives as part of this larger mythopoetic context that we are most likely to expand our consciousness, see what we could not see before, establish the full awareness of how our lives are like all other lives, and head in the direction of living authentically and compassionately. It is in this larger, transcendent view that we discover that the blossom of resurrection and the promise of psychological healing and spiritual growth lies within the seed of pain.

The truth is that our lives *are* mythological and fed by the life-nourishing images that have been described throughout human history. "You've got the same body, with the same organs and energies, that Cro-Magnon man had thirty thousand years ago," Joseph Campbell said in his PBS series about the power of myth. "Living a human life in New York City or living a human life in the caves, you go through the same stages of childhood, coming to sexual maturity, transformation of the dependency of childhood into the adult responsibility of manhood or womanhood, marriage, then failure of the body, the gradual loss of its powers, and death. You have the same body, the same bodily experiences, and so you respond to the same images."[1]

Each of us must live through every moment of an unfolding and ancient human drama. What will we do when our souls are tested and our spirits threatened? We all hold the capacity to live as a hero, to come to our life like a warrior, regardless of the burdens and difficulties we must endure to get home again. Will we be up to the task?

As I was writing this book, I looked for a single story that would embrace and illustrate many of the points I've made. Just as I was thinking about it, my friend Andrea called me. It seems that the day before she called she had had lunch with Ann, a close friend of hers and a woman I met once a few years earlier, while we were both working on a Public Radio fund-raiser. Andrea didn't know I was on a quest for a story, but for some reason she mentioned to Ann that I was writing a book about how suffering in life can set us on a path toward enlightenment and wisdom. Upon hearing the subject of my book, Ann immediately took Andrea's arm and said, "Oh, Kathy must talk with my good friend Jennet Bernert. She's going through a very difficult time with such grace and courage that she glows." Andrea called me the next morning and told me about this conversation. I trust synchronicity—those meaningful coincidences—that the universe delivers with great frequency if only we will pay attention and see them as the gifts that they are. I immediately placed a call to Jennet, who, it turns out, lives very near me in Virginia.

Jennet said that she was both reluctant and eager to talk to me. Her reluctance came from her belief that she was in no way special. She was, she insisted, just a woman who was up against a challenging time in her life and doing the best she could with it. On the other hand, she said, she would be more than happy to talk with me if there was anything in her story that could help even one other person. If that were the case, she reiterated, she would be eager to share her experience. I knew immediately by both her humility and her clearly expressed desire that her story might help someone else and that, when I met Jennet, I would be in the presence of a warrior, a woman on a hero's journey. I was not disappointed.

Jennet and her husband, Larry, a retired psychiatrist, live in a beautiful old two-story house in a Norfolk neighborhood where giant oak trees line the sidewalks and a park borders the edge of the Lafayette River. The streets are quiet and merge into protected cul-de-sacs. You can tell at first glance that this is a great neighborhood for kids. Jennet and Larry have lived in this same house for thirty years and raised two daughters and a son here; all are now adults with families of their own.

Larry answers the door and invites me in. He's trim, gray haired but with a youthful face, and dressed casually in khakis and an oxford cloth shirt. He's most welcoming—I could be coming over for afternoon tea—but there's sadness in his eyes. I meet with Jennet in a glass-walled sunroom that overlooks their well-tended yard and garden. Outside there's a statue of St. Francis, which is near a bird feeder and surrounded by a bed of blooming flowers. It's odd to see outdoor flowers thriving at this time of the year, I think. But it's been unusually warm here. Just yesterday I wore shorts when Dorothy and I walked our mile and a half. The sunlight streams into this room from all directions, making it a brilliant and warm place to talk. The room is so bright that I rearrange my chair to look directly at Jennet without squinting. She's sixty-one but looks fifteen years younger than that. She's dressed casually in a dark skirt and pretty blouse. Jennet is a trim, beautiful woman with short dark hair and clear blue eyes that sparkle with warmth and wisdom. There is a peacefulness about her, and I immediately think that Andrea's friend is right. Jennet does glow with some kind of inner strength, knowledge, or grace. She sits on a couch with only one external clue of the struggle she has told me a little about on the phone and we'll discuss in greater detail today. It is a polished black cane that she used to walk into this room.

Jennet couldn't have asked for a better life, she tells me. She is married to a wonderful man. Their three healthy, adult children are all married to good people who love each other, and they've given her five granddaughters who adore her. Three years earlier Jennet and Larry's oldest daughter, Kathryn, was diagnosed with breast cancer. Jennet explained that Kathryn was only thirty-three and had a one-and-a-half-year-old daughter. It was the most difficult thing that had ever happened in Jennet's life up to that point. But, thankfully, Kathryn recovered and has been healthy ever since. "She handled that with such grace and courage," Jennet says, "that she's set a really tough example that we'll all have to live up to." Sitting in her calm and courageous presence, I quickly sense that Jennet is meeting the call.

Then Jennet moves on to how she discovered her own illness. About a year ago, in the midst of her wonderful life, she noticed some weakness in her left foot, which she thought was a pinched nerve. Jennet's doctor disagreed and believed her symptoms were being caused by post-polio syndrome, since she had had a bout with that disease as a child. Jennet accepted this diagnosis and was learning to live with the fatigue and the muscle weakness in her left foot that she had been told to expect with this syndrome. But soon other symptoms emerged. Jennet explained that she was not just fatigued but chronically exhausted and physically wiped out, something totally out of character for her. Then she began to feel a weakness in her left hand. To learn to better live with her symptoms, in June 1999 Jennet went to the National Rehabilitation Hospital in Washington, which offers one of the world's best programs for post-polio syndrome. More rigorous medical tests showed that she did not have post-polio syndrome, after all, but something far worse. There Jennet was told that she had Lou Gehrig's disease—amyotrophic lateral sclerosis (ALS)—a rapidly progressive, paralyzing, and fatal neuromuscular disease for which there is no known treatment or cure.

"I know what I have," she told me. "My husband is a psychiatrist, so I have a little bit of a relationship with the words that people use, like *denial*. I'm not in denial. I don't have anger. I've had sadness. A deep sadness—mostly because of what it does to my family. That's what brings me to tears. We're a close family, which is a plus. But when you love a lot, then you have a lot to lose."

Jennet and Larry thought about how best to tell their children this devastating news. They waited several months and then told them in mid-October, just a month before my interview with Jennet. "I was getting weaker, and there would have been no way to hide it. I was hoping it would progress a little more slowly. Now all my friends know, too, and everyone has been wonderful, supportive, and compassionate," she said.

The Bernerts have made modifications to their house. They've installed an elevator and a handicapped bathroom. They've ordered a van that can carry a wheelchair, and Jennet has a scooter to help her get around now. "I love my independence," she says. "After all, I'm a Yankee from Massachusetts." She and Larry have done everything possible to prepare their physical environment for every contingency as Jennet's condition worsens and she becomes less able to get around. Barring a miracle, she will need these things. One of the cruelest aspects of ALS is its unpredictable time course. People who suffer with this disease don't know what to expect. Some people experience only minor symptoms for years, while others suffer rapid physical deterioration and die within months. None of her doctors can predict the course of Jennet's illness. ALS is still a mystery, they tell her. She'll just have to take it day by day.

Like a warrior, Jennet is bravely facing the truth about her life. She's actively doing everything possible to make her environment work for her, searching the medical literature and latest information on clinical trials that might offer some hope for her. She says she is prepared to do any reasonable thing to extend the quality of her life. At the same time, she is accepting her fate; and it is her inner changes, her outlook on life, that offer such a courageous model for extracting the gold from the lead of profound suffering. This trial has altered her awareness, changed her consciousness, Jennet says. She's had a *metanoia*—a change of heart. Like suddenly seeing the hidden image in the stereogram, she's transformed. "Before this, I took life for granted. I was hurrying through it like everybody does, zip here, zip there, do this, do that," she tells me. Now I never waste time. Every moment matters to me. I'm not going to feel sorry for myself because every day is the best day of my life now and I can't afford to waste a single one. If I mope around, then I may have wasted the very best day because tomorrow I might not be able to do the things I can do today." Jennet tells me that she's become a better person and that she can deal with the minutiae of life without getting upset. "I'm more loving and can't imagine wasting time being angry or cross. I'm more compassionate. Everything in my life is more precious to me now."

In spite of everything that is happening to her, Jennet tells me that she says "thank you" every day. "I've had a very blessed life. I have a wonderful husband of forty years and a beautiful family. I've traveled. I've danced. I've skied. I've played tennis. I've done it. Yes, I'd like to do those things longer, but if I can't then I'm content to know that I've done more than most. My life has been a remarkable gift and, even now, knowing what I do, I wouldn't trade it for anyone else's."

Jennet insists that she is not a special person in any way nor is she more courageous than anyone else, but she does find her strength in a spiritual, transcendent perspective. Jennet says that it is her strong belief in God that gives her the courage to take each day as it comes. She's on prayer lists with many friends, with fellow members of her First Presbyterian Church, and with her large extended family. She's one of six children.

Jennet says she spends an hour each day meditating, praying, and reading the Bible, something she has tried to do daily for the past eight years, but now she makes it a priority in her day. Two passages, in particular, have become so important to her that she's memorized them. She turns to them when she feels her courage or strength fading: "And not only that, but we boast in our sufferings, knowing that suffering produces endurance, and endurance produces character, and character produces hope, and hope does not disappoint us, because God's love has been poured into our hearts through the Holy Spirit that has been given to us" (Romans 5:3–5). And from Psalm 28 (6–7): "Blessed be the Lord for he has heard the sound of my pleadings. The Lord is my strength and my shield; in him my heart trusts; so I am helped, and my heart exults, and with my song I give thanks to him."

Jennet has told me how she lives each and every moment with the fullness that life has given her, and I believe it, but it's proven beyond a doubt when Larry knocks quietly on the door. "Normally I wouldn't interrupt," he says. "But Ellen wants to give you some good news. It's a boy!" Jennet screams out loud in delight. For a moment our talk about suffering and its gifts disappears and the room is filled with a joyous energy that I can feel in my heart, tingling on my skin. Jennet explains to me that their daughter Ellen has just finished an amniocentesis test and learned that she is pregnant with a healthy boy. So is her daughter-in-law, Amy. Soon there will be two new boys, one due in March, the other in May, in a family that already boasts five beautiful granddaughters. "Amy and Ellen both got pregnant after I was diagnosed with ALS. I knew for sure that God was putting happiness back into this family," she said. I'm feeling emotionally moved by the pure power of her happiness at this good news. She looks me right in the eye and tells me, "No matter how bad this year will be—they tell you, you can live a month, a year, they don't know—but no matter what else happens, this is the year we're getting two new babies. And it's a good thing. Isn't that the best?!"

Jennet has always done handwork and sewing. She's made quilts and Christmas stockings for each of her grandchildren. "My right hand and foot are still pretty good," she says. "I focus on the positive. I look at the things I can still do and not the things I can't. And because sewing is a sit-down job, I believe I'll be able to make quilts for these two new babies. I already have the patterns picked out." She pauses. "Things are going to get worse and it might get harder. I'll accept what's going to happen to me, but until then, I'm going to try hard. I'm not folding my tent to life."

One doesn't have to look into the mythological literature to discover people who are living the hero's journey. Like Jennet Bernert, they're all around us. And we, too, can walk the path of enlightenment and wisdom. For it's how we respond to life's challenges, losses, and suffering that will determine if we are up to the task of creating meaning in our lives, of making the most from the worst, and discovering gold amid the lead of our pain. And one thing is for certain: Each one of us will have many chances to learn the lesson of suffering. Every life will be visited by ample opportunities to grow through the powerful, often savage, teacher that is suffering.

In the thirteenth century, the Sufi mystical poet Rumi elegantly described this truth about life.

This being human is a guest house.
Every morning a new arrival.

A joy, a depression, a meanness,
Some momentary awareness comes
as an unexpected visitor.

Welcome and entertain them all!
Even if they're a crowd of sorrows,
who violently sweep your house
empty of its furniture,
still, treat each guest honorably.
He may be clearing you out
For some new delight.

The dark thought, the shame, the malice
meet them at the door laughing,
and invite them in.

Be grateful for whoever comes,
because each has been sent
as a guide from beyond.[2]

Open the door to your guest house. Say "yes" to all of your life. Choose to live joyfully even in your pain. Love yourself and everyone else. Be present always—alive to every moment. Grieve when you should, fight when you can, accept when you must. But above all, say yes.

Many blessings on your path.

Notes

PART ONE

Introduction

1. Stories based on clinical material have been altered to guarantee anonymity. All identifying details have been changed, though the core point of the story is true and is not a composite. Other stories that identify an individual by first and last names are reported with their full permission or have been taken from published sources.

2. For more information about Mark O'Brien go to his Web site at http://www.pacificnews.org/pacificnews/marko. The documentary film *Breathing Lessons* is available on video from Fanlight Productions, 1-800-937-4113. Also see: A. Tresniowski and Harrison Laird, "No Surrender," *People*, July 14, 1997, 77–78 and Jane Braxton Little, "Breathing Lessons," *Hope*, July/August 1997, 26–33.

3. Mark O'Brien, "Breathing," *Poems from the First Collection.* © Mark O'Brien, July 1988.

4. James Hollis, *Swamplands of the Soul* (Toronto: Inner City Books, 1996), 8.

5. Carl Jung, *Memories, Dreams, Reflections* (New York: Pantheon, 1963), 358–59.

6. ———, "The Development of Personality," *CW*, vol. 17, par. 154. Note: All citations are from *The Collected Works of C. G. Jung.* Herbert Read, Michael Fordham, Gerhard Adler, eds. (Princeton, N.J.: Princeton University Press, 1953–1992).

7. Marion Woodman, *The Pregnant Virgin* (Toronto: Inner City Books, 1985), 152.

8. Carl Jung, "Aion," *CW*, vol. 9ii, par. 415.

9. ———, "Psychology and Religion," *CW*, vol. 11, par. 497.

10. Viktor Frankl, *Man's Search for Meaning* (New York: Washington Square Press, 1985), 163. First published in Austria in 1946.

11. *Ibid.*, 135.

12. Magic Eye is used with permission by Magic Eye Inc. (http://www.magiceye.com). All rights reserved.

The hidden image in the stereogram is of the flying horse, Pegasus. If you did not see it, go back and take another look with this image in mind.

Postscript

July 1999: I'm sitting on the deck with my father and Deanne. Deanne has recovered nicely, though it took a long time before she could sneeze or laugh without chest pains from her broken sternum. Trying not to laugh was the hardest, she said. It took the better part of a year and hundreds of hours of physical therapy but, since May, my dad has been able to leave his wheelchair behind and now gets around just with the help of his cane. Deanne found one he really liked at a local arts-and-crafts show. It is sleekly varnished, and the artist used the natural shape of this piece of wood to help him define what it would become. The handle looks like a duck's head. My father uses it as a prop when he mentors second-graders in reading at the local elementary school. "Mr. Cane loves phonics," he tells them in a ducky voice and they stare wide-eyed, eagerly taking advice from this anthropomorphized stick. A year later, my dad and Deanne haven't changed their point of view that they are both blessed and lucky. Dad says that there are blessings all around and that, in spite of his long recovery and frequent physical pain in his legs and feet, life is extremely good. "After all," he tells me, "how can life be bad when you're in your extra innings."

Chapter One: The Truth about Life—Everyone Lives a Drama

1. "The Color of Roses," by Beth Nielsen Chapman and Matt Rollings. BNC Songs (ASCAP) and Zesty's Zack's Music (BMI). All rights administered by Almo Music Corp. (ASCAP) on behalf of BNC Songs for the World, 1997.

2. Cited in Sogyal Rinpoche, *The Tibetan Book of a Living and Dying* (San Francisco: HarperSanFrancisco, 1992), 24.

3. *Holy Bible: The New Revised Standard Version* (Nashville: Thomas Nelson, 1989), 453–88. Scripture quotations are from the New Revised Standard Version of the Bible, copyright 1989 by the Division of Christian Education of the National Council of Churches of Christ in the U.S.A. Used by permission. All rights reserved.

4. Huston Smith, *The Religions of Man* (New York: Harper Perennial, 1986), 122.

5. Polly Young-Eisendrath, *The Resilient Spirit* (New York: Addison-Wesley, 1996), 13.

6. Dante, *The Inferno*. Translated by Nicholas Kilmer. (Boston: Branden Publishing Company, 1985), VII 82–90.

7. June Singer, *Boundaries of the Soul* (New York: Doubleday, 1972), 9–10.

8. Personal interview. Also see, Richard Jerome and James Jones, "Double Jeopardy," *People*, July 12, 1999, 52–55.

Chapter Two: Lead into Gold, or the Alchemical Process of Making the Best from the Worst

1. Carl Jung, *Memories, Dreams, Reflections* (New York: Random House, 1963), 325.

2. Manly P. Hall, *The Secret Teachings of All Ages* (Los Angeles: The Philosophical Research Society, 1988), CLIV.

3. Personal interview. Also see Karen Weintraub, "A Case for the Disabled," *Virginian-Pilot*, August 8, 1999.

4. Marion Woodman, *The Pregnant Virgin* (Toronto: Inner City Books, 1985), 7.

5. Michael Maier, *Atalanta Fugiens* (first published in Latin in 1617), cited in Jung, "Psychology and Alchemy," *CW*, vol. 12, par. 387.

6. Carl Jung, *CW*, "Alchemical Studies," vol. 13, par. 70.

Chapter Three: Brick Houses and Straw Houses: How Prepared Are We for Hard Times?

1. Alice Miller, *The Untouched Key: Tracing Childhood Trauma in Creativity and Destructiveness* (New York: Doubleday, 1990). Also see some of Alice Miller's other books: *The Drama of the Gifted Child, For Your Own Good, Thou Shalt Not Be Aware*, and *Banished Knowledge*.

2. Cited in Polly Young-Eisendrath, *The Resilient Spirit* (New York: Addison-Wesley, 1996), 64.

3. Cited in Robert Owens Scott, "It's Called Optimism," *Spirituality and Health*, Spring/Summer 1999, 22–25. Also see: Martin E.P. Seligman, *Learned Optimism* (New York: Pocket, 1998).

Chapter Four: Beyond Resilience

1. S. Wolin and S. Wolin, *The Resilient Self: How Survivors of Troubled Families Rise Above Adversity* (New York: Villard, 1993), 6.

2. Kathleen Brehony, *Ordinary Grace* (New York: Riverhead, 1999).

3. "Hero" refers to both men and women.

4. Joseph Campbell, with Bill Moyers, *The Power of Myth* (New York: Doubleday, 1988), 123. PBS also sells the six-part television interviews that Bill Moyers conducted with Joseph Campbell on videocassette.

5. "Patmos," in *An Anthology of German Poetry from Hölderlin to Rilke*, ed. and trans. Angel Flores (New York: Doubleday, 1962), 34.

6. Joseph Campbell, with Bill Moyers, *The Power of Myth*, 123.

7. Schwerin, Mark, "Singing a Song of Triumph over Tragedy," *Battle Creek Enquirer* (Battle Creek, Michigan), November 12, 1997.

8. "Life Holds On," words and music by Beth Nielsen Chapman. © BMG Songs, Inc. (ASCAP). From the CD *Beth Nielsen Chapman*, Reprise, 1990. Used with permission. All rights reserved. Note: Information about Beth Nielsen Chapman, her music, tour dates, and lyrics can be found on her Web site located at http://www.bethnielsenchapman.net. I highly recommend her CDs and seeing her in concert when you can. Both are healing and wonderful experiences.

9. "Sand and Water," words and music by Beth Nielsen Chapman. © 1997 BNC Songs (ASCAP). All rights administered by Almo Music Corp. (ASCAP) on behalf of BNC Songs for the World. From *Sand and Water*, CD, Reprise, 1997. Used with permission. All rights reserved.

10. Ibid.

11. Kerry Dexter, "Beth Nielsen Chapman—The Song's the Thing," *Dirty Linen*, (June/July, 1998), 77.

Chapter Five: Rowing versus Flowing: Luck, Destiny, and Free Will

1. James Hillman, *The Soul's Code* (New York: Random House, 1996), 46.

2. James Hollis, *Swamplands of the Soul* (Toronto: Inner City Books, 1996), 11.

3. Carlos Castañeda, *The Teachings of Don Juan* (New York: Washington Square Press, 1968), 107.

PART TWO

1. Discover a Larger Perspective

1. A light-year is the distance that light travels in a mean solar year (at a speed of 186,000 miles or 300,000 km per second). A light-year is equal to 5,880,000,000,000 miles or 9,461,000,000,000 km. Many thanks to Bruce Hanna, Director of the Pretlow Planetarium at Old Dominion University, for his help in furthering my understanding of this mind-boggling concept.

2. Carl Jung, *Memories, Dreams, Reflections* (New York: Pantheon, 1963), 325.

3. Viktor Frankl, *Man's Search for Meaning* (New York: Washington Square Press, 1952), 168.

2. Turn Toward Compassion and Help Others

4. Information derived from: Diane Tennant, "Out of the Depths Comes Hope," *Virginian-Pilot*, September 22, 1999, A1.

3. Recognize and Stop Self-Imposed Suffering

5. John Lancaster Spalding, *Glimpses of Truth*. (Chicago: A. C. McClurg and Company, 1903).

4. Practice Mindfulness

6. This story is recounted in many places. I particularly like its telling in Jack Kornfield, *Teachings of the Buddha* (Boston: Shambhala, 1993).

7. Jon Kabat-Zinn, *Wherever You Go There You Are* (New York: Hyperion, 1994).

8. William Carlos Williams, "Thursday," in *The Collected Poems of William Carlos Williams, Volume 1, 1909–1939*, ed. A. Walton Litz and Christopher MacGowan (New York: New Directions, 1986), 157.

9. Terry Tempest Williams, *Refuge: An Unnatural History of Family and Place* (New York: Vintage Books, 1991), 52.

10. W. Timothy Gallwey, *The Inner Game of Tennis* (New York: Bantam, 1974).

11. Mihaly Csikszentmihalyi, *Flow: The Psychology of Optimal Experience* (New York: Harper Perennial, 1990).

12. Jon Kabat-Zinn, *Wherever You Go*, 6–7.

5. Grieve

13. Kahlil Gibran, *The Prophet* (New York: Knopf, 1969), 58 (originally published in 1927).

6. Build Good Containers

14. Thomas Moore, *Care of the Soul* (New York: HarperCollins, 1992), 72.

15. Rumi, *The Essential Rumi*, trans. Coleman Barks with John Moyne (San Francisco: HarperSanFrancisco, 1995), 99.

7. Count Your Blessings and Discover the Power of Optimism

16. Theodore Roethke, *The Collected Poems of Theodore Roethke* (New York: Anchor, 1957), 231.

17. Robert Owens Scott, "It's Called Optimism," *Spirituality and Health*, Spring/Summer, 1999, 22–25. Also see: Martin E.P. Seligman, *Learned Optimism* (New York: Pocket, 1998).

8. Find Courageous Role Models and the Hero Within

18. Joseph Campbell with Bill Moyers, *The Power of Myth* (New York: Doubleday, 1988), 126.

19. Carol S. Pearson, *Awakening the Heroes Within* (New York: Harper-SanFrancisco, 1991), 1.

9. Keep a Sense of Humor

20. Candace B. Pert, "The Wisdom of the Receptors: Neuropeptides, the Emotions and Bodymind," *Advances* 3:3 (1986), 8–16. Also see: Pert, *Molecules of Emotion* (New York: Scribner, 1997).

21. Norman Cousins, *Anatomy of an Illness* (New York: Bantam, 1979).

22. Patty Wooten, "Humor: An Antidote for Stress." http://www.takayasu.org/antistress.html.

23. Abraham Maslow, *Toward a New Psychology of Being* (New York: Van Nostrand Reinhold, 1968), 209.

24. Sara Abdulla, *Nature* (Science Update) (London: Macmillan, 1998).

10. Express Your Feelings

25. Pearl S. Buck, *China, Past and Present* (New York: J. Day and Company, 1972), Chapter 1.

26. A. Tennyson, *In Memoriam*. Robert H. Ross, ed. (New York: W. W. Norton & Company, 1973), 6.

11. Silence, Prayer, and Meditation

27. Larry Dossey, *Prayer Is Good Medicine* (New York: HarperSanFrancisco, 1996), 2.

28. Randolph C. Byrd, "Positive Therapeutic Effects of Intercessory Prayer in a Coronary Care Unit Population," *Southern Medical Journal* 81:7 (July 1988), 826–29. Also cited in Dossey, *Healing Words* (New York: HarperSanFrancisco, 1993), 179–86.

12. Come to Your Life like a Warrior

29. Chögyam Trungpa Rinpoche, liner notes, in Cynthia Kneen, *Shambhala Warrior Training* (Boulder, Colo.: Sounds True, audiotapes).

30. Rinpoche, cited in Jack Kornfield, *A Path with Heart* (New York: Bantam, 1993), 222–23.

31. Rinpoche, "Confidence and Compassion," in *The Awakened Warrior*, ed. Rick Fields (New York: Jeremy P. Tarcher/Putnam, 1994), 6.

Conclusion: "Living in the Guest House"

1. Joseph Campbell with Bill Moyers, *The Power of Myth* (New York: Doubleday, 1988), 37. Also see: The six-part PBS television series. Videocassettes are available at many libraries or video stores and can be purchased from Mystic Fire Video, 1-800-727-8433.

2. Rumi, "The Guest House," in *The Essential Rumi* trans. Coleman Barks with John Moyne (New York: HarperSanFrancisco, 1995), 109.

Acknowledgments

✍ Throughout all the seasons of my life—the good times and bad—I am blessed by the surrounding love of my family and friends. This very personal book overflows with your insights, your compassion, your support, your tears, and your laughter. I thank each and every one of you, for I have no greater gift than the love you give me. As William Blake once wrote, "The bird, a nest; the spider, a web; man, friendship." You protect and contain me beautifully throughout all the sweet and bitter times of my life.

To Lisa Ross, my literary agent, manager, friend, lifeline—your unfaltering support and creative energy fuel me every step of the way.

To my friends at Henry Holt and Company: Amelia Sheldon, an editor whose intelligence, insights, and skills crafted this book into a far better one than I could have written alone. To Deborah Brody—editor, promoter, and relentless seeker of a perfect title. John Sterling, Maggie Richards, and Elizabeth Shreve for their enthusiastic support of this book and the philosophy about life that it presents.

To my friends and colleagues in Dr. Michael Pearson's Creative Nonfiction workshop in the MFA program at Old Dominion University—your honest and supportive commentary helped shaped the book and reminded me about the most important three rules of writing—rewrite, rewrite, rewrite. I thank you.

My thanks especially to the men and women whose personal life stories inform this book and bring spiritual ideas down to earth. Your courage, compassion, and aliveness attest to the remarkable human capacity to grow through suffering and to live always with joy and wonder even in the midst of tears. You give us powerful models to follow and remind us that each day comes bearing its own gifts.

Permissions Acknowledgments

About the Author

KATHLEEN A. BREHONY, PH.D., is a Jungian-oriented psychotherapist, personal coach, and public speaker who has delivered hundreds of keynote addresses and presided over numerous workshops and training sessions. She is the author of *Awakening at Midlife* and *Ordinary Grace.* She divides her time between Virginia and California.